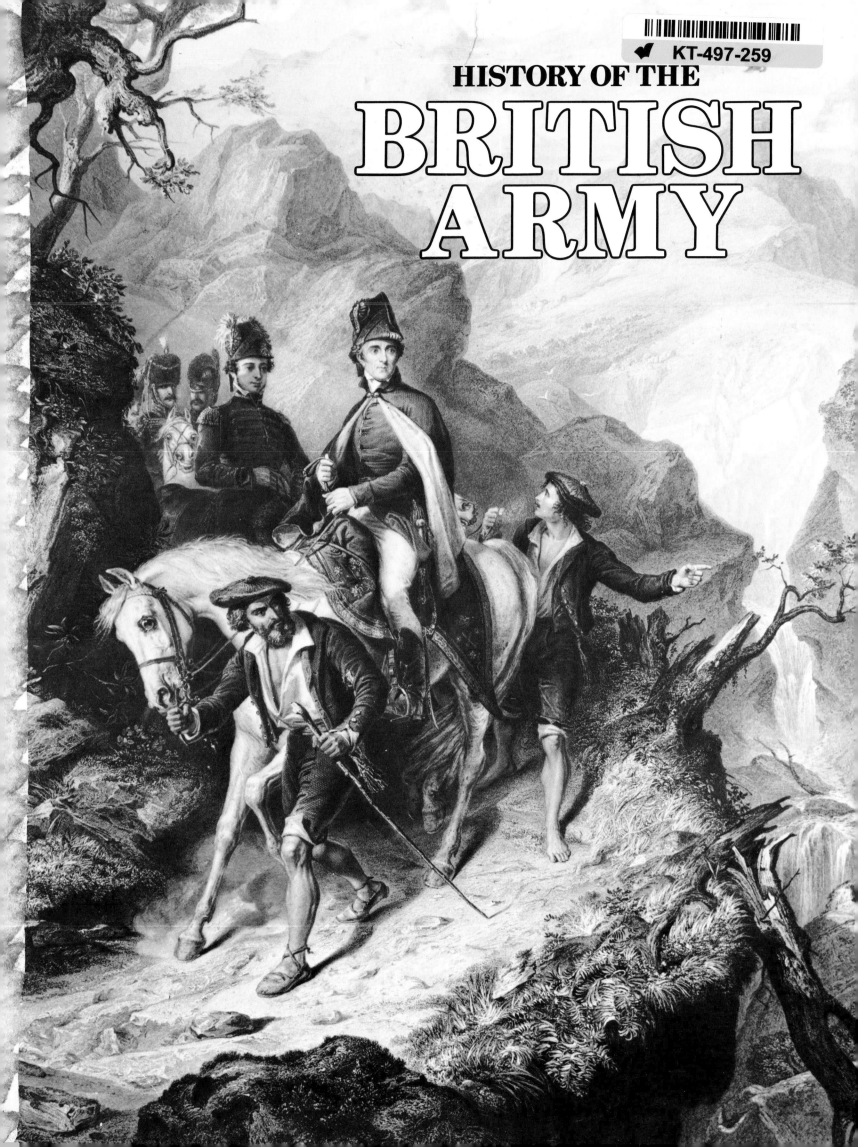

HISTORY OF THE
BRITISH ARMY

HISTORY OF THE
BRITISH ARMY

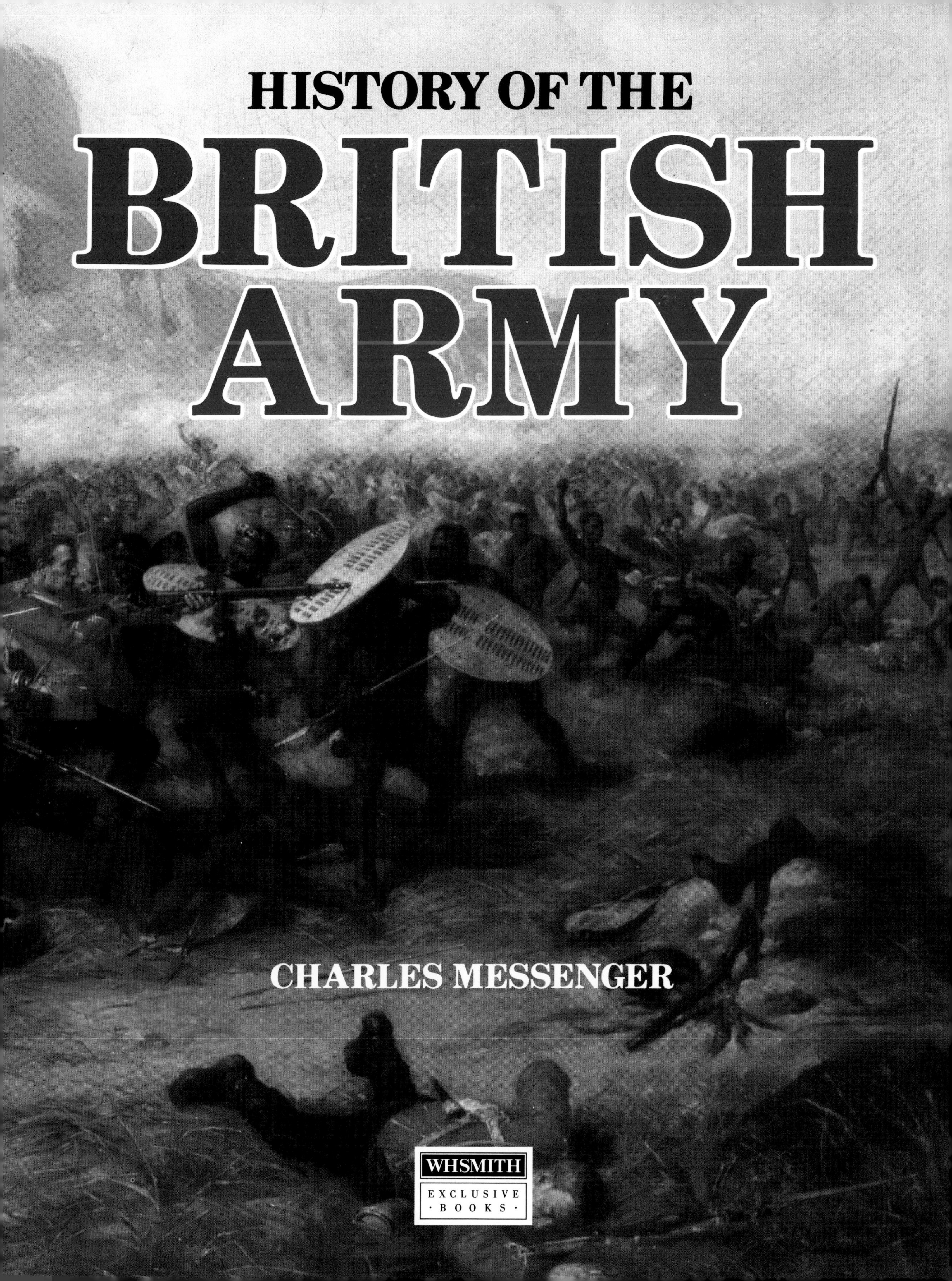

CHARLES MESSENGER

WHSMITH
EXCLUSIVE
· BOOKS ·

This edition produced exclusively for
W.H. Smith & Son Limited
Greenbridge Industrial Estate
Greenbridge Road
Swindon
Wiltshire SN3 3LD

Produced by
Bison Books Ltd
176 Old Brompton Road
London SW5 0BA

ISBN 0-86124-274-2

Printed in Hong Kong

Page 1: Wellington is led over a rocky
mountain path in Spain during the
Peninsular War.
Page 2-3: The last stand of the 24th Regiment
at the Battle of Isandlwhana, 22 January
1879, from the painting by C E Fripp.
This page: North Africa, March 1942. A
newly-arrived Grant tank is tried out by its
crew.

CONTENTS

INTRODUCTION

In 1985 no less than twelve regiments in today's British Army celebrated the three hundredth anniversary of their founding, tracing their ancestry directly back to 18 regiments of horse and foot raised by James II in 1685. Since those days there have been few places in the world that British soldiers have not served in at one time or another, and few years when they have not been in action.

This book relates the story of the British Army from its very earliest days until the mid-1980s. It is a very full history, and inevitably, because of lack of space, much has to be left unsaid. Nevertheless I have tried to cover all aspects, from battles and campaigns to uniforms, equipment, recruitment and training, as well as something of the life that the soldier has lived through the centuries. In this way I hope that the reader's appetite will be whetted to study in greater depth those topics which he or she finds of particular interest.

If there is an overall theme, it is encapsulated in the Regimental Spirit which has been the backbone of the British Army for so long. This concept of 'tribal' loyalty has often been under attack, but has survived and is as strong today as it ever was; it is significant that the US Army, after resisting it for so long, is now adopting a similar regimental system.

Charles Messenger
London, 1985

Above: John Churchill, Duke of Marlborough, seated, and his chief engineer, John Armstrong.

Right: Perhaps the most famous recruiting poster ever, Kitchener in WWI.

Left: The Battle of Gwanga, 8 June 1846, during the Second Kaffir War. The British forces, including the 7th Dragoon Guards, won a comfortable victory.

Overleaf, page 8-9: Cruiser tanks of the 3rd Royal Tank Regiment on exercise in East Anglia in September 1940.

BRITONS

"WANTS
YOU"

JOIN YOUR COUNTRY'S ARMY!

GOD SAVE THE KING

Reproduced by permission of LONDON OPINION

Printed by the Victoria House Printing Co., Ltd., Tudor Street, London, E.C.

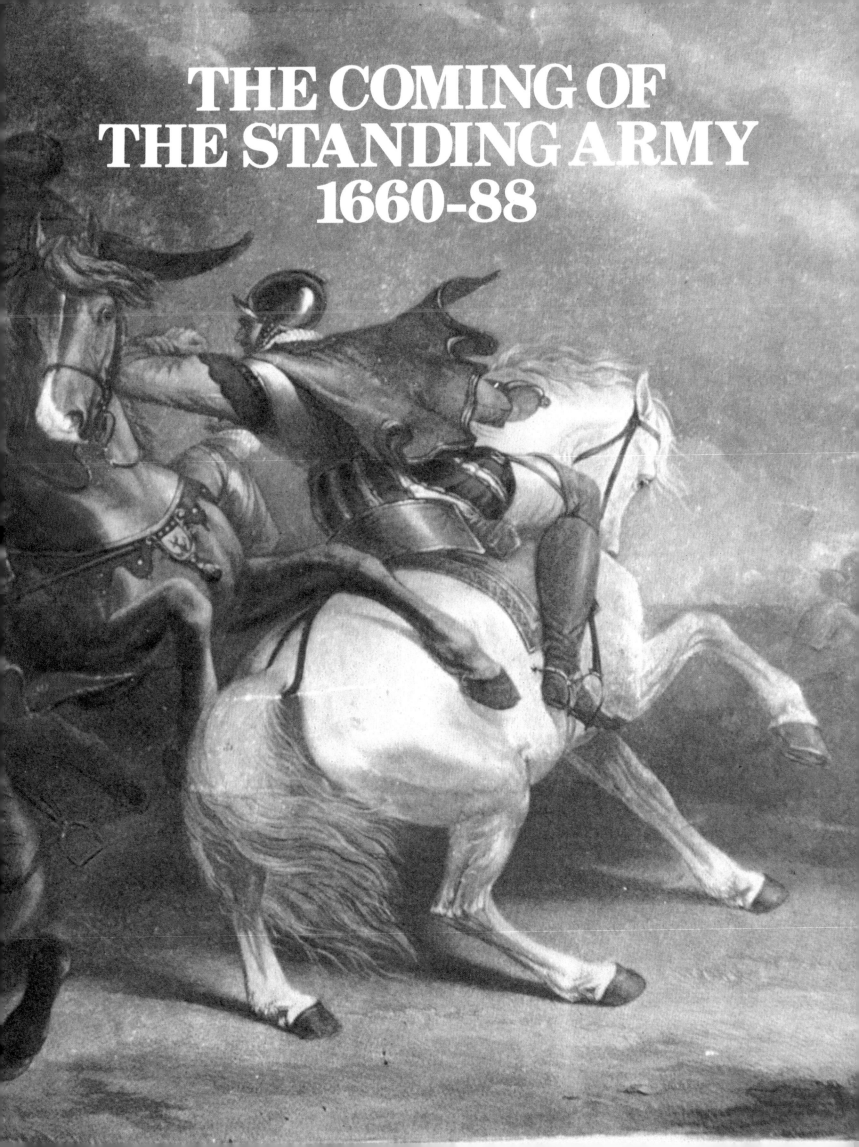

THE COMING OF
THE STANDING ARMY
1660-88

Given Britain's long history, it is in some ways surprising that the British Army as we know it today is only just over 300 years old. Its origins lie in the restoration of the monarchy in 1660 after 11 years of Puritan rule, and Charles II's view that a standing army was needed to protect his throne, maintain order in the country and as a foreign policy tool.

It was the Saxon kings who first organised a recognisable system for the defence of their kingdoms in the face of the pillages of the Vikings. This was the *fyrd*, which was based on the principle that it was a man's obligation to help in the defence of the country in time of emergency. The *fyrd* was a militia, organised on a shire basis, whose call-out was dictated by the king. A further measure was introduced by King Canute in the eleventh century, when he formed a personal bodyguard, mainly composed of mercenaries, the *housecarles*, whose successors were to die at the side of King Harold at the Battle of Hastings in 1066.

The coming of the Normans and the introduction of the feudal system changed the character of the British land forces. Feudalism was based on the idea that the king granted a nobleman his lands in return for his loyalty. This loyalty involved the nobleman making his armed retainers available for the king's service in time of war. The militia principle also continued, but only in terms of volunteers, and it was from this source that the English longbowman, who so influenced the battles of the Hundred Years War against France, was drawn. The system, however, was not reliable in that the king could never be sure of the number of men who would actually rally to his standard and there was often little uniformity in their martial skills. Hence, as was the practice in most European armies at the time, he made much use of foreign mercenaries, usually Germans and Swiss. This became even more important when gunpowder appeared on the battlefield. To handle the early cannon and guns required special skills, which only the professional mercenary, with much practice, could attain.

A further factor was that the nobles, who often had large private armies, had the power to challenge the king, and this was nowhere better illustrated than during the Wars of the Roses in the fifteenth century. When Henry VII took the throne after his defeat of Richard III at the Battle of Bosworth Field in 1485, one of his aims was to dismember what remained of the feudal system, and only a few of his trusted followers were allowed to keep their bodies of armed retainers. The militia was left as the only indigenous force, and reliance on mercenaries became even greater. This was especially noticeable when Henry VII's son, Henry VIII, became king. He found himself involved in war with both the Scots and the French. The militia was sufficient to take care of the former, but the bowmen and billmen, armed with medieval billhooks, with the few light cavalry he was able to recruit, were no match for the modern continental armies, which had now, through continuous fighting, achieved a semi-permanent status. He therefore had to enlist the services of German *Landsknechte*, pikemen who were also proficient in firearms, and cavalry from Burgundy. Three times during his reign Henry raised expeditionary forces to take to France, but after each campaign they were disbanded. It was impossible to keep the Army in being in peacetime since there was not sufficient money in the Treasury to pay it. In any event Henry saw the Navy as being of primary importance and concentrated what financial resources he had on building it up. Nevertheless, he and his father founded two military bodies which still exist today. The first of these was created by Henry VII in 1485 and was the Yeomen of the Guard, the royal household troops of the day, and still responsible for guarding the

Above: The Battle of Chevy Chase (1388), also known as the Battle of Otterburn, between the English and the Scots who were often at war before the union of the two countries.

Previous page: Sir William Rossel at the Battle of Zutphen (1586) as seen by a Victorian artist.

Right: The death of Sir Philip Sydney, paragon of the 16th century gentleman volunteer, at Zutphen in September 1586.

Left: The Battle of Ploermel (1345) against the French in the Hundred Years War gives an idea of the role of foot soldier on the battlefield.

Royal Armoury at the Tower of London. Then in 1537 Henry VIII, realising the importance of weapons technology, lent his support to the newly formed Guild of St George, a City of London livery company charged 'to be overseers of the science of artillerie, that is to witt, long bowes, cross bowes and hand gonnes'. As the Honourable Artillery Company, this formation remains part of today's Territorial Army. At the same time, in order to co-ordinate the development of artillery, which was fast becoming a major weapon of war, the King created the first permanent military department, the Ordnance Department, which was headed by the Master of the Ordnance. This department exists today and the Master-General of the Ordnance is still responsible for the procurement of the Army's weapons systems.

After the short reign of the sickly Edward VI, Queen Mary ascended the throne in 1553 and married Philip of Spain. Militarily it was a disastrous reign for England in that Calais, her one remaining possession on the continent of Europe, was lost. Nevertheless in 1558, the last year of her reign, Mary reorganised the militia system, which had undergone little change since the time of Edward I in the thirteenth century. It was now laid down that all men between the ages

Above: Roundhead uniforms of the Civil War.

Below: Drill with the pike, which still played an important role in 17th century warfare.

and England soon found herself at war with the Spanish, who were determined that the Roman Catholicism of Mary should be restored. The exploits of Drake, Grenville and others, including the defeat of the Spanish Armada in 1588 and the 'singeing of the King of Spain's beard' at Cadiz in 1587, might make one think that this was entirely a naval war, but this was not so. Throughout much of the period there was war in the Low Countries, the traditional 'cockpit of Europe' between the Protestant Dutch and their Spanish overlords. For a time Elizabeth had stopped short of open war with Spain, but sent money and individual volunteers to help the Dutch. Indeed it was a tradition of the time for Englishmen to serve with foreign armies in order to gain military experience. After the assassination of the Dutch leader, William the Silent, in 1584, it seemed that Spain might regain her Dutch territories, while an invasion of England was increasingly likely. To bolster the Dutch an expeditionary force under the Earl of Leicester was dispatched to the Continent and the militia put on a war footing. It was now that those veterans with experience of foreign wars became invaluable, and many were invited to raise companies of volunteers for service with Leicester, who was appointed Lieutenant and Captain-General. These captains of companies were paid to raise their men, but were often crooked: dishonesty among officials was commonplace at the time. To obtain men to serve overseas was very difficult, and many of those recruited were the dregs of society, described by Shakespeare as

of 16 and 60 were liable to serve in time of war and, dependent on the wealth of the individual, were responsible for providing so much equipment in terms of armour, weapons and horses. Lords-Lieutenant were appointed to co-ordinate each county militia, although initially, so that they should not provide a threat to the Crown, they were only given office on a temporary basis in time of emergency.

Mary was succeeded by her sister Elizabeth

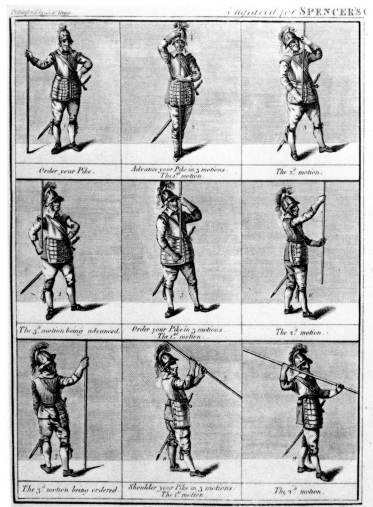

Engraved for SPENCER'S *New* HISTORY *of* ENGLAND.

Order your Pike.

Advance your Pike in 3 motions. The 1ˢᵗ motion.

The 2ᵈ motion.

The 3ᵈ motion being advanced.

Order your Pike in 3 motions. The 1ˢᵗ motion.

The 2ᵈ motion.

The 3ᵈ motion being ordered.

Shoulder your Pike in 3 motions. The 1ˢᵗ motion.

The 2ᵈ motion.

The 3ᵈ motion being Shouldred.

Port your Pike in 3 motions. The 1ˢᵗ motion.

The 2ᵈ motion.

The 3ᵈ motion being Ported.

Charge your Pike.

Advance your Pike.

Shoulder your Pike in 3 motions. The 1ˢᵗ motion.

The 2ᵈ motion.

The 3ᵈ motion being Shouldred.

Plate 1 of the OLD ENGLISH PIKE EXERCISE.

'. . . slaves as ragged as Lazarus . . . discarded unjust serving-men . . . revolted tapsters, and ostlers tradefallen; the cankers of a calm world and a long peace.'

Nevertheless, it was through this and subsequent expeditions that a form of recognisable military structure began to evolve. The commander needed a staff to assist him and hence a number of new titles came into being. Colonels-General of infantry and cavalry were appointed; the Master-Gunner held an important post, and there were also the Forage-Master, Carriage-Master and Trench-Master, each responsible for a particular aspect of waging war. The Sergeant-Major-General deployed the army to its battle positions, while the High-Marshal took responsibility for discipline, the lay-out of camps, and movement away from the actual battlefield. The regiment, which was made up of a number of companies, each of approximately 100 men, became the basic tactical unit, and was commanded by a colonel with a lieutenant-colonel to assist him. Every month a muster of the men of each company was undertaken, and it was on these that the supply of pay, equipment and food was based, the soldiers usually being paid every six months. The muster office under the Muster-Master was responsible for collating these musters, but they were seldom accurate as the captains of companies invariably entered false names so that they could make money. There was no standard uniform, although the government at times laid down the form that it should take. Thus in the 1570s the infantry were supposed to have blue coats, while troops in Ireland were to wear 'a sad green'. The provisioning of the Army was done through civilian contractors, who were equally as corrupt and inefficient, and practice differed widely from theory. In spite of the administrative problems, however, the English soldier began to establish a reputation in Europe, and, under the influence of the military innovator Maurice of Nassau, under whom English troops fought, adopted more formalised tactics.

With the death of Elizabeth I in 1603 and the accession of James I, war with Spain ended and the militia slipped back into its old peacetime habits. Musters were held on only one day in every summer month, and became regarded as 'matters of disport and things of no moment.' Only the Trained Bands of London took their soldiering at all seriously. Nevertheless, parties of volunteers continued to be sent to the Continent to fight in the wars still raging there, especially the Thirty Years War, which swept back and forth across Europe from 1618 to 1648. These volunteers were, however, divorced from the domestic land forces. The latter had reached such a low state that when Charles I called out the northern Trained Bands in order to impose the Anglican Church on the Scots, a contemporary witness described them as 'very raw, our arms of all sorts naught, our victuals scarce and provisions for horses worse. . . . there never was so raw, so unskilful, and so unwilling an army, brought to fight.' Not surprisingly, they fared badly and Charles's reputation, which was coming under increasing attack from Parliament, was severely dented.

War between King and Parliament seemed ever more likely and in 1642 it eventually broke

out. In general terms, at the outset the King had the support of the nobility and landed gentry, while Parliament drew its support from the towns and cities. Apart from the Trained Bands of London, who provided the backbone of the early Parliamentarian armies, both sides were quickly disillusioned by the low standards of the militia and turned to other ways of raising men. King Charles granted commissions to men to raise regiments, but his purse was limited and often colonels and captains formed units at their own expense. Pay and provisioning of the Royalist armies also suffered from this defect and they were forced to live off the land. Parliament, on the other hand, having the merchant class behind it, was able to establish its troops on a

Above: Cavalier or Royalist Civil War uniforms. They were more elaborate than those of their opponents (opposite).

Left: General Monck, later 1st Duke of Albemarle, whose march from Coldstream in 1660 secured Charles II his throne.

much sounder administrative foundation. Many units on both sides, however, refused to serve outside their own areas and the command structures were inefficient, which meant that the early campaigns were waged with little coordination between separate forces. In spite of a leavening of continental veterans, the early battles were noted for the military inexperience shown. The one thing that neither side lacked, however, was courage on the battlefield.

While the Parliamentarians seemed to have many advantages, one thing they lacked was good cavalry. The Royalists had the dashing Prince Rupert, a veteran of both the Dutch and Swedish wars, to lead their horse, and it soon made an impact. The Royalist cavalry's great failing, however, was that it could not pull up after a charge and hence in a battle it was a 'one time only' weapon. This sign of ill discipline was noted by Oliver Cromwell, a country squire who commanded the cavalry of the Eastern Association, one of Parliament's armies. His men were yeomen, farmers and squires from East Anglia, who had a significant edge in quality over the average soldier on either side. Cromwell instilled in his men a discipline that was not seen elsewhere, much of the secret behind which lay in the fact that all ranks shared a religious fervour. Cromwell's force was also well equipped and promotion was by merit. The concept quickly spread, and by the spring of 1645 the New Model Army had a strength of 22,000 men, a third of them cavalry. The latter comprised regiments of

Opposite, top: This view of the Battle of Naseby gives a good idea of how armies deployed for battle in the mid 17th century.

Opposite, below: Oliver Cromwell at Marston Moor (1644), a victory for the Parliamentarians.

Below: King Charles II, founder of today's British Army.

horse armed with swords and pistols, who fought mounted, and dragoons, named after the short French musket they used, the *dragon*, who were mounted infantry. The regiments of infantry, each divided into 10 companies, were two-thirds musketeers and one-third pikemen. The New Model Army first proved itself in its defeat of the King's forces at the Battle of Naseby in July 1645, and then in the later campaigns in Scotland and Ireland. The King himself was beheaded in January 1649, and the Commonwealth came into being. During the 1650s this gradually made itself more and more unpopular with the people. They resented the endless taxes they had to pay to maintain a large standing army and, after Cromwell's death in 1658, a return to monarchy became inevitable. Nevertheless, before the Restoration, the New Model Army was sent to the Continent and, allied to the French, played a leading part in defeating the Spanish at the Battle of the Dunes at Dunkirk in 1658.

A key factor in Charles II's accession to the throne in 1660 was the Commonwealth Army of Scotland under General Monck, which marched south from Coldstream in May 1660. As a reward the King appointed Monck Captain-General, but the 40,000-man army which he now commanded was beginning to become restless, not having been paid for some time, Charles therefore decided to disband it and revert to the old militia system. In 1661 a small anti-monarchist uprising halted the disbanding, but by then only two regiments were left, the Lord General's Regiment of Foot, which was Monck's own regiment, and the Lord General's Troop of Guards. The King now decided that these, together with two other regiments, which had been with him in exile, should be formed into two regiments of foot guards and two troops of horse guards for the permanent protection of the throne. They became the 1st Foot Guards, later the Grenadier Guards, the 2nd Foot or Coldstream Guards, the King's Own or 1st Troop of Life Guards and the Duke of York's or 2nd Troop of Life Guards. The two last-named are today's Life Guards. At the same time, a former Commonwealth regiment of horse was reconstituted to become the Royal Regiment of Horse, later the Royal Horse Guards. Further regiments were also raised specifically for overseas service because Charles II's bride had brought the colony of Tangier as part of her dowry. Two regiments were formed to garrison the colony: the Tangier Horse, which, when it returned to England in 1684, was redesignated the Queen's Royal Regiment of Dragoons, later shortened to the 1st Royal Dragoons, and the Tangier Regiment of Foot, later the Queen's Regiment of Foot, or the 2nd Foot. The last-named were nicknamed Kirke's Lambs after their rumbustious colonel, Percy Kirke, the last Governor of Tangier, who had a reputation for hard living. Jostled by a drunken soldier in the street one morning, his only reaction was to comment: 'God damn me, the fellow has a good morning's draught already!'

Of the regiments constituting Charles II's army, which by the end of his reign in 1685 had grown to 16,000 men organised into four regiments of horse and eight of foot, one has a more unusual history and is today the British Army's oldest regular regiment. The Royal Scots,

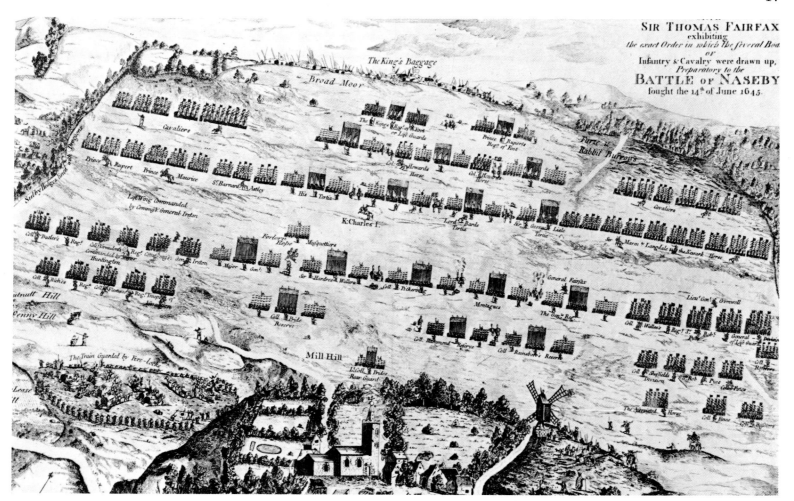

SIR THOMAS FAIRFAX
exhibiting
the exact Order in which the several Bod
of
Infantry & Cavalry were drawn up,
Preparatory to the
BATTLE of NASEBY
fought the 14th of June 1645.

formerly the 1st Foot, owe their origins to Sir John Hepburn who obtained the authority of Charles I to raise a regiment to fight for the French King Louis XIII. Elements of an even older mercenary formation, said originally to have been founded by Charles III of France in 882 as the Garde Ecossaise, joined them, and they became known as the Régiment d'Hebron. They came back to England in 1661, and were first called the Dumbarton Regiment. To this day the Royal Scots jealously guard their long history and take much pride in their nickname of Pontius Pilate's Bodyguard.

Besides the regular regiments in England and those serving overseas, there were also garrisons in Scotland and Ireland, which was going through one of its quiet periods and was under the remnants of Cromwell's Army, who had sworn allegiance to the King without objection. Those serving overseas tended to be officers who had seen service with foreign armies and were the true professionals. The officers serving with the regular regiments in England were of a different breed, who obtained their commissions through their social connections with the Court. Very quickly the practice of purchasing commissions crept in, which was to be the foundation of officer selection in the British Army for the next two centuries, and those selling their commissions were ordered by the monarch to give one shilling (5 pence) in the pound to the newly founded Royal Hospital at Chelsea for veteran soldiers. Many officers were wild young sparks and more than once the monarch was forced into personal involvement with their affairs. He deprived the Earl of Mulgrave of his Colonelcy of

The Buffs (3rd Foot, and so called from the colour of the facings on their uniforms) for wooing his niece Princess Anne. He was also caused considerable embarrassment by his bastard son, the Duke of Monmouth, who, with some other military noblemen, beat up a beadle of the watch (the policemen of the day) so badly that he died. The fact that Monmouth was of royal blood meant that he escaped punishment for this crime. A third type of officer, generally an ex Civil War Royalist, made up the static garrisons and also commanded the militia, over whom there was a continual battle for control between king and parliament. The organisation of regiments had changed little since the New Model Army, and the command structure was also very much the same as in Elizabethan days.

Charles II was secretly a Roman Catholic, but only revealed his true faith on his deathbed. He was succeeded by his brother James who had no such scruples about his religion. During his brother's reign, Roman Catholics had been banned from holding commissions in the Army and Royal Navy, but James soon began to flout this law. The country at large became unhappy over the way in which he appeared to be enforcing Roman Catholicism. Matters quickly came to a head in June 1685, when the Duke of Monmouth landed in the West Country and was proclaimed King Monmouth by the local population. The local militia proved useless, some actually siding with Monmouth. Regular regiments were brought across from Holland and, along with London-based regiments, overwhelmed Monmouth's rabble of peasants at Sedgemoor, near Bridgwater in Somerset. The realisation that

Above: The garrisoning of Tangier was the British Army's first taste of defence of Empire. The painting, by Dirck Stoop shows a review of the garrison in 1683.

Right: The 2nd Foot or Coldstream Guards parading on Horse Guards, London c1680.

there might well be other threats to his throne and the poor performance of the militia caused James to increase immediately the size of the standing army, and later that same year no less than seven regiments of horse, two of dragoons and nine of foot were added to the order of battle, more than doubling the Army's size. The cost of maintaining this large force, together with fears that the influx of Roman Catholic officers might cause James to use the Army as a tool of absolute rule, caused Parliament to grant the King only half the money he needed to maintain it. In a fit of fury James therefore prorogued Parliament, not summoning it again during his reign. The Army increasingly resented the flood of Catholic officers, and when the officers of the Princess Anne of Denmark's Regiment (later the 8th Foot and today's King's Regiment) refused to admit them, the King cashiered the colonel and five captains.

Eventually overtures were made to James's Protestant eldest daughter, Mary, who was married to William of Orange. Hearing of William's intention to land in England, James raised 12 more regiments, and the Army now stood at 40,000 men. William landed at Torbay in Devon in November 1688 with 24,000 men and James moved his Army to meet him. Many of the senior commanders, including John Churchill the future Duke of Marlborough, now deserted James and went over to William.

James, realised that he had lost the support of the Army and fled to France, but was determined to regain his throne.

CONTINENTAL CAMPAIGNING 1689-1714

No sooner had William and Mary ascended the throne than the Declaration of Rights was passed, making it illegal for the King to maintain a standing army in peacetime. At this time there were no barracks in England, apart from those in the permanent forts, and officers had the right to billet their troops in private houses. This was understandably unpopular, although appreciated by the soldiers themselves, who could eat and drink at their hosts' expense. The Declaration of Rights stated that no householder could have troops billeted on him without his consent. Later, by the 1703 Mutiny Act, Constables or Justices of the Peace were confined to housing troops in inns, or other places 'selling brandy, strong-waters, cyder or metheglin to be drunk on the premises.' While this seemingly encouraged the soldier to drink, William strove to tighten up discipline and introduced the Continental punishments of the lash and the wooden horse, where the victim was made to sit astride two boards at a sharp angle. But if Parliament hoped that the large standing army, now swollen with William's Dutch troops, would be disbanded, events were quickly to prevent it.

The first threat to William and Mary's position came from Scotland. An over-enthusiastic reaction to their accession from the Presbyterian Scots produced a Catholic backlash from the Highland clans. William sent an army north, which fought the Highlanders under John Graham of Claverhouse, Viscount Dundee, at the Battle of Killiecrankie. Dundee was killed, but his name remains immortalised in British Army music in 'the Cavalry Canter of Bonnie Dundee.' No sooner had this resistance been crushed than a threat arose from another quarter. James II had gathered a small French army and landed in Ireland, where the still predominantly Catholic officered army was likely to support him. Within a few weeks he had laid siege to the Protestants in Londonderry, a town which ever since has been a symbol of Ulster Loyalism. Although the Royal Navy raised the siege in July 1689, William's army in Ireland was able to do little more

than hold on to the Protestant enclave in Ulster. Poorly trained, ill equipped and badly supplied, it proved no match for James' Frenchmen. The next year, therefore, William was forced to send across a much larger army of English, Dutch and Danish troops, who defeated James at the Battle of the Boyne in July 1690. James' army was driven southwards, but not until 1691 was all resistance crushed after a series of sieges. James had by now returned to France, and William was free to concentrate on wider issues.

William III's accession had meant that England was now automatically allied to Holland and more deeply embroiled in the affairs of Continental Europe than hitherto. The dominant power was France under Louis XIV, the Sun King, who had his eye on the Spanish crown. The King of Spain was dying and had no direct heir, and Louis wished to put his younger grandson on the throne. Fearful that this would upset the balance of power in Europe, the Austrian Empire, Prussia and Holland combined to thwart it, and England found herself on their side. Once more Flanders was to be the battleground, and a contingent of 7000 troops under Lieutenant General John Churchill, now Earl of Marlborough, was sent to serve under the Dutch while the fighting in Ireland was still going on. Churchill's time in command was, however, to be short-lived. He had been increasingly resentful of the preferment given to Dutch officers in the British service, and had entered into correspondence with James II's court in exile. Through the indiscretion of Churchill's wife Sarah, this came to the ears of William, who dismissed Churchill from the Army and even had him locked up for a few weeks in the Tower of London on suspicion of treason. William now increased the British force in Flanders by 10,000 men and took personal command of the Anglo-Dutch forces.

Warfare at this time was dominated by sieges. The famous French engineer Vauban had made such an impact on the design of fortresses that they played a major part in military strategy. Indeed, it was William's capture of the fortress of

Right: The British Army's oldest regiment, The Royal Scots (left) at the Battle of Steenkirk, 1692. A famous incident in which Colonel Sir Robert Douglas recovers a captured colour and returns it to his men before he is himself shot and killed.

Previous page: King William III at the Battle of the Boyne, July 1690.

Centre right: A flintlock musket c1700. Brown Bess, as it was called, would change little for the next 100 years.

Below right: King William III at the siege of Namur (1695), many regiments' first Battle Honour.

Below: William III's troops defeat those of James II at the Boyne in July 1690, as seen in a contemporary engraving.

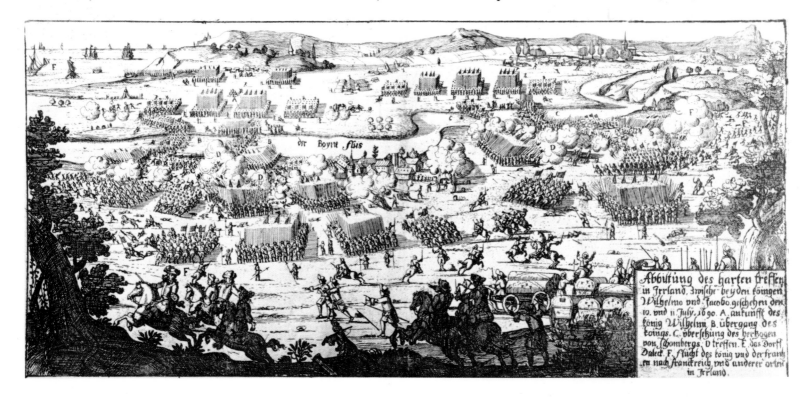

Namur in 1695 which proved the high point of the war, and is the earliest battle honour carried on the colours of a number of regiments. Otherwise, during the campaigning season, which lasted from spring to autumn, the opposing armies manoeuvred and occasionally fought pitched battles. At Steenkirk in 1692, the British contingent distinguished itself by breaking through the French line, but the remainder of the allied army was too slow to reinforce this success, and William was forced to retreat. Making the basic military mistake of taking up a defensive position with a marshy stream to his rear cost William another defeat at Neerwinden the following year. Neither side, however, had the strategic flair or the material superiority to force a decisive result, and the war gradually petered out, ending with the Treaty of Ryswick in 1697. Yet, while British generalship was not especially distinguished, the regimental officers and rank and file more than proved their courage and steadiness.

William now had a well-seasoned army, but because Britain was finally at peace Parliament insisted that it be run down and many regiments were disbanded. It was not long, however, before war clouds loomed once more.

Charles II of Spain finally died in 1701 and nominated the Sun King's grandson as his successor. The Grand Alliance of Austria, Holland and Britain was resurrected and by the end of

1701 British troops were once more in Flanders. Selected to command them was the Earl of Marlborough, now restored to favour as 'General over all Our Foot Forces'. Marlborough's first task was to agree with his allies as to what the British contribution should be. This was fixed at 40,000 men, which meant that the Army had once more to be expanded, and many of those regiments disbanded in 1697 brought back into being. Parliament, however, was hesitant and war was not actually declared until Louis had gone so far as to announce that he recognised James II's son, known in Britain as the Old Pretender, as James III and the rightful King of Britain. Before British troops actually went into action William III died after a fall from his horse, which had tripped over a molehill. The Jacobites, supporters of James, drank to 'the little gentleman in black velvet' as they also toasted the Sovereign by passing their glasses over a glass of water to signify the 'king over the water' ... meaning James who was overseas. This practice was prevented in Army messes by ensuring that all extraneous glasses were removed from the table before the toast to the monarch was drunk, a procedure which continues to this day.

James II's other daughter Anne was now crowned Queen. It so happened that Marlborough's wife Sarah was her confidante, which was to be of immeasurable help to him during the next few years. Likewise, one of his daughters had recently married the son of Sidney Godolphin, the Treasurer, who would also be a vital ally. On her accession in March 1702, Queen Anne signified her regard for Marlborough by appointing him not just Master-General of the Ordnance, but Captain-General as well, thus giving him far greater powers over the Army than any officer previously.

Marlborough began his campaigning in the

early summer of 1702. The Dutch Army had already been defeated and Holland was in grave danger from the French under Marshal Boufflers. With an Anglo-Dutch army of 60,000 men, of whom only a fifth were British, Marlborough's intention was to attack. Twice he managed to manoeuvre Boufflers into a disadvantageous position, but each time he was thwarted not by the enemy but by the Dutch civil deputies who were accompanying the army and were fearful that a pitched battle might bring about its destruction. Nevertheless, Marlborough was able to capture three fortresses, including Liège. This was as well since elsewhere the enemy had driven back the Austrians from the Rhine, and a British combined naval-military expedition to Cadiz was a disaster. If 1702 had been frustrating for Marlborough, 1703 was worse. Every time he

Above: Artillery on the march in Marlborough's time, from a contemporary engraving.

Above right: Blenheim (1704). Marlborough (right) looses his cavalry on the French.

Left: Medal struck to commemorate the victories of Marlborough and Eugene.

Right: A sergeant urges on a civilian wagoner (from the Wyendael Tapestry on public display at Blenheim palace).

wished to launch an offensive against the French he was thwarted by the Dutch and all he could show for his efforts was the capture of two minor fortresses. Meanwhile the French and their allies were now directly threatening Austria and Marlborough realised that unless he could give direct support there was a danger of Austria being knocked out of the war.

The campaign of 1704 was a military classic which is often cited as a supreme example of good generalship. Marlborough managed to persuade the Dutch that for the sake of the alliance as a whole it was vital to concentrate on the Moselle in order to deflect French attention from Austria. Once there, he then slipped eastwards and in six weeks had covered 250 miles, arriving on the Danube near Ulm. This march was in itself a masterpiece of organisation and revealed only too clearly Marlborough's good administration – a much ignored principle of war, at least in the British Army of the time. Captain Robert Parker of the Royal Irish Regiment, who served under Marlborough:

'As we marched through the countries of our allies commissaries were appointed to furnish us with all manner of necessities for man and horse: these were brought to the ground before we arrived and the soldiers had nothing to do but to pitch their tents, boil their kettles, and lie down to rest. Surely never was such a march carried on with more order and regularity and with less fatigue.'

The army used to begin the day's marching at three in the morning and halt for the day at about

Right: After Blenheim. A
grenadier with a captured
French colour.

Right: After Blenheim. A grenadier with a captured French colour.

9 am. Every fourth or fifth day would be set aside for rest. Thanks to Marlborough's friendship with Godolphin, there was never any problem in ensuring that the money was available for the purchase of supplies, and, unlike in previous wars, Marlborough was able to issue an edict forbidding plundering of any form; the penalty was death by hanging. Nevertheless the British soldier would still commit crimes, although not to the extent painted by another of Marlborough's officers, Lieutenant-Colonel John Blackader of the Cameronians. A zealous Puritan, he constantly bewailed the evilness of soldiers in his diaries: '. . . the English army are sinners exceedingly before the Lord'; but he was a fine and very brave regimental commander, whose soldiers would follow him anywhere.

As the march continued, detachments from the German states joined the army, and various dignitaries appeared to inspect the British troops. At Mainz the Elector Palatine inspected the infantry and remarked that 'all these gentlemen are dressed for the ball', such was the good condition of their clothing and accoutrements. Likewise Prince Eugene, commanding the Austrian Army, when inspecting the British cavalry declared: 'Money, which you don't want in England, will buy clothes and fine

horses, but it cannot buy that lively air I see in every one of your troopers.' That 'lively air' came from the fact that every soldier was conscious that Marlborough was constantly thinking of his wants, even ensuring that every man had a new pair of boots before entering enemy territory; this gained him the nickname of Corporal John.

At Ulm, Marlborough was joined by the Margrave of Baden's army and the enemy withdrew south of the Danube. Marlborough was determined to bring him to battle before he could be reinforced from the Upper Rhine and engaged him near the town of Donauworth on the evening of 2 July. It proved a bloody battle, but a victorious one for the Allies. Those who fell included eight generals and 28 brigadiers and colonels. Eighteenth-century battles were no respecters of rank. Yet after the battle Marlborough's attention, as Dr Francis Hare, his Chaplain-General, wrote, '. . . was now employed about sending the wounded away to hospital.' It was also the custom for soldiers' wives to accompany their husbands on campaign, the numbers being regulated by each regiment, a practice which continued until after the Crimean War. Those whom the battle had widowed Marlborough encouraged to nurse the wounded. He also arranged free passage back to England for those widows wishing to go home.

The Margrave of Baden now went off to invest the fortress of Ingolstadt, to Marlborough's displeasure; but this is one of the problems of coalition warfare when there is no overall commander, and in this case he and the Margrave had been taking turns to command day about. At the same time the French were reinforced from the Upper Rhine, and they and their Bavarian allies resolved to attack the weakened opposition. They recrossed the Rhine and moved against Prince Eugene. Marlborough, however, was able to join his ally before the French could attack, and their combined forces advanced westwards, coming across the enemy taking up positions around the village of Blenheim.

The style of battle which was about to be fought would change little during the eighteenth century. It involved three arms – infantry, cavalry and artillery. The first-named was the 'workhorse' and was organised into regiments. Most of them consisted of a single battalion, which was the tactical unit in battle, but a few, such as the Guards, had more. Some regiments, as we have seen, had a geographic title, but most were called after the Colonel of the Regiment. A present-day

Below: 'Corporal John' receives the surrender of the French Marshal Tallard.

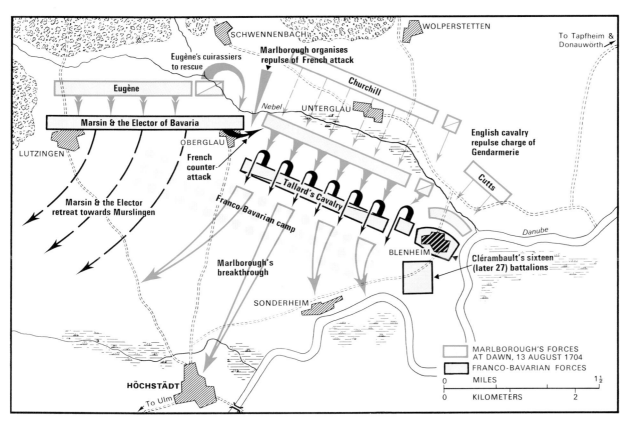

Labels within the map:

SCHWENNENBACH
WOLPERSTETTEN
To Tapfheim & Donauworth

Eugène's cuirassiers to rescue

Marlborough organises repulse of French attack

Eugène

Churchill

Nebel

UNTERGLAU

Marsin & the Elector of Bavaria

English cavalry repulse charge of Gendarmerie

OBERGLAU

LUTZINGEN

French counter-attack

Cutts

Marsin & the Elector retreat towards Murslingen

Franco-Bavarian camp

Tallard's Cavalry

Danube

BLENHEIM

Marlborough's breakthrough

Clérambault's sixteen (later 27) battalions

SONDERHEIM

HÖCHSTÄDT

To Ulm

MARLBOROUGH'S FORCES AT DAWN, 13 AUGUST 1704

FRANCO-BAVARIAN FORCES

0   MILES   1½
0   KILOMETERS   2

Left: Map of the Battle of Blenheim.

Below: Blenheim village. The cavalry begin their decisive charge.
(All pictures on this page show details of the Blenheim Tapestry which is displayed in the Green Writing Room at Blenheim Palace).

example of this is the Green Howards. At one stage in the eighteenth century they were commanded by a Colonel Howard, but so were the Buffs. It was therefore decided that to differentiate between the two they should be called the Green Howards and the Buff Howards after the colours of their uniform facings. In 1712 regiments of the line – those outside the Guards, who were the monarch's household troops – were allocated numbers based on their seniority, but it was not for some years that the practice of calling them after their colonels died out.

The battalion was organised into one grenadier and 12 line companies, each having a strength of some 60 men. When deploying for battle they would form a line of companies, the grenadiers being split equally on the flanks and the line companies drawn up in a predetermined order, with the colonel's own company and that of his second-in-command, the lieutenant-colonel, in the centre. They would be drawn up in three ranks, with the colours of the regiment to the centre and in the rear. The line companies would then be split into four Grand Divisions, each of which was broken down into four platoons. The 16 platoons so formed would then be redivided into three 'firings' of six platoons each, which were so distributed that the battalion could produce a volley of fire all the way along its front. This was unlike the French, who fired by ranks rather than platoons, but contemporary British accounts reveal that the British system resulted in a heavier weight of fire. The firearm used by all armies was the flintlock musket, which required 24 separate evolutions to load it, and the average rate of fire was two rounds per minute with an extreme range of 250 yards. Sergeants retained the pike or halberd, which was used to correct the aim of the firers, as did the escort to the colours. All movement was regulated by the beat of a drum. The main object was to win the

fire fight and then go in with the bayonet. If faced by cavalry, the infantry then formed a square, which gave them all-round protection.

While the infantry wore the enemy down, the cavalry were held back for the decisive moment of 'shock action' which would carry the day. The British cavalry were still made up of two basic types – horse and dragoons.. Regiments were made up of some six to eight troops, each comprising 50-60 men. In battle, however, like the infantry, the cavalry regiment reorganised itself into two or three squadrons, each of a number of troops. While in most Continental armies the cavalry fought with sword and pistol (apart from the dragoons, who retained their mounted infantry role), Marlborough was not a believer in firearms where the cavalry were concerned, limiting his men to three charges of powder and ball for each campaign, and this specifically for guarding their horses when at grass. The age-old problem of controlling the cavalry in a charge was overcome by restricting them to a fast trot, usually by two squadrons abreast in two ranks. Marlborough, however, was a great believer in retaining a large cavalry reserve for the *coup de grâce*, and this was one of the secrets of his success on the battlefield. Once the enemy had been broken, it was then the cavalry who carried out the pursuit.

The artillery of the time was organised in three distinct groups – field, garrison and siege. Field artillery ranged in calibre from 24-pounders (the weight of the cannon ball) down to one- and even half-pounders. Marlborough's artillery train, however, contained few pieces larger than 16-pounders, and the most common was the 12-pounder with a range of 4500 yards. There was no formalised artillery corps or regiment at the time, and the Royal Regiment of Artillery, as we now know it, was not established until 1716. Gunners were formed into companies, usually 30

Above: Blenheim. The Scots Dragoons (now the Royal Scots Dragoon Guards) in dismounted action.

Below: The capture of Gibraltar in 1704.

Above: The 3rd Regiment of Horse (now 1st the Queen's Dragoon Guards) charges at Ramillies.

Above right: The ignominy of defeat. Almanza, 1707.

in each, for a campaign, and the horses to draw the guns, and their drivers, were contracted from civil life. Faced with the prospect of action, the latter would often become unwilling, and infantry had to be used to ensure that the movement of the guns was properly carried out. Indeed the Royal Fusiliers was raised by James II in 1685 specifically for this task as 'Our Royal Regiment of Fusiliers, also Our Ordnance Regiment.' On the battlefield the guns were usually grouped into batteries of six to nine guns, and sited on high ground in order to achieve their maximum firing range. Although generally deployed on the flanks, lighter pieces would be moved forward of the infantry at the beginning of the battle in order to cover their final preparations. Often, too, they would be manhandled about the battlefield to critical points. While artillery did not yet have the importance that it would attain a century later, it was becoming increasingly effective as pieces became easier to handle.

The battle about to be fought at Blenheim was very typical of its day and of Marlborough's tactics, which were, in essence, to make preliminary attacks on both wings in order to force the enemy to weaken his centre, and then make the decisive attack there. Although he was attacking, Marlborough was of slightly inferior strength, having 50,000 men and 60 guns against 60,000 and 120 guns. The enemy had, however, made a fatal mistake in holding their centre with cavalry only. Eugene's Austrians attacked the French left, and this became a battle of attrition, as the fighting ebbed and flowed across the marshy River Nebel. Casualties were high, but Eugene succeeded in his task of pinning down the enemy left, even though, as he said afterwards: 'I have not a squadron or a battalion which did not charge four times at least.' On the right the fighting centred on the village of Blenheim itself, which the French had fortified. The task of attacking it was given to one of Marlborough's able lieutenants, Brigadier General Lord Cutts, known as Salamander on account of his fire-eating character. The story was much the same, with Cutts making repeated attacks, but the French were compelled to reinforce and gradually the centre became weaker. Finally, in the early evening, Marlborough decided that the moment had come and launched his main attack of 90 squadrons, supported by 23 infantry battalions and most of his guns. Countercharges by the French cavalry made no impression, and by 7 pm it was over, with the enemy right encircled and the remainder retreating as fast as they could pursued by the cavalry. In all, the Franco-Bavarian casualties were some 38,000 men, including 14,000 prisoners, while the Allies lost 4500 killed and 8000 wounded.

As a result of this momentous victory, the Bavarians were knocked out of the war and the Allies well established on the west bank of the Rhine for an invasion of France. While British troops made up only a quarter of the Allied army at the battle, their performance and, more especially, that of Marlborough himself established their reputation in Europe as a formidable fighting force.

The year 1704 had also brought success to British arms elsewhere when Admiral Rooke captured Gibraltar from the Spanish. Apart from its value as a naval base, Gibraltar would also become known intimately to succeeding generations of British troops, who provide the garrison to this day.

Marlborough hoped to capitalise on the successes of 1704 with an invasion of Alsace and Lorraine, designed to turn the French flank. The Dutch deputies, however, refused to release the necessary troops. He was then forced to dash back to Flanders when Marshal Villeroi made a swoop on Liège. Marlborough foiled this and then tried to draw his opponent into battle, but each time he was poised to attack he was, as in 1703, thwarted by the deputies who refused to allow him to do so. Meanwhile a British force under the Earl of Peterborough landed in Spain and rallied the eastern provinces to support the Austrian contender to the throne. The year 1706, however, was marked by another of Marlborough's great battles, when he inflicted a severe defeat on Villeroi at Ramillies. The result of this was the capture of a number of fortresses and the securing of the whole of Brabant and Flanders. In Spain, too, Peterborough continued to make progress. The bad weather in Flanders prevented any positive results in 1707, while in Spain the Allies suffered a bloody reverse at Almanza, although the British contingent did not disgrace itself, and the 9th Foot, later the Royal Norfolk Regiment, earned their Britannia cap badge for the gallant way in which they covered the Allied retreat.

The year 1708 was better. After a very wet spring the weather improved, and a French army of 100,000 men advanced on Flanders once more. Marlborough summoned Eugene to join him and, after the French had captured Ghent, the opposing forces met in a classic encounter battle at Oudenarde on the River Scheldt on 11 July. On this occasion Marlborough reversed his normal tactics, and won what many consider his most brilliant victory by two perfectly co-ordinated attacks on the wings which encircled the enemy, causing 20,000 men lost, including 9000 prisoners, as against only 3000 Allied casualties, of which the British lost a mere 230. Marlborough now wanted to carry out an ambitious amphibious operation on the River Somme, but the Dutch would not hear of this, so he contented himself with laying siege to Lille, which finally fell at the end of the year. The French attempted to negotiate peace during the winter, but the terms were unacceptable to the Allies, and the fighting continued the following year with Marlborough's victory at Malplaquet on 9 September. Here he chose a direct frontal attack against an enemy who had had several days to prepare his defences, and it was only the tenacity of his troops which brought about eventual victory, but at a cost of a fifth of their number. The fact that Marlborough was not well at the time accounted for his lack of tactical subtlety.

By this time Marlborough was losing his support at home. Queen Anne and the Duchess had fallen out, and a new Tory administration had come to power and was eager to find ways of making peace with the French. Maintaining two armies abroad, Marlborough's and Peterborough's, was putting a severe strain on the Treasury. Manpower was also a problem: the United Kingdom did not operate conscription for the army, although the Royal Navy employed the press gang. At the beginning of the war, enlistment was theoretically voluntary, and parties from the various regiments toured the country looking for likely recruits. These were given a

Above: Marlborough (on the white horse) and his staff at Ramillies, a painting by Laguerre.

Top right: Every cavalryman's dream – the pursuit after Ramillies.

Centre right: Marlborough's last major victory – Malplaquet, 1709.

Right bottom: The King's Carabiniers (now the Royal Scots Dragoon Guards) clash with French cavalry at Malplaquet.

bounty of one shilling, which was known as 'taking the King's [Queen's] Shilling'; unscrupulous recruiters were not above getting a man drunk and then forcing a shilling on him. This did not provide anywhere near the number of men required for the expanding wartime army, hence Parliament decreed that all unemployed men could be compulsorily enlisted. Even this did not produce enough men and a short three-year term of service was introduced. This again, while slightly improving the situation, did not solve the problem, and the country was forced to rely to a large extent on foreign mercenaries, usually from the German states. Parliament's continued refusal to countenance conscription was through fear of creating a large military force in the hands of the monarch, and the British Army would remain 'voluntary' until 1916.

Marlborough's final campaign took place in 1711, and some of his old brilliance was seen in his forcing of the seemingly impregnable Ne Plus Ultra (thus far and no further) defence lines without losing a man, and the capture of Bouchain, while keeping a very much larger French army at bay; but on New Year's Day 1712 he was accused of misappropriating public funds and was dismissed by the Queen. It was a sad end to the career of one of Britain's greatest soldiers. Superb tactician and strategist, an outstanding diplomat, whose personality kept often difficult allies together, and a first-class administrator, he rightly deserves his place among the Great Captains of War, and those regiments who fought with him proudly carry the names of his battles on their colours to this day. As Captain Robert Parker said of him: 'He never fought a Battle which he did not gain, nor laid siege to a Town which he did not take.' Few generals have been able to boast such a record.

WINNING AN EMPIRE 1715-89

The War of the Spanish Succession had been brought to an end by the Treaty of Utrecht of 1713, which marked the beginnings of Britain's empire. She came away from the war with Gibraltar, Minorca, Nova Scotia and Newfoundland in her possession, but they had to be garrisoned. The British Army was already being run down even before the Treaty of Utrecht was signed. From a strength of 70,000, together with an additional 12,000 in the Irish establishment, it had fallen to 47,400 by the beginning of 1713, of whom only 25 per cent were stationed in the United Kingdom. In 1714 the establishment was set at 18,000 men, of whom two-thirds were to be stationed in Flanders or the colonies. Indeed it was officially not called 'the Army' but merely referred to as 'guards and garrisons' in order to dispel ideas that there was in fact a standing army. The garrisons themselves were small and scattered, often in no more than company strength and seldom more than a battalion, and were kept out of the public eye as much as possible. In the absence of an organised police force they were used to quell civil disorders, but this merely served to make them even more unpopular with the country at large. Yet before the Army was finally to become immersed in the long peace that followed the end of the War of the Spanish Succession, it was to experience one more brief spell of active service.

Throughout all this time the Old Pretender had remained in France, waiting for an oppor-

tunity to seize the throne that he thought was rightfully his. Queen Anne died childless in August 1714 and, in order to secure the Protestant succession, the Elector of Hanover, a great-grandson of James I through his mother, was invited to take the throne and was crowned George I. Even during Anne's final illness, Jacobite agents had been frequenting London's coffee-houses to try to woo Army officers to their cause, but with little success. George I, however, was initially very unpopular on account of his Germanic ways and lack of English, as well as because of fears that he would immediately embroil Britain in another continental war. Now seemed the moment for the Old Pretender to strike. In August 1715 the Earl of Mar raised the Jacobite standard at Braemar, seized the Scottish east coast ports and began to advance southward. The Government reacted by quickly reactivating no less than 26 additional regiments, and also bringing 6000 troops across from Holland. Lacking any artillery, the rebels were not able to capture any of the major towns in Scotland and, with their forces divided into three, they were defeated in detail, although one column succeeded in reaching as far south as Preston in Lancashire. By the time the Old Pretender himself had landed in Scotland in January 1716, the rising was virtually over, and the new regiments were disbanded once more.

Peacetime soldiering had little to commend it for most. Much of the time of the rank and file was

Top, far left: George Daraugh of Rich's Dragoons (now the Queen's Royal Irish Hussars), commissioned by George II on the field of Dettingen for gallantry.

Above left: King George II at Dettingen, 1743.

Pages 32/33: Second Jacobite Rebellion. Battle of Prestonpans, September 1745.

Left: 'You fire first, Sir.' Fontenoy, 1745. The incident was not entirely an example of polite behaviour. The unit holding its fire ready to fire second could expect to gain a tactical advantage.

Far left: Defeating Jacobites and Spanish troops at Glenshiel (1719), the Scots Dragoons (now the Royal Scots Dragoon Guards) and Colonel Clayton's Regiment of Foot (now the Prince of Wales's Own Regiment of Yorkshire).

Above: The defeat of Bonnie Prince Charlie's forces at Culloden, 16 April 1746. Note the detachment of 42nd Highlanders (now the Black Watch) in the foreground.

Right: Clive of India.

taken up with drill, but then at the time this was the very lifeblood of soldiering, without which a unit could not hope to survive on the battlefield. This, however, filled only part of his day, and during the remainder he was often left to his own devices. Since recreational pursuits were not organised, all that was left was the bottle, and, encouraged by the fact that soldiers were billeted in inns, drunkenness was very much part of the military way of life. This and the severe punishments meted out in cases of ill discipline brutalised the soldier; but then in many ways it was a brutal age. In theory his pay was reasonable by the standards of the day. He received two shillings and sixpence per day if he was a cavalry trooper, one shilling and twopence if a dragoon, and eightpence if an infantry private. But out of this he was expected to pay for his food, lodging and equipment, which included that of his horse if he was a cavalryman. These expenses and other, often unofficial stoppages left him with very little to spend on his own pleasures. In terms of uniform he was subject to a two-year cycle. In the first year he received a new coat, a waistcoat, breeches, a pair of strong stockings, two shirts with neckcloths and a hat. During the second year his coat would be converted into a waistcoat and he would receive a new one, as well as a change of other clothing. In practice, though, he would often find himself issued with old worn clothing instead, the resultant profit lining the pocket of his colonel or captain. They in their turn were being sold short by the civilian clothing contractor, and the government, in order to keep the costs of the Army to the minimum, was dunning them all.

For the officer there was not much encouragement to take his profession seriously. Within the regiment there was little for him to do and hence for much of the time he took leave of absence, whether officially authorised or not. Many bright young sparks would spend their time in London and, as a character in a contemporary play said when asked to give proof of his military prowess: 'I had lodgings in Charing Cross; I kept a bank at a gaming table; I have broke windows with field officers and have been tossing subalterns in blankets.' Gambling gave bored officers something of the excitement of the battlefield, but a milder form was to take out a life insurance policy on another officer, and a number of insurance brokers specialised in this form of risk.

Duelling was another diversion, which plagued the Army well into the nineteenth century, as it did civilian life as well. It was for this reason that the topics of women, politics and religion were banned in officers' messes, a rule that remained in force until recent times, because they were the three subjects most likely to inflame tempers.

Only a minority of the Army was stationed at home and those battalions posted to the colonies would expect to remain overseas for a very long time. Thus the 38th Foot (later the South Staffordshire Regiment) were sent to the West Indies in 1706 and remained there for almost 60 years. While their colonel was deprived of his commission for managing to avoid going, many officers faced with the prospect of a long overseas tour managed to exchange into other regiments, albeit for a financial consideration. Nevertheless there were dedicated regimental officers who were prepared to go with their men, who of course had no choice in the matter. The West Indies was the worst station of all. The insanitary conditions in which the troops lived made them especially vulnerable to yellow fever, and regiments were quickly decimated. It was service here that inspired some officers to compose a drinking song which ran as follows:

Cut off from the land that bore us,
Betrayed by the land we find,
When the brightest have gone before us,
And the dullest remain behind,

There is no time for repentance,
'Tis folly to yield to despair,
When a shudder may finish a sentence,
Or death put an end to a prayer.

So stand with your glasses steady,
'Tis all we have left to prize,
Quaff a cup to the dead already,
And one to the next who dies.

Army life during this period was not, however, entirely stagnant. Artillery had been organised on a permanent basis in 1716, and in 1722 became the Royal Regiment of Artillery. Likewise, although military engineers had been recognised as specialists in their own right since 1683, it was finally in 1717 that they were given formal recognition and placed, along with the Royal Artillery, under the Ordnance Office, although their officers did not begin to receive the King's Commission until 1757. The enlisted men in the military engineers were kept as a separate organisation, forming companies of military artificers. It would not be until 1856 that the Corps of Royal Engineers, as we now know it, was formed from these two branches. The officers of the two 'scientific' corps, unlike the remainder of the Army, were appointed and did not purchase their commissions, and in 1741 the Royal Military Academy Woolwich, affectionately known as The Shop, was founded in order to carry out artillery and engineer officer training, a task it continued until the outbreak of war in 1939.

The long peace began to crumble when in 1739 a trade squabble broke out with Spain, called 'the War of Jenkins' Ear' after an English sea captain who allegedly had his ear torn off by the Spaniards. Although it was essentially a naval war, an amphibious expedition against the

Spanish port of Cartagena in New Grenada, South America was planned. Ten regiments of marines and seven regiments of foot were raised, but it took a long time to bring the expedition to fruition, and it did not arrive off Cartagena until March 1742. Dissension between the naval and military commanders, along with an outbreak of yellow fever, did not help, and the attack itself met with a bloody repulse.

Above: North America. Combining with the Royal Navy in the capture of Louisburg, 1745.

Left: A soldier of the 42nd Regiment of Foot (the Black Watch), the first Highland Regiment.

Meanwhile war had broken out once more on the continent of Europe. Once again it was over the succession to a throne, this time Austria's. The old Emperor, Charles VI, had died in 1740 and had no male heir. His daughter Maria Theresa succeeded, but the French, who had hoped that their ally the Elector of Bavaria would be chosen, invaded Silesia. The British Prime Minister, Walpole, tried desperately to keep his country out of it, but concern to protect Hanover and general war fever proved too much for him, and in 1742, with the country once more at war, he resigned. This time the British were allied with the Dutch and the Austrians against the French, the Spanish, with whom Britain was at war anyway, and the Prussians, led by the youthful Frederick, soon to become one of the most famous soldiers of all times. An army of 62,000 men was raised, 16,000 of whom went to Flanders under Lord Stair. The latter was even more frustrated in his dealings with the Dutch than Marlborough had been, and little occurred in this theatre during 1742. Consequently for the 1743 campaign Stair took his contingent into Germany, where he joined King George II, who like Stair was a veteran of Marlborough's campaigns, having been present at the Battle of Oudenarde, and who assumed overall command, the last time that a British monarch would personally lead his troops in battle. They clashed with the French at Dettingen on 26 June.

Mistakes on the French side, combined with the steadiness of the infantry, turned impending defeat into victory. Indeed the French commander, Marshal Noailles, likened the Allied infantry to a wall of brass 'from which there issued so brisk and well sustained fire that the oldest officers owned that they had never seen anything like it, incomparably superior to our own.' While there were no medals in those days to reward individual acts of gallantry, the King commissioned Trooper George Daraugh of the 4th Dragoons in the field, and Trooper Thomas Brown of the King's Own Dragoons was given an even more signal honour. During a battle with the French horse Brown saw his regimental standard slip from the hand of the wounded cornet who was carrying it. As he tried to recover it he was attacked by a Frenchman, who cut off two of his fingers and seized the standard. Brown's terrified horse now bolted to the rear of the French cavalry but, undeterred, Brown found the gendarme once more, killed him and retook the standard. Locking it between his knee and

the saddle, he fought his way back through the French, suffering no less than seven wounds to his face and body. This illustrates not only the regard that all ranks of a regiment had for their standards, guidons and colours, but also the toughness of the soldiers of those days, and Brown was knighted on the field of battle by the King himself.

Little else happened during 1744, but the next year the King's son, the Duke of Cumberland, who was in command of the Allied army in Flanders, clashed with the very experienced Marshal Saxe at Fontenoy, south of Tournai. Cumberland somewhat foolishly attacked the French, who were superior in numbers and well entrenched, and was beaten back with heavy losses, although the French too suffered badly. It was at this battle that a somewhat apocryphal story originated, which illustrates something of the gentlemanly way in which eighteenth-century battles were often fought. A British infantry column led by Lord Charles Hay came across a French column. Both halted, and the

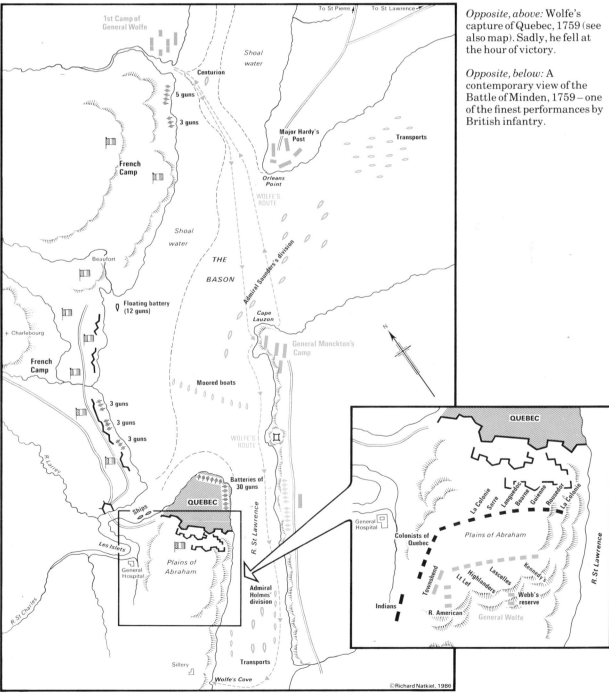

Opposite, above: Wolfe's capture of Quebec, 1759 (see also map). Sadly, he fell at the hour of victory.

Opposite, below: A contemporary view of the Battle of Minden, 1759 – one of the finest performances by British infantry.

© Richard Natkiel, 1986

Above: East India Company troops drilling at Bombay, 1767.

Above right: James Wolfe and his officers on the eve of taking Quebec.

officers doffed their hats to one another. Hay then toasted the French with his flask and called upon his men to cheer the enemy. Hay is then supposed to have said to his opposite number, although he afterwards denied it: 'Sir, be good enough to open fire.' The Frenchman replied: 'No sir, we never fire first' and then promptly did so.

Immediately after Fontenoy, trouble blew up nearer home. In June 1745 Charles Edward Stuart, son of the Old Pretender and known as the Young Pretender or more popularly as Bonnie Prince Charlie, landed in the Highlands of Scotland with a few companions and the clans flocked to him. Before the scattered Army garrisons could be concentrated, Prince Charles had occupied Edinburgh, won a victory at Prestonpans, and moved south across the border. In London panic set in, and the Duke of Cumberland and many regiments were recalled from Flanders. The Jacobites, who had reached Derby, decided to withdraw. Cumberland followed them and eventually brought them to bay at Culloden Moor near Inverness in April 1746. The severity with which Cumberland put down the rebels in the aftermath earned him the name of Butcher; among the measures he introduced was that the Highlanders were to be denied the right to wear the kilt, and all existing tartans were suppressed. It was this that gained one Highland Regiment, the first to be formed, its current title. The 42nd Highlanders had been raised originally in 1729 to help keep the peace in Scotland. They had campaigned under Cumberland on the Continent, but also had to change their tartan, adopting the present green and black. It being dark, they called themselves in Gaelic *Am Freiceadan Dubh* or the Black Watch to distinguish themselves from *Saughdeoran Dearg* or the Red Soldiers of the English. Such was the government's distrust of the Highlanders, though, that it would be some 30 years before other Highland regiments were raised.

The War of the Austrian Succession dragged on until 1748, when it was brought to an end by the Treaty of Aix-la-Chappelle. In the meantime the war had taken on another dimension, that of colonial rivalry between Britain and France in both India and North America. In India both countries had trading posts run by their national East India Companies. In order to defend them they had both European and native troops paid for by the companies, and also enlisted the aid of local rulers. During the 1740s the French, under their Governor Dupleix, were in the ascendant, but slowly the British began to fight back. Three characters in particular came to the fore, and their military exploits were notable for the fact that they were consistently vastly outnumbered by their foes. Major Stringer Lawrence was in command of the East India Company's troops at the time, and his achievements are succinctly summarised underneath his bust in Westminster Abbey: 'For Discipline established, Fortresses protected, Settlements extended, French and Indian armies defeated and Peace restored in the Carnatic.' One who left his lowly clerk's desk to join Lawrence was Robert Clive, who proved to be a natural soldier. In 1751, with a party of just 300 men, he captured the capital of Chanda Sahib, Nabob of the Carnatic, who was under the influence of the French, and held it for two months against a vastly superior enemy. At the Battle of Plassey in 1757 his 3500 men put 50,000 to flight, and he went on to become the first Governor-General of India, although he was later accused of bribery. The final character was the now almost forgotten Major Thomas Adams, who with just 3000 men fought four major actions and captured two major forts and 500 cannon, defeating an army of 40,000, all in four months, and retired to Calcutta to die of exhaustion. Long after he had been buried came news that he had been promoted Brigadier General for his achievements.

In America the French, centred on Quebec, were trying to prevent the British from expanding their colonies westward over the Alleghenies. Because of the vast tracts of forest and the great lakes communications were very bad, and both sides tried to establish their influence by building forts. At the time the British were reliant on local colonial militias, but thwarted in their attempts to build a fort on the Ohio and seeing the French succeed in building Fort Duquesne there, the Government decided to send a regular force under General Braddock to force the issue. Authority was also given to raise two regular regiments from among the colonists themselves, one of which was later to become one of the British Army's first rifle regiments. Originally called the 62nd Loyal North American Provincials, its title was shortly afterward changed to the 60th (Royal American) Regiment of Foot and later the 60th King's Royal Rifle Corps. Braddock, however, met with early disaster, when shortly after his arrival in 1755 his column was ambushed on its way to Fort Duquesne by the French and their Red Indian allies. Although he had put out scouts his red-coated infantry were easy targets, and the trees made their volley firing ineffective. Braddock himself was killed, but one of the survivors was Colonel George Washington, whose Virginia Militia had taken part in the abortive expedition to the Ohio the previous year. As a result of this the 60th Foot was turned into a light infantry formation, armed with the long American hunting rifle and dressed in the soft leather clothing worn by the frontiersmen.

It was inevitable that these colonial struggles should spill over into Europe and in 1756 the Seven Years War began. This time Prussia, Britain and Russia sided against France and Austria. Britain's initial fear was that France would invade her; there were not sufficient troops in the country and, given the poor state of the militia, Hanoverian and Hessian troops had to be brought across to defend it. The loss of Minorca that year, however, brought a new Prime Minister to office: William Pitt The Elder, later Lord Chatham, who was to become one of Britain's finest war ministers. He immediately reorganised the Army, sending the German troops home, and enlarging the standing army in Britain to 30,000 men by raising a second battalion for each regiment. The Royal Artillery and the engineer branch were also enlarged. Furthermore, he reformed the militia so that it could take

an effective part in the defence of the country, charging the Lord-Lieutenant of each county with the provision of 1600 men, who would serve a three-year term. There was a mandatory one month's training per year and the militia could be called upon to serve anywhere in the country.

Nevertheless matters continued to go badly, with the Duke of Cumberland, who had a small army in Hanover, being forced to come to terms with the French when they invaded, and the loss of further forts in Canada. Only Clive's victory at Plassey and Frederick the Great's at Rossbach and Leuthen brought any cheer. In 1758 the situation improved, the French being driven out of Hanover, and in Canada three separate thrusts on Quebec, Montreal and Fort Duquesne made good progress. Pitt could spare few troops to help Frederick and subsidised him with money instead, although by the end of 1758 he had been able to send a sizeable contingent to Germany. It was 1759, however, which was to be the *annus mirabilis*. At sea Admiral Hawke destroyed a French fleet at Quiberon Bay, while on 1 August an Anglo-Hanoverian army under the Duke of Brunswick decisively defeated the French at Minden. This battle was noteworthy in that it was not the cavalry under Lord George Sackville (afterward Minister for War and the Colonies during the American War of Independence) but six battalions of British infantry who delivered the decisive attack. Supported by the Hanoverians and artillery, they unusually succeeded in brushing aside the French cavalry and breaking their line. As it happened they had passed through a rose garden on their way to the battlefield and had plucked flowers to wear in their hats. The descendants of these regiments continue to celebrate Minden Day each year by continuing the custom of 'Minden Roses'. Another British force under General James Wolfe captured Quebec the following month. In a brilliant night operation they surprised the French under Montcalm by landing from the St

Above: Close quarter fighting at the Battle of Bunker Hill.

Left: Private of the picket or duty company of the 11th Foot (now the Devonshire and Dorset Regiment) c1771.

Above: Cornwallis surrenders to the Americans at Yorktown, 1781.

Below: General Sir George Elliot, commander of the garrison, and his staff at the great siege of Gibraltar during the American War of Independence.

By 1760 the British Army establishment was larger than it had ever been – 120,000 men and 20,000 embodied militia. The Government was also paying for the services of 55,000 German troops. During that year the victories continued. Amherst captured Montreal and in India Sir Eyre Coote defeated the French at Wandewash, the French power in both regions being broken. In Germany there was victory at Warburg. Here the cavalry redeemed its failure at Minden with a brilliant charge, during the course of which the commander, the Marquis of Granby, lost his wig. This occurrence is still recognised through several public house signs and the expression 'to go bald-headed into things.' The Treaty of Paris of 1763 finally brought the war to an end and resulted in a vast consolidation and expansion of Britain's empire, all of which needed to be policed and defended.

The large wartime army was run down to a strength of 45,500, of which 16,000 men were earmarked for overseas garrisons, 12,000 remained in Ireland and 17,500 in mainland Britain. It was, however, from the colonies that the next trouble arose. The American colonists had been growing increasingly discontented. They were governed from Westminster, 4000 miles away, and especially resented the fact that taxes were imposed on them without representation in parliament. Furthermore they were not allowed to trade independently. The war that became ever more likely eventually burst into flame in April 1775, when General Gage, commanding the British troops in Boston, sent out a detachment to Concord to seize some arms being stored by the militia there. When it reached Lexington the militia opened fire and, using trees and hedgerows as cover, drove the troops back into Boston. The Americans now tried to bottle the British up in the town. To foil this, the British

Lawrence river at the foot of the formidable Heights of Abraham, scaling them and then defeating the French on the plain in front of the city. Sadly Wolfe himself fell at the hour of victory. He was only in his early thirties but had already established his reputation as a military commander. He had been commissioned at the age of 14, a not unusual occurrence in those days, when commissions were even bought for babes in arms, and was adjutant of his regiment at Dettingen at the age of 16. (Indeed, Cornet John Floyd saw action with Eliott's Light Horse [later the 15th Hussars] at the age of 13 at the Battle of Emsdorf in June 1760. He took part in no less than five cavalry charges on that day and then obtained two years' leave of absence to complete his schooling.) As for Wolfe such was the esteem in which he was held that thereafter the regiments with him at Quebec wore a double line of black in their gold braid as a sign of mourning.

attacked the strongly fortified Breed's Hill outside Charlestown on the peninsula in Boston Harbour. Twice the British infantry were thrown back by the colonists, only capturing the hill on the third attempt because the Americans had run out of ammunition. Even then, as General Burgoyne noted: '. . . the retreat was no flight; it was even covered by bravery and military skill, and proceeded no further than to the next hill [Bunker's Hill], where a new post was taken.' The colonists would not be easy to defeat.

The Americans appointed the experienced George Washington to be their overall commander, but he found it an uphill struggle to get the scattered groups of men throughout the Thirteen Colonies to co-operate in a concerted overall plan. The British also had organisational problems. The command and control structure was ungainly, to say the least. Sackville, now Lord Germain, the same man who had failed to charge at Minden, conducted the overall strategy from London, in his capacity as Secretary of State for the Colonies, in concert with the Commander-in-Chief in America. The other commanders in America were never clear whether they should be taking orders from Germain or from the Commander-in-Chief. This confusion, together with the time it took for orders from London to reach the field commanders, hardly increased the chances of victory. The British Government, instead of sending immediately regular reinforcements from Britain, relied on the local recruitment of loyalists to provide the numbers of men needed, and when this failed had to call on German mercenaries, although these did prove to be good troops, especially the Hessians.

During 1776 the American Benedict Arnold drove into Canada and took Montreal, but was turned back when he tried to capture Quebec. General Howe, having decided to evacuate Boston, concentrated 30,000 men at New York. A plan was now gradually evolved whereby Howe would advance north to Albany and link up with Burgoyne coming south from Canada. At the beginning of 1777 Washington defeated a British force under Cornwallis at Trenton and secured New Jersey. Howe decided that he must defeat Washington first before going north to join Burgoyne. In June Burgoyne set forth, unaware that Howe was still heavily engaged against Washington. By October Burgoyne had reached Saratoga, 100 miles north of his objective, but his men were exhausted by the long march and their supplies had almost given out. Surrounded by General Gates' troops, they had no alternative but surrender. Lieutenant Colonel John Hill of the 9th Foot tore his regiment's colours from their staffs, loath to compound the disgrace that he felt, and hid them in his baggage while he was a prisoner until he was exchanged in 1781, when he presented them to King George III, who promoted him for his pains. Saratoga encouraged the French, still smarting from their defeats in the Seven Years War, to join the Americans, and a contingent under Lafayette was sent out to help them. In 1779 both Spain and Holland also joined the Americans, and Britain found herself isolated in Europe. These additions to the American strength were more than welcome, for in spite of Saratoga the Americans had been hard pressed in the north, with Washington forced to spend the miserable winter of 1777-78 at Valley Forge. In 1779 the British turned their attention to the southern states and won a string of victories, but the various commanders disagreed on the strategy to be followed to regain the initiative in the north. The eventual result of this lack of co-ordination was that Cornwallis found himself shut up in Yorktown. He hoped that he would be relieved by a British fleet, which never arrived, and on 17 October 1781 he too was forced to surrender.

Yorktown marked the end of the fighting in America, and the American colonies were effectively lost, although this was not finally confirmed until 1783, when the Treaty of Versailles ended the war. Elsewhere the fighting continued. Franco-Spanish might resulted in the seizure of a number of West Indian islands from the British, but Admiral Rodney destroyed the French fleet under de Grasse at the Battle of the Saintes near Dominica in 1782 and partially restored Britain's military influence in the Caribbean. Nearer to home, Minorca was lost once more, but in a four-year siege, which lasted until the formal end of the war, Gibraltar held out against the French and Spanish. Nowhere was the tenacity of the British soldier, constantly under bombardment and on virtually starvation rations, better tested. Even today this test of endurance and fortitude is commemorated in the Castle cap badge of the Royal Anglian Regiment, whose ancestor, the 12th Foot (Suffolk Regiment), was with the garrison throughout.

While Gibraltar seemingly restored the reputation of the British Army, it should be remembered that the British Army did win several victories in North America, and although the American colonists proved to be a doughty opponent, it was the higher direction of the war and the weight lent by the colonists' European allies which really decided the issue. Within a few years, however, Britain was to find herself involved in the longest European conflict that she had experienced since the Hundred Years' War four centuries previously.

Below: A British success – the recapture of the island of Jersey from the French, January 1781.

THE NAPOLEONIC ERA
1789-1815

Above: The Duke of York, much maligned Commander-in-Chief of the Army.

Previous page: The Battle of Famars, May 1793.

Below: A satirical view by Cruikshank of the Fencibles. The original caption is, 'Hampshire Fencibles protecting their Bacon.'

Inevitably, with the coming of peace once more in 1783, the Army contracted in size, this time to 52,000 men, higher than the establishment fixed after the Seven Years War. Even after the loss of the American colonies, however, 6400 men were needed in India, where fighting continued almost unceasingly as the British attempted to widen their influence over the native rulers. More serious was the grave deterioration in the state and efficiency of the troops at home. The post of Commander-in-Chief was left vacant and the Secretaries of State were hopelessly inefficient. Recruiting was well down, perhaps not surprisingly since the rates of pay had not changed for over 100 years, and new equipment was in short supply because of government parsimony. Abuses of the purchasing system flourished. Sir Walter Scott, the eminent Victorian novelist, wrote of this period: 'We know ourselves of one fair dame who drew the pay of captain in the —— Dragoons and was probably not much less fit for the service than some who at that period actually did duty.' Likewise a satirist advised officers: 'If the major or adjutant advises you learn the manual, the salute or other parts of the exercise . . . you may answer, that you do not want to be a Drill-sergeant or corporal – or that you purchased your commission and did not come into the army to be made a machine of.'

In spite of this some thought was given to a future war in Europe. In 1788 Colonel (later General Sir David) Dundas published his *Principles of Military Movement.* Influenced by the tactics of the colonists, the British Army had adopted very much looser formations than hitherto, and Dundas argued that these would not stand up to disciplined European troops. A more rigid drill like that of the Prussians was required, and also a standard manual of tactics. While he ignored the value of light infantry in

America, much of what Dundas said made sense, and four years later his suggested drills were officially adopted. While many criticised their rigidity, they undoubtedly contributed to the steadiness that the infantry of the line would display in the years to come.

Meanwhile events in France were taking on a sinister air. The economic burden of the almost ceaseless wars which France had been waging over the past 100 years had fallen increasingly on the common people, who saw themselves becoming increasingly poor while the aristocracy grew richer. Discontent grew and finally exploded on 14 July 1789, when the Paris mob stormed the fortress of the Bastille, for so long the hated symbol of the monarchy. Within two years Louis XVI had fled Paris and been arrested, and this, combined with the revolutionary fervour which was now beginning to sweep Europe, made sovereigns fear for their thrones. Accordingly Austria and Prussia declared war on the new republic and invaded it but their highly disciplined armies were turned back by the seemingly mob-like French revolutionaries at Valmy in September 1792. The Prime Minister William Pitt the Younger, son of the Earl of Chatham, was determined to keep Britain out of the war but now the revolutionaries declared that they were prepared to 'liberate' other countries suffering under the 'yoke of repression' and occupied Belgium and Savoy, threatening Britain's ally Holland. Then in January 1793 Louis XVI was guillotined, and France declared war on Britain and Holland.

To bolster her ally, Britain sent a small expeditionary force to Holland under the King's second son, Frederick Duke of York. Here they were joined by 20,000 German mercenaries, giving the Duke a force of 27,000 men, which was to operate in conjunction with Austrian and Dutch forces.

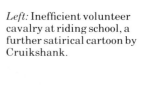

The Allies, however, each selected a different objective, Pitt ordering the Duke of York to capture Dunkirk. Its fortifications proved no match even for the Duke's ill-equipped siege train. He did not, however, have sufficient forces to invest the town properly, and was soon forced to withdraw to Ostend by a relieving force. There was a unique occurrence at one of the skirmishes which preceded the siege. At Famars in May the 14th Foot was faced by a superior French force. The French were playing the famous revolutionary air *Ça Ira*, and the Colonel of the 14th ordered his band to play the same air: 'Come along my lads, we'll break them to their own damn tune!' This they did, and the present regiment, the Prince of Wales' Own Regiment of Yorkshire, retains *Ça Ira* as its Quick March, the only march gained on the battlefield. For the next year, 1794, Pitt decided to reinforce the Duke with a further 10,000 men. Among them was the 33rd Foot, then commanded by the young Arthur Wellesley. In the meantime an Allied expedition against

Left: James Gillray's view of the Duke of York's campaign in the Low Countries. The Duke eats heartily, served by starving soldiers.

Toulon, designed to bolster the French Royalists, met with failure, a major contribution being made by the French artillery commanded by one Napoleon Buonaparte.

The 1794 campaign in the Low Countries went no better than that of 1793, despite the reinforcements. By the end of the year the Duke had been driven out of Holland and, singularly ill-equipped to spend the winter in the open, he withdrew his army to Hanover, where the Hanoverian General Walmoden wrote to the Duke: 'Your army is destroyed: the officers, their carriages, and a large train are safe, but the men are destroyed.' The message was plain, and in April 1795 the remnants were withdrawn to England.

This pointless expedition is still commemorated in the nursery rhyme:

The Grand Old Duke of York,
He had ten thousand men,
He marched them up to the top of the hill
And he marched them down again.

Yet the fault lay not with the Duke but with the shoddy tool that he had been given to carry out his task. Its failings were summed up by the Duke's Adjutant-General in Flanders, Major-General Sir James Craig:

'That we have plundered the whole country is unquestionable; that we are the most undisciplined, the most ignorant, the worst provided army that ever took the field is equally certain: but we are not to blame for it . . . there is not a young man in the Army that cares one farthing whether his commanding officer, the brigadier or the commander-in-chief approves his conduct or not. His promotion depends not on their smiles or frowns. His friends can give him a thousand pounds with which to go to the auction rooms in Charles Street and in a fortnight he becomes a captain. Out of 15 regiments of cavalry and of 26 infantry which we have here, 21 are commanded literally by boys or idiots . . . we do not know how to post a picquet or instruct a sentinel in his duty; and as to moving, God forbid that we should attempt it within three miles of an enemy.'

Typical of the young officers of the time was the celebrated Regency dandy Beau Brummell, who was a captain in the 10th Light Dragoons. Happy enough to serve with his regiment while it was at Brighton, the favourite watering place of the Prince Regent with whom he was very friendly, he felt forced to resign his commission when he heard that it was to be moved. As he said to the Prince Regent: 'I really could not go. Think, your Royal Highness – *Manchester!*'

Appointed Commander-in-Chief on his return from the Continent, the Duke of York was determined to institute reforms. While he could not end purchase, he at least insisted that officers were not to be allowed to purchase their next promotion step without spending a minimum length of time in their present rank. He stopped the custom of unofficial leave of absence and that of officers communicating direct with Ministers. He also instituted a system of confidential reports in order to judge whether an officer was worthy of promotion. Furthermore, he realised that one of the major failings in Flanders had been a lack of competent staff officers. Too often commanders had selected their staffs from their personal friends and relatives, with no thought as to the military prowess of the individuals con-

cerned. On the suggestion of Lieutenant Colonel (later Major-General) John Le Marchant, he instituted a military college at High Wycombe in 1799 at which officers could study at their own expense. It was Le Marchant, too, who drew up the first sword exercises for cavalry – all too often in Flanders cavalrymen had cut their horses' heads instead of the enemy. In 1802 an academy was opened for aspirants for commissions in the non-scientific arms, to be run along the same lines as Woolwich, and in 1812 this moved from Great Marlow to its present home at Sandhurst. Other reforms included the formation of a Royal Corps of Artificers, responsible for building fortifications, and the replacement of civilian drivers in the Royal Artillery by soldiers of the Royal Corps of Artillery Drivers. The Duke also turned his attention to the neglected art of light infantry, and instructed Sir John Moore to set up a training camp at Shorncliffe in Kent. The British Army owed him a great debt, and it was more than unjust that he was forced to resign in 1809, when his name became linked to a scandal involving an ex-mistress, Mary Anne Clarke, and the trafficking of commissions, even though he personally was not guilty of any malpractice.

No immediate attempt was made to send another army to the Continent. Indeed by 1797 Britain stood alone, all her allies apart from Portugal being knocked out of the war, and the French occupied the Low Countries, the Rhineland and northern Italy, which had been conquered as a result of a brilliant campaign by Napoleon Buonaparte. Even the Mediterranean

was barred to the Royal Navy for a time. At home there was an invasion scare when a small French force landed at Fishguard in South Wales, but they were seen off by the local militia, who fired their buttons when they ran out of ball. The following year the French tried another invasion, this time through Ireland, but the Irish rebels rose before the French could arrive. Although they had some success against the local militia, a regular force under General Lake, including militia from the mainland, put paid to their hopes, crushing them at the Battle of Vinegar Hill.

That same year Napoleon took an expedition to Egypt, and Pitt managed to persuade the Austrians and Russians to resume the fight. Horatio

Above: The evacuation of the Helder, November 1799, after the inconclusive Anglo-Russian expedition to Holland.

Opposite: The Irish rebels are defeated at Wexford, 1798. They were no match for disciplined troops.

Below: Sir Ralph Abercromby's forces landing to remove the French from Egypt, 1801.

The Battle of Alexandria, 21 March 1801.

Nelson succeeded in re-entering the Mediterranean, and defeated Napoleon's fleet at Aboukir Bay, off the Egyptian coast. Minorca was recaptured and the kingdom of Sicily entered the war on the Allied side. The year 1799 opened with much promise. The Austrians drove the French out of northern Italy and, with the Russians, invaded Switzerland, then held by the French. An Anglo-Russian expeditionary force was also landed in Holland, on the Helder Peninsula. It came to nothing, however, the numerous waterways and dykes being ideal defensive terrain, and the expedition was re-embarked. A series of plans for amphibious operations was also drawn up, and 80,000 troops were retained in Britain for this purpose. In the event only two expeditions were launched, against Cadiz and Ferrol, and both were failures, to a large extent because of the age-old problem of naval-military co-operation. Napoleon's army remained beleaguered in Egypt, but he himself returned to France, and in 1800 decisively defeated the Austrians at Marengo in Italy, while Moreau annihilated another Austrian army in Germany at the Battle of Hohenlinden.

Only in the Mediterranean and India could the British take any comfort. A force under the elderly but still very competent Sir Ralph Abercromby was landed in Egypt in 1800 and the following year, even though badly outnumbered, defeated the French and their Turkish allies at the Battle of Alexandria. It was here that the 28th Foot (now the Gloucestershire Regiment) earned both their Sphinx cap badge with 'EGYPT' inscribed underneath and the small back badge which they still wear on their headdress. Faced with a sudden French cavalry charge, they had no time to form a square, and the rear rank was given the order 'Right about face!' Back-to-back they repulsed the charge. Malta also fell into British hands, to become a vital naval base for the next 150 years. In India, meanwhile, the future Duke of Wellington was winning his spurs, sent there with his regiment, still the 33rd Foot (now called The Duke of Wellington's Regiment), at the beginning of 1797. His brother Richard had been appointed Governor-General and the task facing him was what to do with the aggressive ruler of Mysore, Tippoo Sahib, who was known to be in French pay.

Wellington found himself, with his 33rd, commanding a contingent of native troops provided by the Nizam of Hyderabad. He was to co-operate with two other forces, one under General Harris, whom Wellington would accompany, and the other under General Stuart. The task was the seizure of Tippoo Sahib's base at Seringapatam. It was very indicative of the style of campaigning in India in those days that the train accompanying Harris and Wellington, whose total fighting strength was about 40,000 men, comprised 150,000 followers and 120,000 transport animals

– donkeys, horses, bullocks, and elephants. In May 1799 Seringapatam was finally taken after nine days fighting and the troops indulged in an orgy of looting, one of the macabre items found being a mechanical tiger, with which Tippoo Sahib used to torture his victims. Wellington remained in charge of Mysore for the next four years. In 1803 he was involved in war against the Maharattas. He seized the fortress of Ahmednaggar in a manner which caused a Maharatta chief to remark: 'These Englishmen are strange people, and their general a wonderful man. They came here in the morning, looked at the pettah wall, walked over it, killed all the garrison, and returned to breakfast.' His crowning moment came, however, in September 1803 at Assaye, when with 20,000 men he decisively defeated an enemy 50,000 men strong. He had three horses shot under him and his orderly was killed, but retained his coolness, one of his great characteristics in battle, throughout. He always considered Assaye to be his greatest battle. Eighteen months later he returned to England, his reputation as a general firmly established.

Back in Europe, the Second Coalition had by now collapsed in the face of French successes in 1800 and 1801 and Britain once more stood alone, but after almost 10 years of war the country was weary and Pitt decided to come to terms with Napoleon, who was now undisputed master of France. The Treaty of Amiens was signed in 1802 and the country was able to pause for breath while checking to see whether 'Boney' really wanted peace.

An unusual and interesting experiment was taking place at this time. In the spring of 1800, as a result of experience gained in the Helder and elsewhere, an Experimental Corps of Riflemen had been formed at Horsham in Sussex to provide a skirmishing force of marksmen to cover both advance and retreat. They were dressed in bottle-green uniform, taken from the German *jägers*, and armed with the Baker rifle, which had an effective range of up to 500 yards. Drawn from 15 regiments, the Corps represented the cream of the army in Britain. Apart from their distinctive uniform and the fact that they were armed with the rifle, as opposed to the smoothbore musket, they were notable for their novel attitude to discipline. Colonel Coote Manningham, their commanding officer, laid down in his standing orders that:

'Every inferior, whether officer or soldier, shall receive the lawful commands of his superior with deference and respect, and shall execute them to the best of his power. Every superior in his turn, whether he be an Officer or a Non-commissioned Officer, shall give his orders in the language of moderation and of regard to the feelings of the individual under his command; abuse, bad language or blows being positively forbid in the Regiment.'

This ran entirely counter to the Prussian-style discipline of the Army in general. Coote Manningham also laid down that every man was to be encouraged to use his initiative rather than

Above: The storming of Montevideo, February 1807. Whitelocke's expedition would, however, end in disaster.

Below: Cruikshank's view of the Militia at drill, 'The Auckward Squad,' contrasts with the picture of Pitt, opposite.

merely be an unthinking automaton. For the first time in the British Army the officers were to encourage their men to play sport. A regimental library was set up, along with a school for reading, writing, geometry and arithmetic, to encourage riflemen to qualify themselves for promotion. Regimental medals for Good Conduct, Long Service and Special Merit were also instituted. Rifle companies took part in the expedition to Ferrol and the Battle of Copenhagen in April 1801, when Nelson neutralised the Danish fleet.

When war broke out once more in 1803, the Experimental Corps of Riflemen was retitled the 95th (Rifle) Regiment (it was later called the Rifle Brigade) and brigaded with two other battalions, the 43rd and 52nd Foot (later 1st and 2nd Battalions The Oxfordshire and Buckinghamshire Light Infantry), under Sir John Moore at Shorncliffe to form the famous Light Brigade. Moore built on Coote Manningham's philosophy, instituting command by bugle, which would carry farther than voice, and adopting a new style of marching designed 'to bring down the feet easily without shaking the upper part of the body'. Fieldcraft and skirmishing through fire and movement were also emphasised.

Another welcome reform at this time was the abolition of the pigtail. Up until then soldiers had worn their hair in a pigtail, but it also had to be dressed in a mixture of flour and water, which was very time-consuming. In 1805 this was finally done away with and the soldier merely had to keep his hair short. The old custom is still, however, commemorated by one regiment today. The Royal Welch Fusiliers were at sea when the order was promulgated and were the last regiment to carry it out. Every member of the regiment continues to wear the 'Flash', a bunch of five 9-inch-long black ribbons attached to the back of the collar to signify the black leather bag in which the pigtail used to be placed to protect the uniform from grease and powder.

During the years 1803-5, Britain was under continuous threat of invasion by Napoleon, and once again she had to look to her reserve forces to help bear the burden of defending her shores. In the 1790s two further forces had been raised. The first were the Volunteers, raised by private subscription. They considered themselves socially superior to the militia, in which service was mandatory, and many drew away from it. The Regular Army was desperately in need of recruits, but could not draw them automatically from the militia, which was a separate organisation. A partial solution to the problem was the Fencibles. They were raised as part of the Regular Army, but strictly for the duration of the war and for home service only. The militia itself was also divided into two parts – the Old Militia, embodied for the duration, and the New or Supplementary Militia which was to be called out in emergencies only. All these forces were combined into the Army of the Reserve, and by 1805 the country had no less than 450,000 men under arms, which created an enormous problem in arming them. After Nelson's victory at Trafalgar in October 1805, the threat of invasion receded and the reserve forces were wound down. From then on, however, a form of conscription was introduced in that the Regular Army at

various times called on the militia to furnish it with manpower, and indeed 40 per cent of its recruits came from this source.

The removal of the invasion threat meant that Britain could turn once again to regaining the initiative on land by sending expeditionary forces overseas. The early expeditions were marked, however, by the lack of a coherent overall strategy. In the autumn of 1805 a force was dispatched to the River Elbe in Germany in an ultimately unsuccessful attempt to clear the French out of Hanover. Half of the force was made up of mercenaries, who became the King's German Legion and were to fight well in Spain. With Napoleon's defeat of Austria at Ulm in October 1805 and of Prussia at Jena and Auerstadt exactly a year later, both countries sought terms, and the British force, now isolated, returned to England. A second force of 7000 men was sent to join the Russian and Neapolitan army in southern Italy, with the object of cooperating with the Austrian army in the north of the country. This force, however, had to withdraw to Sicily after the Austrian surrender. From here an expedition was mounted to regain Naples which was the first dent to the seeming invincibility of the French armies.

On 4 July 1806 just over 5000 men under Major-General Sir John Stuart clashed with 6500 Frenchmen under General Reynier at Maida. The French tactic at this time, which had proved so effective against other European armies, was to advance *en colonne* against the weak point in the enemy's line and to keep on attacking until the line broke. Stuart, however, deployed his men in long thin lines, which meant that they could bring more firepower to bear than the densely packed French and also take them in the flank. As the French columns advanced, the British held their fire until the enemy were at 100 yards distance, at which range the musket could be highly effective, and exchanged two or three volleys. The British then advanced to 70 yards and fired another volley, 30 yards and a volley and then they charged with the bayonet. This was too much for the French, who broke and ran, leaving a quarter of their strength dead or prisoners. As a French officer afterwards wrote: 'Such a thing has not been seen since the Revolution!' Yet the French would not change their tactics, and the 'Thin Red Line' would time and again prove an effective antidote. Lack of cavalry, however, meant that Stuart was not able to follow up his victory, and the fact that there were 50,000 French troops in southern Italy eventually forced him to withdraw from the mainland.

Another force was sent to the Cape of Good Hope, and the Dutch colony there was taken. Disaster, however, struck another expedition under General Whitelocke in South America. The idea was to foment revolt in Spain's colonies. While Montevideo was captured, Whitelocke was forced to surrender when attempting to capture Buenos Aires, and was lucky to be allowed to evacuate his men in safety from the country. Although the whole idea was poorly conceived, it was Whitelocke himself who had to pay the penalty and he was cashiered. More success was gained in another operation against Denmark in 1807. After Copenhagen had been bombarded

Right: A recruiting sergeant, identified by the ribbons in his hat, and some likely prospects.

Far right: Sir John Moore, as painted in 1805 by Sir Thomas Lawrence.

Below: The 10th Hussars (now the Royal Hussars) at Benevente during the retreat to Corunna.

Denmark left the war. A force under Sir John Moore spent six weeks sailing up and down the Swedish coast, hoping to land and co-operate with the Swedish Army, but the mad King Gustavus could not decide on how it should be employed and it sailed home. At the beginning of 1808, however, Napoleon sent an army to occupy the country of his supposed ally, Spain, towards which he had become increasingly dictatorial. The Spanish people raised the standard of revolt, and called for British help to remove the French. The moment had come at last for a coherent strategy.

In early July 1808 the future Duke of Wellington, still then Arthur Wellesley, was at Cork preparing for another expedition to South America when he was ordered to take his 12,000 men to Spain instead. Here he was joined by a further 5000 men already in the Mediterranean. Sir John Moore too, who had only just arrived back from Sweden, was ordered to take his force to the Peninsula. Wellesley's troops landed first on 1 August at Mondego Bay, near Oporto in Portugal. He now discovered that he had been placed at the bottom of a highly complex command structure. Two elderly generals, Sir Hew Dalrymple and Sir Harry Burrard, were placed at the top, Moore occupying the position of third-in-command. Then came another four generals and finally Wellesley. Nevertheless as the first to arrive he was to continue preparations to advance on Lisbon and clear the French under Marshal Junot out of Portugal. As Wellesley wrote to the Duke of Richmond: 'I hope that I shall have beat Junot before any of them arrive, then they will do as they please with me.' Having disembarked his force and been joined by expected reinforcements, Wellesley began his advance within a few days of landing and on 17 August had his first brush with the French at Roliça and drove them back. Four days later Junot, having moved out of Lisbon to drive Wellesley back into the sea, met him at Vimiero. His attacks on Wellesley's positions were disjointed and ill-

Right: Map of the major campaigns in the Peninsular War.

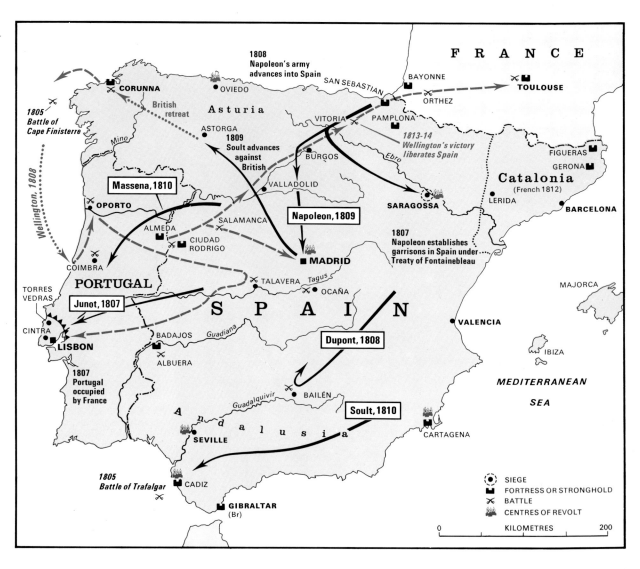

Below: A wounded piper of the 71st Foot (now Royal Highland Fusiliers) plays his comrades forward at Vimiero, 1808, one of Wellington's first victories in the Peninsula.

prepared, and were beaten off with little difficulty. Wellesley now wanted to pursue the French to Lisbon and beyond, but Burrard would not countenance this and the army remained where it was. Dalrymple now arrived, and at the same time the French, now in a precarious position, proposed that they should be allowed to evacuate Portugal. This was agreed to, and the French were embarked in British ships under the Convention of Cintra. There was an outcry in Britain and Portugal, and Dalrymple and Burrard were removed from command. Wellesley

too, as a signatory to the Convention, was sent home, which left Moore in command.

Moore had some 32,000 men and now planned to advance into Spain, hoping to co-operate with the Spanish army. Unfortunately at this juncture Napoleon, fresh from making peace with Prussia, chose to come to Spain himself with an army of 120,000 men. The Spanish were quickly broken, and Moore, having been forced to divert part of his force to cover Lisbon, found himself isolated and was forced to withdraw. The epic retreat to Corunna began on Christmas Eve 1808. In the bitter Iberian winter and with the French constantly harrying the British troops, it was to prove a severe test of endurance. Moore himself described something of the problem:

'At this season of the year in a country without fuel, it is impossible to bivouac; the villages are small, which obliges us to march by corps in succession. Our retreat therefore becomes much more difficult.'

A German commissary officer:

'Every minute a horse would collapse beneath its rider, and be shot dead. The road was strewn with dead horses, bloodstained snow, broken carts, scrapped ammunition, boxes, cases, spiked guns, dead mules, donkeys and dogs, starved and frozen soldiers, women and children.... The road frequently followed a zigzag course along the very edge of a precipice.... We waded through snow and mud over the bodies of dead men and horses. The howling wind as it whistled past the ledges of rock and through the bare trees, sounded to the air like the groaning of the damned.'

To the ordinary soldier, with the victories of Roliça and Vimiero behind him, the retreat made little sense and all were caught up in a sullen rage. Discipline suffered, and Moore wrote of his army: 'I can say nothing in its favour except that when there was a prospect of fighting the Enemy, the men were then orderly, and seemed pleased and determined to do their duty.' The burden of the fighting rested with the rearguard, which was composed of the Light Brigade, now commanded by General 'Black Bob' Craufurd. He commanded it with a rod of iron, on one occasion even halting to have three men flogged in spite of the fact that the enemy was close at hand. Without his leadership there is no doubt that the army would have disintegrated long before it reached its objective. Rifleman Harris, who served under him, later wrote: 'I do not think I ever admired any man who wore the British uniform more. . . .' Eventually, on 11 January 1809, the army reached Corunna where the fleet was waiting. Before embarkation could take place, however, the French had to be turned back. The tattered remnants finally had the chance they had been waiting for and drove the French off. Sadly, Moore himself was mortally wounded, but his army was able to get aboard the ships and sail back to England.

Within a few months the British army returned to Portugal. Wellesley, who had quickly overcome the slur on his name for his part in the Convention of Cintra, convinced Castlereagh, the Secretary of State for War, that Portugal could be held against the French with the help of a Portuguese army. Accordingly in April 1809 he returned with an army of 23,000 men. Three French armies were carrying out a converging advance on the Portuguese capital, Lisbon, and Wellesley saw his first task as removing this threat. In conjunction with the Portuguese he drove Soult out of northern Portugal, and then turned east to tackle Marshal Victor. For this he needed the co-operation of a Spanish army under General Cuesta, and he was also frustrated by lack of money. The troops had not been paid for some time and looting was rife. Victor was now reinforced, and Wellington with 20,000 men found himself up against 46,000 at Talavera at the end of July. For two days the battle raged before the French withdrew, suffering 7300 casualties to the British 5400. Although created Viscount Wellington for this victory, there was little that he could do to capitalise on it. The Spanish proved increasingly intractable, and another French army under Soult was threatening him from the south. Furthermore his men were almost starved of food. He therefore withdrew to the frontier of Portugal and then to the northern part of that country, where he spent the winter. While there Wellington constructed a line of fortifications between the River Tagus and the sea, the Lines of Torres Vedras.

Wellington was a master tactician. He had an especially good eye for country and the art of always being in the right place on the battlefield. What is often forgotten, however, is that he was a very sound logistician, and his victories in Portugal and Spain were won as much by this as by his skills on the battlefield. It was not so much that he was an innovator, more that he had a liking for order which was essential given the

still cumbersome command structure of the time. He did not have overall control over a number of vital elements in the army. His artillery chief was merely an adviser and was answerable to the Master-General of the Ordnance rather than to Wellington; likewise his chief engineer. His supplies and transport came under the Commissary-General, who operated on behalf of the Treasury. Given the bad state of the roads, as well as the inhospitable nature of the terrain, which Wellington recognised early on, a good logistic system was vital. During 1809 he was much frustrated

THE OLD SAUCY SEVENTH,

Or Queen's Own Regt. of Lt. Dragoons.

COMMANDED BY THAT GALLANT AND WELL KNOWN HERO,

Lieut. General HENRY LORD PAGET.

YOUNG Fellows whose hearts beat high to tread the paths of Glory, could not have a better opportunity than now offers. Come forward then, and Enrol yourselves in a Regiment that stands unrivalled, and where the kind treatment, the Men ever experienced is well known throughout the whole Kingdom.

Each Young Hero on being approved, will receive the largest Bounty allowed by Government.

A few smart Young Lads, will be taken at Sixteen Years of Age, 5 Feet 2 Inches, but they must be active, and well limbed. Apply to SERJEANT HOOPER, at

N. B. This Regiment is mounted on Blood Horses, and being lately returned from SPAIN, and the Horses Young, the Men will not be allowed to HUNT during the next Season, more than once a week.

BOOTH AND WRIGHT, PRINTERS, NORWICH.

Above: A typical recruiting poster. The Saucy Seventh are now the Queen's Own Hussars.

Below: 'Steady the Drums and Fifes!' by Lady Butler. the 57th Foot (later Middlesex, but now part of The Queen's Regiment) at Albuera, 1811, where they gained their 'Diehard' nickname.

Above: One of the most famous feats of arms of the Peninsular War. After being cut off by enemy cavalry, Captain Ramsay's troop of the Royal Horse Artillery limbered up their guns and charged to safety. Fuentes d'Onoro, 5 May 1811.

by the lack of co-operation from his commissaries, but from 1810 onward he had an excellent Commissary-General in Robert Kennedy. The army's main supply base was Lisbon and from here everything had to be brought up by mule train and bullock cart driven by locally recruited Portuguese. Wellington realised only too well that 'a soldier with a musket cannot fight without ammunition and that in two hours he can expend all he can carry.' The secret was the establishment of intermediate depots.

The soldier himself carried a heavy burden. In his large knapsack he had three pairs of shoes, with an extra pair of soles and uppers, spare socks, a shirt, his greatcoat and a blanket. Every six men were issued with a camp kettle, which they took it in turns to carry strapped on to the knapsack. At the hip he had a haversack containing a clasp knife, fork, spoon, tin mug and other personal items, together with three days' rations – the daily ration being 1 pound of beef and 1 of biscuit. In addition he had a filled water bottle, hatchet, musket – the Brown Bess, which had changed little over the past 100 years – bayonet and 80 rounds of ammunition. The officers, of course, were better off, but Wellington waged a constant battle over the amount of baggage they brought with them. It was not uncommon for them to arrive at their regiments with up to 10 baggage animals but Wellington reduced this to one animal for every two subalterns. As a result regiments did not run messes in the field, but each company's officers messed together, pooling their slender resources, which were often not more than the basic issue ration. Although the Duke was very strict in most matters, in officers' dress he was not. Elaborate waistcoats, hats adorned with plumes and luxurious moustaches were popular, but helped to maintain morale, as

Montgomery recognised when he commanded the Eighth Army nearly 150 years later. Only one aspect seems to have stuck in the Duke's gullet and that was the carrying of umbrellas on active service, a particular penchant of the Guards. He considered umbrellas 'not only ridiculous, but unmilitary.'

Until 1811, when tents were introduced, officers and men slept the night in the open, relying on their greatcoats and blankets. Nevertheless it was generally a very fit army. There were, of course, exceptions. Most of the survivors of the retreat to Corunna were sent to Walcheren off the Dutch coast in 1809 as part of an abortive plan to attack Antwerp and seize the Scheldt; 7000 men died and 14,000 had their health permanently ruined through malaria. For those wounded on the battlefield medical treatment was still basic. If badly wounded a soldier would more often than not expect to die, since it might be 24 hours or more before he was discovered. If he could walk he dragged himself to the rear, hoping to find the regimental surgeon. There were no anaesthetics, and surgery consisted either of probing the wound to extract a ball or fragments of metal, or, more often than not, amputation. Vinegar was the only antiseptic, and wounds often turned gangrenous, or the victim succumbed to typhus caused by lice. Convalescents were housed at the Peninsula Army's main depot at Belem on the outskirts of

Left: Royal Military Academy, Woolwich, 1810. Cadets and a typical barrack room.

Lisbon until they were fit enough to rejoin their regiments. Belem was also suspected by the fighting troops of holding many who preferred the fleshpots of Lisbon, such as they were, to active service. These individuals were dubbed 'Belem Rangers', as a century later they would be called 'base wallahs.' Nevertheless Dr McGrigor, the Duke's medical chief, was in many ways an enlightened man. One of his major innovations was the introduction of prefabricated hospitals, which could be set up near the battle area to ensure that the immediate treatment of the sick and wounded could take place under some form of shelter. The Duke, however, rejected his proposal to introduce the French idea of ambulances in which to carry the wounded.

Below: Contemporary view of Fuentes d'Onoro. Note the horse artillery in the centre.

Above: The storming of Ciudad Rodrigo, 9 January 1812.

Right: One of Wellington's most able divisional commanders, 'Daddy' Hill, who was Commander-in-Chief of the Army 1828-42. He wears the Peninsula Gold Cross around his neck.

In terms of the overall organisation of the Peninsular Army, Wellington introduced the division, and the army eventually consisted of five divisions, together with the Light Division, the successor to Craufurd's Light Brigade. Divisions consisted of two or three brigades, each normally of three or four battalions. It was also at this time that a recognisable staff system began to be introduced. Each brigade had a Brigade Major to assist the commander, a title which disappeared only in the early 1980s in favour of Brigade Chief of Staff in order to make the position more intelligible to Britain's NATO allies. Brigade and divisional commanders relied on aides-de-camp (ADCs) to carry messages about the battlefield, as did Wellington. He himself began to use his Quartermaster-General, Sir George Murray, more and more as a Chief of Staff. He also had a Military Secretary, who took much of the burden of the routine correspondence, although no letter ever left his headquarters without his personal approval. Yet it was often the voluminous and petty correspondence from London which irritated him. A believer in simple and straightforward administrative systems, he regarded much of this correspondence as inessential and merely serving to confuse and hinder. As he once complained to the Secretary of State for War:

'My Lord, If I attempted to answer the mass of futile correspondence that surrounds me, I should be debarred from all serious business of campaigning. . . . So long as I retain an independent position, I shall see no officer under my command is debarred by attending to the futile drivelling of mere quill-driving from attending to his first duty, which is and always has been so to train the private men under his command that they may without question beat any force opposed to them in the field.'

It is a message that every staff officer should have pinned above his desk.

A crucial factor in the success of Wellington's campaigns was the importance he placed on intelligence. The main source of this came from his British scouts led by Major Colquhoun Grant, of whom the Duke said 'he was worth a brigade to me.' These officers operated in uniform behind the enemy lines, sending back reports to the Duke. They co-operated with the Spanish guerrillas, who played a major role, especially in their frequent captures of French couriers. A further source was a number of Irish priests who were studying in seminaries in Portugal and Spain. Wellington was never, however, able to break the ciphers which the French often used, although many efforts to do so were made. Apart from the need to gain knowledge of the enemy's intentions and dispositions, Wellington also had to construct his own maps, since there was a dearth of them. This was a task largely carried out by his engineer officers, who relied heavily on the information given to them by patrols. The British soldier, however, with his constant interest in alcohol, tended to remember villages not by their names or layout but by the quality of wine to be found there!

The campaign of 1810 saw Wellington threatened by Massena, who, having captured the fortresses of Ciudad Rodrigo and Almeida, advanced down the River Mondego. At Busaco, on 26 September, Wellington turned on him and inflicted a short and bloody blow; once again controlled volley firing and timely bayonet charges proved more than a match for the French columns. Massena abandoned the main route and moved through the mountains round Wellington's left flank. It was now that the Lines of Torres Vedras came into their own. Wellington was able to retire behind them in good order, and Massena, finding it impossible to keep his men supplied, pulled back to Santarem. Both sides now stayed put until the new year, Wellington and his officers indulging in much foxhunting, several packs of hounds being brought out from England for this purpose.

In January 1811 Soult succeeded in capturing another important Spanish fortress, Badajos. In March a Spanish army threatened Victor who

was besieging Cadiz. Included in it was a British contingent of 5000 men who fought a gallant but costly action at Barrosa. On the day of this battle Massena suddenly pulled back to north of the Mondego. Wellington quickly followed up and fought a number of successful minor actions but he now began to have supply difficulties, so stopped and settled down to recapture Almeida. At the same time he sent Beresford with an Anglo-Portuguese force to recapture Badajos. At the beginning of May Massena attempted to raise the siege of Almeida, and there was three days' severe fighting at Fuentes d'Onōro, marked by several British cavalry charges. Wellington's men held firm, and Massena withdrew to Ciudad Rodrigo, Almeida falling once more into Allied hands. Wellington now hurried off to reinforce Beresford, who was being threatened by Soult. Before he arrived, however, Beresford had already fought the Battle of Albuera, repulsing the French but losing 40 per cent of his British troops. It was here that the 57th Foot (Middlesex Regiment) earned their nickname of the Diehards, having been exhorted by their colonel, as he lay mortally wounded, to 'Die hard, my men, die hard.' The regiment lost 423 men out of 570 engaged, and the day after the battle one of the drummer boys went to collect rations for his company and held out his cap to carry them in. He was the only survivor.

Wellington now tried to take Badajos, but his siege train was totally inadequate. The French threatened him with a superior force, so he abandoned the siege and moved north to Ciudad Rodrigo, where he experienced the same problem. With a large number of sick and shortage of money he now withdrew in order to pause for breath. At the end of the year the French decided to occupy Valencia, and troops were sent from Ciudad Rodrigo for this purpose. Wellington

quickly saw his opportunity and invested the fortress at the beginning of January 1812.

Siege warfare had changed little over the past three centuries. Once a fortress had been invested it was mainly a question of pounding away with artillery until a breach had been made. Meanwhile trenches would be dug forward to as close to the walls as possible so that the attacking force had the minimum of open ground to cross. The attackers themselves were led by what was

Below: The 88th (Connaught Rangers), 'The Devil's Own', storming the citadel at Badajos, 5 April 1812. This supposedly diversionary attack in fact won the battle, succeeding when the main assault failed.

called the Forlorn Hope, a small body of hand-picked volunteers responsible for securing the breach so that the main body could pass through. It was every dashing young officer's desire to lead a Forlorn Hope, but the chances of survival were not good. Ciudad Rodrigo itself, with its now weakened garrison, fell in ten days, although the final attack cost the 3rd and Light Divisions over 1000 casualties, including the Light Division's commander, Craufurd. The fortress captured, the British troops embarked on an orgy of looting, many, crazed by drink, turning on their officers who tried to restrain them. Not until well into the next day was order restored, with the chief culprits being flogged.

Flogging could often end in the death of the victim, a punishment of 500 lashes being not uncommon. As to how it felt, William Lawrence of the 40th Foot (the Prince of Wales's Volunteers (South Lancashire)) has left an account of what happened when he was awarded 400 lashes for absenting himself for 24 hours when on guard in 1809:

'. . .I was told to strip, which I did firmly, and without using the help that was offered me, as I had by that time got hardened to my lot. I was then lashed to the halberds, and the colonel gave the order for the drummers to commence, each one having to give me 25 lashes in turn. I bore it very well until I had received 175, when I got so enraged with the pain that I began pushing the halberds, which did not stand at all firm (being planted on stones), right across the square, amid the laughter of the regiment. The colonel I suppose thinking then that I had had sufficient "ordered the sulky rascal down" in those very words. Perhaps a more true word could not have been spoken, for indeed I was sulky. I did not give vent to a sound the whole time, though the blood ran down my trousers from top to bottom. I was unbound, and a corporal hove my shirt and jacket over my shoulder, and conveyed me to hospital. . . .'

For the majority of victims once was enough to reform them – Lawrence was promoted sergeant four years later – but there was always a small element of 'hardened criminals' who would come up before the halberds time and again.

Wellington now turned south to recapture Badajos, laying siege to it on 17 March. The final assault took place three weeks later. Again casualties were heavy, including six generals wounded and four battalion commanders killed. Again too there was an orgy of looting in the immediate aftermath. During this two young Spanish sisters who had had their jewellery ripped off by soldiers threw themselves on the protection of some officers of the 95th Rifles. One of them was Captain Harry Smith, who shortly afterwards married the younger sister, Juanita, who accompanied her husband for the remainder of the war and quickly became the darling of the army. Ladysmith in South Africa is named after her.

With the two main frontier forts now in his hands, Wellington could advance into Spain, and on 22 July he fought Marmont at Salamanca and drove him back. He entered Madrid in triumph in the middle of August. Then, leaving half his army there, he moved north and besieged Burgos. The French, however, had not been idle and moved against both Burgos and Madrid. Outnumbered, Wellington retired to winter in Portugal, but, as had happened before, his troops, after their recent victories, did not take to withdrawal and discipline broke down.

By now Napoleon had fought his disastrous campaign in Russia, and all Britain's erstwhile Continental allies were rallying against him. While the French army in Spain still outnumbered the Allies by two to one, it was by now so tied down by the guerrillas that it could not concentrate superior forces against Wellington. His moment had now arrived, and he began his final advance in mid May 1813. The French under Napoleon's brother Joseph were forced back by a series of imaginative manoeuvres and only when they reached Vitoria was there a battle. Here Joseph was forced to fight in a disadvantageous position and would have been entirely surrounded if one of Wellington's two simultaneous enveloping moves had been properly pressed home. As it was the French lost their guns, 150 in all, and their baggage train. This provoked another outburst of looting, which caused the Duke to write in exasperation:

'The night of the battle, instead of being passed in getting rest and food to prepare them for the pursuit the following day, was passed by the soldiers in looking for plunder. The consequence was, that they were incapable of marching in pursuit of the enemy, and were totally knocked up. The rain came on and increased their fatigue, and I am quite convinced that we have now out of the ranks double the amount of our loss in the battle. . . .'

Among the items of booty acquired was a silver chamberpot belonging to Joseph, reputedly given to him by his brother. It fell into the hands of the 14th Light Dragoons, and the 14th/20th King's Hussars' officers drink champagne out of it to this day. Yet in spite of his immediate frustrations, the Duke could take consolation in the fact that the French now gave up Spain, and to commemorate Vitoria, Beethoven wrote *Wellington's Victory*. By the end of the year Wellington was in the Pyrenees and poised to enter France.

Above: A sketch of Wellington made by an officer at Badajos.

Opposite, above: Breaking the French at Vitoria, 21 June 1813.

Opposite, below: The American War. The British victory at Queenstown, 13 October 1813.

Below: Wellington supervises the crossing of the Bidassoa, close to the western end of the Pyrenees, October 1813.

Above: The Baker rifle, with which the 60th and 95th Rifles (now the Royal Greenjackets) were armed in Wellington's day.

The Peninsula was not, however, the only theatre of war in which the British Army had been engaged during this time. Mention has already been made of the disastrous Walcheren expedition of 1809, and a sizeable garrison had also been maintained in Sicily. Part of it eventually went to the Peninsula, but the remainder campaigned in northern Italy during 1814. In the West Indies, in a series of well-conducted operations, the French- and Dutch-owned islands had been captured. Ceylon was also captured from the Dutch, but the garrison left there was later massacred. On the other hand, both Mauritius and Java were captured and subjugated. In India there had been another campaign against the Maharattas. There was also another expedition to Holland in December 1813 as part of an Anglo-Prussian plan to capture Antwerp. The Prussians, however, failed to carry out their part in

the plan, and although the British contingent managed to enter Bergen-op-Zoom, they were driven out again. There was also fighting in North America. Exasperated by British interference with her trade with France, America declared war in June 1812. American attempts to overrun Canada failed, but British operations against the United States were equally unsuccessful. A force occupied Washington for a while, but withdrew after setting light to all the public buildings, including the house of the President, which was then painted white to hide the damage and has been known as the White House ever since. Six thousand Peninsula veterans under Pakenham tried to seize New Orleans, but were beaten back by Andrew Jackson, later President of the United States, with heavy loss, including Pakenham killed. By this time, December 1814, peace had already been signed.

Right: The death of Sir Edward Pakenham at the Battle of New Orleans.

The 1814 campaign in Europe saw Napoleon driven back into France by the combined forces of Russia, Prussia and Austria, although many historians consider that in view of the massive superiority of forces against him this was one of his most brilliant campaigns. In the meantime Wellington pushed through the Pyrenees, reached Bordeaux in March and then turned east and defeated Soult one final time at Toulouse on 10 April. Napoleon abdicated and was sent in exile to the island of Elba, while Wellington, now a hero of all Europe, represented Britain at the peace settlement in Paris and then at the Congress of Vienna, which was to settle the affairs of post-war Europe. As at the end of past wars, the hardened and highly experienced Peninsular Army was quickly broken up. Some regiments were sent to America, where the war was still raging, and a small contingent was sent to the Netherlands to support the King, who had assumed sovereignty over Belgium. Of the remaining regiments, many were now disbanded, and the militia and other reserve forces stood down.

On 26 February 1815 Napoleon escaped from Elba, landed near Cannes on the French Riviera and began a triumphant march northwards, reaching Paris on 20 March. His veterans of the *Grande Armée* flocked once more to his standard and within a few weeks he had raised an army of 360,000 men. The Allies, still in conference at Vienna, agreed that he must be crushed once and for all, and pledged themselves to raise 500,000

men. The Austrian and Russian contingents would not, however, be ready until July, and the burden would in the meantime rest on the Prussians under Marshal Blücher and the Anglo-Dutch under Wellington.

As soon as he heard the news in Vienna, Wellington wrote to the Prime Minister, Lord Liverpool, recommending that the army be sent immediately to the Netherlands. When he arrived at Brussels at the end of March he was horrified by what he found. Six weak cavalry regiments and 25 battalions of infantry, many of them below strength, as well as only 42 guns, had been all that Liverpool could provide, and many of the ranks were filled with young and raw recruits. Only six battalions had served in the Peninsula and even they had lost many of their veterans. As he wrote to Lord Stewart at the beginning of May:

'I have got an infamous army, very weak and ill-equipped, and a very inexperienced staff. In my opinion they are doing nothing in England. They have not raised a man; they have not called out the militia either in England or Ireland; are unable to send me anything. . . .'

Yet at least his Peninsula veterans welcomed him. Whey they first arrived in Belgium they found the Prince of Orange in command, and Sergeant Wheeler of the 51st Foot (King's Own Yorkshire Light Infantry) expressed the concern of all: 'Wellington is the man that must lead us on. He is looked to by the remnant of the old

Left: The square of the 28th Foot (now the Gloucestershire Regiment) receives French cavalry, Quatre-Bras, 16 June 1815.

Right: Waterloo, 18 June 1815. The defence of the farm of Hougoumont by the Foot Guards.

Below: Waterloo. French cavalry and infantry attacking a British square. Wellington left foreground.

Peninsular army a hundred times a day.' When it was confirmed that Wellington would command, Sergeant Wheeler joyfully recorded: 'Glorious news! Nosey has got command! Won't we give them a drubbing now!'

Napoleon aimed to deal with his opponents one by one, as he had with much success in 1814. Wellington recognised this and also that Napoleon's eyes were turned on Belgium. While he needed to guard his lines of communication to Ostend, he also agreed with Blücher that should Napoleon try to separate them he would turn his back on Ostend and join him. He believed that Blücher and he could defeat Napoleon on their own, as he told Thomas Creevey, the eminent diarist. While the two talked, a British infantryman came into view. 'There,' the Duke said. 'There, it all depends upon that article

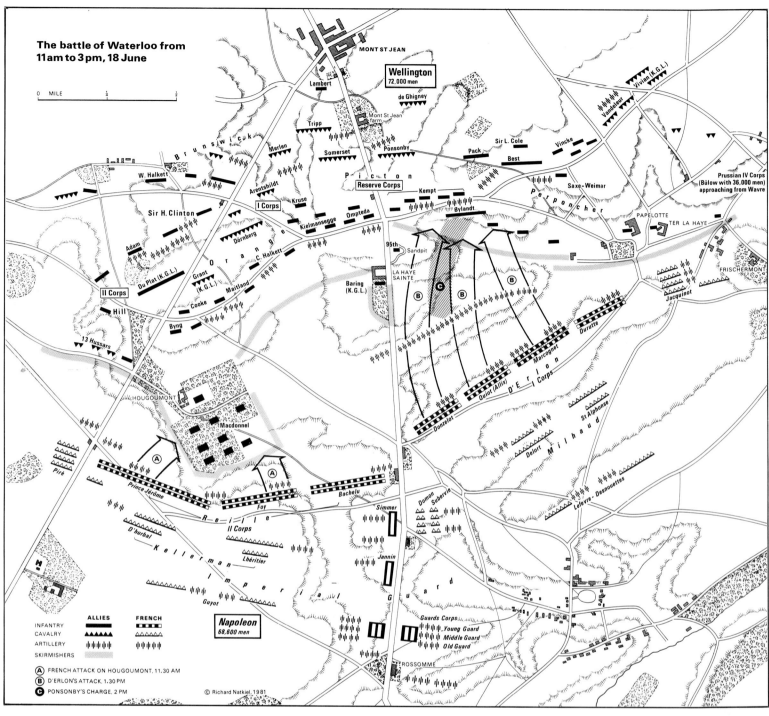

The battle of Waterloo from 11am to 3pm, 18 June

0   MILE   ¼   ½

MONT ST JEAN

Wellington 72,000 men

Lambert

de Ghigney

Vivian (K.G.L.)

Vandeleur

Mont St Jean Farm

Tripp

Somerset

Ponsonby

Pack

Sir L. Cole

Vincke

Merlen

Best

Saxe-Weimar

W. Halkett

Picton

Reserve Corps

Kempt

Perponcher

Prussian IV Corps (Bülow with 36,000 men) approaching from Wavre

Brunswick

Arentshildt

Bylandt

PAPELOTTE

TER LA HAYE

Sir H. Clinton

Kruse

I Corps

Kielmansegge

Ompteda

Orange

Dornberg

95th

Sandpit

FRISCHERMONT

Adam

C. Halkett

LA HAYE SAINTE

B

C

B

B

Jacquinot

Grant (K.G.L.)

Maitland

Baring (K.G.L.)

Du Plat (K.G.L.)

II Corps

Cooke

Byng

Durutte

Hill

Marcognet

13 Hussars

D'Erlon I Corps

Quiot (Allix)

Donzelot

HOUGOUMONT

St Alphonse

Macdonnel

Delort

Milhaud

A

Piré

A

Bachelu

Domon

Subervie

Lefevre-Desnouettes

Prince Jérôme

Simmer

Foy

Reille

II Corps

Picton

D'hurbal

Lhéritier

Jannin

Guard

Kellerman

Imperial

Guyot

Guard

Guards Corps

Young Guard

Middle Guard

Old Guard

Napoleon 68,600 men

ROSSOMME

ALLIES   FRENCH

INFANTRY
CAVALRY
ARTILLERY
SKIRMISHERS

A FRENCH ATTACK ON HOUGOUMONT, 11.30 AM
B D'ERLON'S ATTACK, 1.30 PM
C PONSONBY'S CHARGE, 2 PM

© Richard Natkiel, 1981

whether we do the business or not. Give me enough of it, and I am sure.' Their depredations in the Peninsula may have caused Wellington to state that his troops were 'the scum of the earth,' but he recognised their worth as soldiers.

By June 1815 Wellington had gathered an army of 93,000 men with 192 guns, of whom the British contingent, which included the King's German Legion, made up 40 per cent. Of these Wellington decided to detach 17,000 men to Hal in order to guard his right flank and also be prepared to act in the event of a Buonapartist insurrection in Belgium. Blücher's army, which was also in Belgium, and on the Duke's left, had 120,000 men and 312 guns. Napoleon had formed a striking force of 124,000 men and 370 guns, and by advancing between Wellington and Blücher hoped to drive them back along their divergent lines of communication. On 15 June he moved, crossing the River Sambre by Charleroi and catching the Allies by surprise. Next day he drove the Prussians back at Ligny, while Well-

ington held Ney at Quatre-Bras. On 17 June Wellington withdrew his troops in good order to Waterloo, a position he had already identified as a suitable place to fight, while Blücher moved back to Wavre, covered by Grouchy and a large French detachment. Not until he received a message from Blücher confirming that he would move across from Wavre to join him did Wellington finally make up his mind that he would fight at Waterloo. An Allied army of 68,000 men, including 21,000 British, faced 72,000 Frenchmen. Wellington's frontage was 4200 yards and it was a question of holding on to this until Blücher could arrive, which was expected to be at some time in the afternoon.

The battle of Waterloo has been described many times. In essence it began at 1130 hours with an attack on the farm of Hougoumont on Wellington's right flank, which was held. Napoleon now massed his artillery and bombarded the Allied lines, after which D'Erlon's corps attacked Wellington's left centre. Wellington used his

cavalry to counter-attack and the French replied in kind. At about 1500 hours there was a lull, and then Ney tried to capture the farm of La Haye Sainte forward and in the centre, but failed. Further French cavalry charges followed, with British countercharges but by now the Prussians were beginning to appear and threaten Napoleon's right flank. Ney finally took La Haye Sainte and then, conscious of the increasing Prussian presence, Napoleon realised that he must bring about a quick decision and launched the flower of his army, the Imperial Guard, at Wellington. The attack failed. Napoleon, covered by the Old Guard, began a withdrawal, which quickly became a rout. Four days later Napoleon abdicated once more and was sent to the remote island of St Helena, where he died in 1821.

The individual soldier could, amid the swirling smoke, see little of what was happening, but a selection of personal experiences gives a very good feel for what the battle was like. Sergeant Morris of the 71st Foot (Highland Light Infantry) recalls the French cuirassiers coming

'. . . at a gallop down upon us. Their appearance, as an enemy, was certainly enough to inspire a feeling of dread – none of them under six feet; defended by steel helmets and breast-plates, made pigeon-breasted to throw off the balls.'

Captain Mercer of the Royal Horse Artillery speaks of his

'limbers and ammunition wagons, some of which were totally unhorsed, and others in sad confusion from the loss of their drivers and horses, many of them lying dead in their harness attached to their carriages. I sighed for my poor troop – it was already but a wreck.'

Sergeant William Lawrence of the 40th Foot was ordered to help guard his regiment's colours:

'This . . . was a job I did not at all like; but still I went as boldly to work as I could. There had been before me that day 14 sergeants already killed and wounded while in charge of these colours, with officers in proportion, and the staff and colours were almost cut to pieces.'

Dawson Kelly of the 73rd Foot (2nd Battalion the Black Watch) on the final attack by the Imperial Guard:

'They . . . kept up a confused and running fire, which we did not reply to, until they reached nearly on a level with us, when a well-directed volley put them into confusion from which they did not appear to recover, but after a short interval of musketry on both sides, they turned about to a man and fled.'

Finally, Sergeant Ewart of the Scots Greys recalls how he captured the Eagle of the French 45th Regiment, a feat for which he was afterwards commissioned:

'[The Eagle bearer] thrust for my groin – I parried it off, and . . . cut him through the head . . . one of their Lancers threw his lance at me but missed . . . by my throwing it off with my sword . . . I cut him through the chin upwards, which cut went through his teeth. Next I was attacked by a foot soldier, who, after firing at me, charged me with his bayonet; but . . . I parried it and cut him down through the head.'

Wellington had 15,000 casualties, Blücher 7000 and the French 25,000, all within an area of not much more than two square miles. This more than anything illustrates the intensity of the battle, and it was above all the steadiness of the British soldier during the long day's pounding which brought victory in the end. Never had the stock of the British Army stood so high.

Above: The camp of the 2nd Foot Guards (Coldstream) in the Bois de Boulogne, Paris, after the Waterloo campaign.

Opposite: Map of Waterloo.

Below: 'The Battle of Waterloo' by Sir William Allen RA.

THE LONG SLEEP?
1816-56

For 100 years after 1815 Britain was only involved in one European war and the main role of the British Army quickly shifted to defence of the Empire. The large wartime army was quickly run down, and by 1820 its strength was 100,000 men, compared to 500,000 in 1814, with half based in Britain, 20,000 in India and the remainder scattered about the world in colonial garrisons. Indeed, the force at home would have been reduced even further if it had not been for the industrial unrest which swept the country in the wake of the Napoleonic Wars. The Army still retained its constabulary role, which it would not surrender until the middle of the century, with the establishment of borough and county police forces. Much of this policing was carried out not by the Regular Army but by the locally raised volunteer Yeomanry. While some of these units were well disciplined, others were not. The principle of minimum force, as is now generally applied to civil unrest, was not necessarily recognised in those days. A classic example was the Peterloo Massacre of 1819, when the local Yeomanry charged a radical meeting in Manchester, making free play with their sabres, leaving 11 dead and many wounded. Such actions did not make the Army popular with large sections of the population. In the higher echelons of society there was also an illogical feeling that the Army must be kept out of public view, yet if isolated there was the danger that it might become a political power. In 1816 Lord Lynedoch proposed to found a military club in London. Lord Folkestone objected, saying that it would be

'an institution of which I cannot speak with too much reprobation, where military men alone are admitted and where of course the general topics of conversation must be of a military nature.'

He viewed it as the first step towards forming a military government. The Duke of Wellington approved, however, and in 1817 laid the foundation of what was to become the United Services Club in Pall Mall.

Once again the Army was split up into small detachments, seldom more than a battalion in strength, and the divisional and brigade system broken up. One difference was that the soldiers were now housed in barracks.

'The usual construction of a soldier's barrack-room is an oblong apartment, having a door at one end, with a fire-place at the other, with rows of iron bedsteads on either side, which are folded up with the beds in the day-time; there are also tables and benches. This oblong chamber serves as a dormitory, a dining-room, and washing-place for the women.'

The women referred to were the wives of soldiers, who did the laundry for the men, both married and single. By the 1817 Regulations, four married women in each troop or company of 60 men were permitted to live in the barrack rooms, usually in a curtained-off corner. Not until 1838, however, was any extra furniture provided for them. The other families had to subsist as best they could in lodgings, but only in 1851 was any form of lodging allowance paid. Overcrowding in barrack rooms was often very bad – indeed a convict enjoyed 1000 cubic feet of air, while a soldier had to make do with 300-400 cubic feet. Not surprisingly, sickness rates were often very high. The monotony of the diet, now one pound of bread and three-quarters of meat daily, did not help, and, since there were no professional cooks in the Army, it was often badly prepared. The wartime short service enlistment was quickly rescinded, and the soldier was now back on a straight 21-year term of service. A private was still paid one shilling a day, but continued to see little of this because of stoppages. The lash still remained the main punishment, apart from imprisonment in the regimental cells, but public outcry against it became increasingly vehement, and in 1851, 100 out of 132 regiments had not used it once during the year. Drink continued to be the one way that the soldier could escape the monotony of life, and the existence of regimental canteens encouraged this. Nevertheless, by 1840 determined attempts were being made to wean soldiers away from alcohol. Sport became in-

Left: The Peterloo Massacre of 1819 did little to enhance the popularity of the Yeomanry.

creasingly organised, with games pitches being laid out in barracks. Regimental libraries were started, and schoolmasters appointed to instruct both the soldiers and their children. Regimental temperance societies were also formed.

The 1840s saw rewards being introduced on a much wider scale. Apart from private regimental rewards, decorations and medals had been awarded to officers only. The first break with this rule came during 1816-17 with the issue of the Waterloo Medal to all ranks who had fought there and a year given towards pension for the Other Ranks. The Peninsula veterans were understandably aggrieved that their service was not so recognised, but the Duke of Wellington viewed the Waterloo Medal as a 'one-off' case. The East India Company, however, began to issue its own medals, beginning with one to commemorate the Burma Campaign of 1824-26, followed by another for Jellalabad in 1842: a further medal was issued by Shah Shoojah, the British nominee to the Afghan throne, for the capture of Guznee in 1839. British as opposed to East India Company regiments which had taken part could not be excluded, and Queen Victoria took the step of authorising the issue of campaign medals from then on. In 1847 the Military General Service medal for 1793-1814 was finally sanctioned, with 29 bars for individual battles and engagements for those veterans who were still alive; a counterpart for service in India during 1799-1826 was issued by the East India Company in 1851. In 1830 William IV had also instituted the Long Service and Good Conduct Medal, to be awarded to soldiers with 21 years service of impeccable conduct, and this was followed shortly afterwards by the institution of Good Conduct badges for every seven and then five years' service, with an award of an extra penny per day for each badge.

For the officers the purchase system still reigned supreme. The prices for each step were regulated – at the time of the Crimean War an infantry ensigncy cost £450 (at 1850 prices) and an infantry lieutenant colonelcy £4540, while the cavalry equivalents were £840 and £6175, and those in the Foot Guards £1200 and £9000 – but prices over the odds were often paid. Thus Lord Lucan, who commanded the Cavalry Division in the Crimea, was said to have paid £25,000 for command of the 17th Lancers. If an officer retired he was allowed to take the proceeds of selling out with him. However, if promoted above the rank of lieutenant-colonel he lost his investment. Often a commanding officer might offer to sell out in return for a financial consideration from the field officers and captains in his regiment. This would enable some of them, unless one was prepared to purchase, to be promoted at little personal cost. Indeed, it was possible to work one's way up the promotion ladder without paying, although it took longer unless the regiment was on active service and suffering casualties. This was why a popular toast in the mess was to 'a bloody war or a sickly pestilence.' In the Royal Artillery and

Below: 'Up before the halberds,' a cartoon published in 1820. Offenders were, however, only stripped to the waist.

Royal Engineers, which did not have purchase, promotion was very slow, and it was not unusual for an officer to serve 25 years before promotion to captain. In the increasing debate over the merits of purchase, avoiding this delay was one of the main arguments of those in favour of retaining it. An officer could leave the active list by going on half-pay, which was the fate of many in the post-1815 rundown. Theoretically this gave the Army a ready reserve in the event of another expansion. However, the victims could scarcely keep themselves on the very modest retainer paid to them, which had not changed for 100 years, and many went abroad, where of course they were not immediately available to rejoin the Colours. Many, too, sought to augment their incomes by becoming parsons. During the peace, however, a number placed themselves voluntarily on the half-pay list but remained on the promotion list, which worked against those still on the active list in that it merely slowed down the rate of promotion.

Promotion itself, through purchase or not, carried anomalies. One was that the ranks of Guards officers equated to higher ranks in the rest of the Army. Thus a Guards captain was equivalent to a lieutenant colonel and was paid as such. This meant that the chance of reaching general rank was very much higher in the Guards. As Lord Hardinge noted: 'The Guards' system of rank over the Line gives to 7 Battns of Foot Gds 70 Lt Colonels – reared in London, trimming up to the rank of Major General. In the Line of 120 Battalions ⅓ dispersed in our Colonies, we have 140 Lt Cols toiling upwards for the same reward!' One way of bringing on promising Line officers was to have them transferred to the Guards, and some 450 benefitted from this in half a century. Nevertheless, promotion to the rank of general was very slow, because many generals remained on the half-pay list. Thus in 1837 there were four generals for every 1000 men, but there were active posts for

only a quarter of them. It is hardly surprising that those appointed in command of expeditionary forces were often elderly and out of date. Another system of reward for officers was that of brevet rank, which gave the officer a higher rank in the Army than in his regiment. This could produce farcical situations. Sir Winston Churchill recounted that in one garrison an officer settled an old score with his commanding officer by dint of holding a higher brevet rank. When appointed to command a brigade during manoeuvres, he had great delight in ordering his commanding officer to take his regiment home. Nevertheless, brevet rank would last well into the 1960s in the Regular Army, and still exists in a very small way in the Territorial Army.

Yet there was a growing realisation that promotion by purchase or vacancy was not necessarily being given to those that merited it, and a significant proportion of officers were not up to the standards expected for their rank. Passing in and out examinations were introduced at both

Above: Men of the 2nd Life Guards in dress and undress uniform in the Guardroom of Horse Guards, 1831.

Below left: Royal Horse Artillery firing their 9-pounders at Woolwich, 1843. Royal Military Academy in the background.

Woolwich and Sandhurst, the one passport to a commission without purchase in the non-scientific arms, and the syllabus taught at each was tightened up. By 1850 an examination was also introduced for promotion to captain. This covered military administration and the handling of a company and, for those commissioned from 1849 onwards, a wide-ranging academic portion, including history, geography, mathematics and the first six books of Euclid. Although too late to have much influence over the conduct of the Crimean War, this did much to raise the professionalism of the army officer. A noticeable indication of this was the introduction of a number of military journals in which officers of all ranks could air their views. Foremost among them were the *Naval and Military Gazette, United Service Gazette* and *United Service Journal*, the house publication of the United Service Institution, which, as the Royal United Services Institute for Defence Studies, celebrated its 150th anniversary in 1982.

There were, however, a number of scandals in cavalry regiment officers' messes, which did little for the reputation of the officer corps as a whole. The 10th Hussars gained a very bad reputation for snobbery among its officers. One young officer who did not fit in was victimised and the Press got to hear of it. The regiment also offended local society in Dublin where it was stationed, and the

story goes that a gentleman asked one of the dandified officers of the 10th to dance with a certain young lady. 'Oh, trot her up and down a bit and let's see how she goes', was the reply reminiscent of the procedure at a horse sale, which led to 'The Tenth don't dance' becoming a popular catch-phrase. More notorious was James Brudenell, seventh Earl of Cardigan, who having purchased command of the 15th Hussars in 1832 was determined to make it the finest regiment in the Army. A row with one of his officers over new stable jackets for his troop also reached the ears

Above: The charge of the 3rd Light Dragoons (now the Queen's Own Hussars) at Ferozeshah, 1845, during the First Sikh War.

Below: Last stand of the 44th Foot (later the Essex Regiment and now part of the Royal Anglian Regiment) at Gandamak during the disastrous First Afghan War.

of the Press, and the fact that the Earl was in the habit of taking down the conversations of his officers in the orderly room without their knowledge led to his removal from command. Undeterred, he purchased the 11th Light Dragoons (later Hussars) and his overbearing manner once again caused ructions. He nursed a particular dislike for 'Indian' officers, those who had seen service in India, although he was not alone in this and some even referred to Wellington as a 'Sepoy General.' An argument in 1840 with one 'Indian' officer in his regiment again reached the Press and brought down the wrath of the Commander-in-Chief on Cardigan's head. Yet his regiment remembered him ever afterwards by wearing the cherry-coloured trousers which he instituted, earning the nickname of the Cherrypickers.

The main reason for the rift between officers of the army at home and those who had served in India was that the latter continued after 1815 to see much active service. On their return to Britain they tended to be disparaging about the amateur efforts of their counterparts, who had not had the opportunity to experience battle. This was understandably resented, especially since the style of campaigning in India was considered likely to be very different from that of a European war.

The organisation of the army in India up until the time of the Indian Mutiny in 1857 was complicated in that there were two separate armies. The East India Company's army, known as 'John Company's army', was organised on British lines, with Indian regiments and a few locally recruited Europeans under command, wearing similar uniform to the British Army, albeit with a few indigenous touches. It was split up among the three Presidencies into which British India was then divided, Bengal, Madras and Bombay. Its officers were educated at its own academy at Addiscombe in Surrey, and there were no cross-postings with the British Army in India. The latter maintained an organisation divorced from that of the Company troops, but combined with them when on campaign.

Throughout this time the British were gradually expanding their power in the region. During 1815-16 there was war against Nepal, whose tribesmen were constantly raiding northern India. It was a hard-fought campaign, and at the end each side had developed a respect for the other which has lasted to this day. Although Nepal retained its independence, volunteer battalions were raised from the tribesmen to serve John Company, and their descendants, today's Gurkha regiments, form a proud part of both the British and Indian armies. During 1824-26 the Bengal Army, with four British Army regiments and some artillery, waged war against the Burmese, who had been encroaching into the eastern part of Bengal. Although it gained the areas of Assam, Cachon, Manipur, Chittagong and Arakan – names that would become very familiar to the Fourteenth Army over 100 years later – the First Burmese War is chiefly remembered for the appalling administration of the troops. No less than 85 per cent of the British troops who took part died, 95 per cent of them from disease.

The attention of the authorities in India was being drawn increasingly to the North-West Frontier and Afghanistan beyond it, which the Russians might use as a springboard to invade India. In 1837 the Russians incited the Persians to attack Herat on the border with Afghanistan, and the Governor-General of India, Lord Auckland, sent an expeditionary force to the country in 1839, intending to place a ruler sympathetic to the British on the throne. The incumbent was successfully deposed, and Shah Sooja installed. Garrisons were left at Kabul and Kandahar, and the force returned to India. Although there was some trouble from Dost Mohammed, the former ruler, during 1840, the situation looked brighter the following year, and plans were put into operation to relieve some of the garrisons. That of General Sale at Kabul began its march back to India in October, but then Afghanistan rose in revolt. General Elphinstone, an elderly incompetent who had spent 25 years on the half-pay list, was in overall charge, and mistakenly thought he had obtained safe passage across the Khyber Pass. In fact his 4500 men were constantly harried, and only Jellalabad, garrisoned by the 13th Foot (Somerset Light Infantry), held out and waited for Elphinstone's men to appear. One man, Dr William Brydon, the sole survivor of the column, struggled through the gates of the fort, which continued to hold out until relieved in April 1842. The 13th Foot was paid special honours by the troops in India and became known as the Illustrious Garrison for producing the only gleam of light in an otherwise disastrous undertaking.

Finally there were the two Sikh Wars of the 1840s caused by anarchy in the Punjab spilling over into Company territory. The first campaign of 1845-46 brought the cavalry to the fore, and the 3rd Light Dragoons (later Hussars) carried out a celebrated charge at the Battle of Mudkee, which caused the Sikhs to call them 'The Devil's Children' and the rest of the Army 'The Mudkee Wallahs'. Victories at Ferozeshah and Sobraon followed, and the Sikhs were driven back across the River Sutlej. The Second Sikh War of 1848-49 saw further victories, and the Punjab became part of British India. Trouble now arose once again in Burma, where British merchants were being treated increasingly badly. In April 1852 a small expedition of 5700 men was sent to Rangoon, and from there proceeded up the Irrawaddy. A number of towns including Prome and Pegu were captured and the whole of the Burmese coastline fell under British rule.

India, however, was not the only colonial theatre in which British troops were engaged. In West Africa there was war against the Ashantis during 1824-26. The British force was made up of native troops and the Royal African Corps, formed from convicts as an alternative to imprisonment. The concept of raising locally enlisted corps was now widespread as a means of keeping colonial garrisons up to strength in order to deal with unrest. South Africa too was the scene of much fighting, with three campaigns against the Kaffirs, who were constantly threatening Cape Colony, in 1834-35, 1846-47 and 1850-53. There were also problems with the original Dutch settlers, the Boers, who did not think the British were giving them enough protection against the Kaffirs, yet at the same time resented their rule. The result was the Great Trek, with the Boers

gradually moving northwards over the Drakensberg mountains and the British establishing control over Natal. This did not solve the problem, as the British would find some years later.

The problem of matching manpower to colonial commitments was only partly solved by locally raised forces such as the Royal African Corps and the Royal Canadian Rifles. Another solution was to encourage men to take their discharge while serving in the colonies and then form a militia for local defence. It was, however, recognised in the 1830s that a root cause was the high mortality rate in regiments serving abroad. The 92nd Highlanders (2nd Battalion Gordon Highlanders), for example, lost no less than 860 men, women and children from disease in Jamaica during 1819-27. Two medical officers, Dr Henry Marshall and Lieutenant AM Tulloch, were commissioned to carry out a study and published their results in 1837. They concluded that tour lengths in tropical climates must be reduced and barracks resited away from obvious disease areas and redesigned. It was now laid down that no

regiment should serve overseas for more than 10 years, and although in practice it was not possible to meet this requirement entirely, by 1848 no regiment had been abroad for more than 12 years, and the health of the Army overseas improved dramatically.

Britain had hoped to keep out of European squabbles, but this was not wholly possible. By 1850 Russia was casting covetous eyes over the Ottoman Empire, especially the Balkans. Under the pretext of protecting Christians there she sent troops to occupy the provinces of Moldavia and Wallachia. In 1853, in retaliation, Turkey declared war, but early reverses made it seem to Britain and France that Russia would seize the whole of the Ottoman Empire and upset the balance of power. In March 1854 an Anglo-French military expedition was therefore sent to the Crimea as a means of propping up Turkey.

In spite of the numerous reforms carried out since 1815, the British Army was singularly ill-prepared to fight a war against a European enemy. The rifle regiments were now armed with

'The Devil's Children' – 3rd Light Dragoons at Mudkee, 1845.

the Minié rifle, which although still a muzzle loader had a faster rate of fire than the old Brown Bess, and three times the effective range; but the majority still had the Brown Bess, albeit using the percussion principle, and artillery was still also smoothbore. In 1847 the Limited Enlistment Act had been passed, reducing the term of enlistment to 10 years with the infantry and 12 with the cavalry, with a re-enlistment provision of 11 or 12 years, but there were no indications that this was attracting more or better recruits. Tactically there had been virtually no change, apart from making the Thin Red Line even slimmer by reducing it from three ranks to two. (In practice two rank formations had often been used previously although regulations called for three.) More serious was the fact that few of the generals had had any practice in commanding large bodies of troops in the field because of the break-up of the division and brigade structure. A belated effort was made in 1853 to bring together a division's worth of troops for manoeuvres, but

Left: Royal Artillery river crossing c1850.

Right: 'Three Cheers for Her Majesty!' The Scots Fusilier Guards (now Scots Guards) at Buckingham Palace ready to depart for the Crimea.

Below: Lady Butler's painting, 'The Roll Call' shows Grenadier Guards after the hard-fought Battle of Inkerman.

this merely showed up the defects. As the *Naval and Military Gazette* put it:

'We have treated, tried and found defective, much that we fancied perfect in the organization, training, clothing, equipping and arming of all branches of the Service.... We have seen, too, how easily mistakes can be made through ignorance of the first principles of manoeuvre, and through inexperience in those officers who are the best instructed in the theory of strategy and tactics.'

It was not just the commanders but also their staffs who were guilty. There had still been little attempt to introduce formalised staff training, and the general view was that experience was the best teacher.

Under the command of the 66-year-old one-armed Lord Raglan, the Master-General of the Ordnance – who had seen no action since Waterloo, where he had been one of Wellington's ADCs – 26,000 men and 66 guns joined the French contingent of 30,000 men and 70 guns at Varna

on the Black Sea. Cholera and dysentery quickly struck. Rather than see their men waste away, Raglan and St Arnaud, the French commander, decided to take their forces across the Black Sea to capture the Russian naval base at Sevastopol and destroy the fleet there. With little intelligence as to the Russian strength they landed at Kalamatia Bay to the north of Sevastopol. The Russians were posted in a strong position on top of an escarpment overlooking the River Alma, and using little imagination Raglan launched his troops in a frontal attack on 20 September 1854. The French, however, managed to manoeuvre cannon up in an enfilade position, using a track which the Russians had failed to cover, and the position was taken at a cost of 2200 Allied casualties, the Russians leaving 5700 dead on the battlefield. No attempt to follow the enemy up was made, and the Allies now realised that Kalamatia Bay, being wholly exposed, was entirely unsuitable for landing supplies. They therefore re-embarked, the British landing at Balaklava and the French at two small ports farther west. The Russians moved to counter-attack Raglan, and the result was the Battle of Balaklava, fought on 25 October. It is perhaps a British characteristic that it is the blunder of that day which is chiefly remembered, not the two highly successful actions which preceded it.

Balaklava itself was garrisoned by 3000 Turks, 1000 marines and the 93rd Highlanders (Argyll and Sutherland). The Russians launched a cavalry attack, which was repulsed by the Thin Red Line of the 93rd (this incident is the origin of the phrase). Another body of Russian cavalry was sighted and General Scarlett's Heavy Brigade, made up of the 2nd and 6th Dragoons and 4th and 5th Dragoon Guards, were ordered to charge them, even though the enemy was several times their number. The eminent Victorian military historian Colonel Hamley who was present described what happened:

'There was a clash and a fusion, as of wave meeting wave, when the head of the column encountered the leading squadrons of our brigade, all those being engaged being resolved into a crowd of individual horsemen, whose swords rose and fell and glanced. So for a minute or two they fought, the impetus of the enemy's dense column carrying it on and pressing our combatants back for a short space; till the 4th Dragoon Guards, coming clear of a wall which was between them and the enemy, charged the Russian flank, while the remaining regiment of the brigade went in, in support of those which had first attacked. Then – almost, it seemed, in a moment and simultaneously – the whole Russian mass gave way and fled, at speed

Right: The Battle of Alma. Crossing the river, the Guards commence their long uphill attack.

and disorder, beyond the hill, vanishing behind the slope some four or five minutes after they had first swept over it.'

Lord Cardigan's Light Brigade (4th and 13th Light Dragoons, 8th and 11th Hussars, 17th Lancers) was standing by and 'champing at the bit' to complete the task that the Heavy Brigade had performed so brilliantly. Raglan, however, was keeping it in reserve and used infantry to follow up the success, but not surprisingly they

moved too slowly. In the meantime the Russians were taking away some guns from captured redoubts formerly held by the Turks. Raglan therefore ordered the Light Brigade to 'advance rapidly to the front – follow the enemy and try to prevent the enemy carrying away the guns.' The message was passed to Lord Lucan, commanding the Cavalry Division, by a Captain Nolan, one of Raglan's staff officers, who, over-excited, urged Lucan to attack immediately. The only guns Lucan could see from his position were at the

Below: 'On into the valley of death . . .', the Light Brigade at Balaklava.

head of a valley, where the main Russian position was, but Nolan was insistent. Lucan then rode over to Cardigan and ordered him to attack these, assuring him that he would support him with the Heavy Brigade. Thus the Light Brigade charged and amid the concentrated fire of the guns actually reached them. By that time only 50 men were left mounted, and the remnants were forced to retire, including Lord Cardigan who had led the charge throughout and now went back to remonstrate with Lucan, whom he loathed, for failing to support him. Of the 673 men who made the charge, 113 were killed, many more wounded and a number made prisoner. As a French observer, General Pierre Bosquet, remarked: 'C'est magnifique, mais ce n'est pas la guerre.' It is magnificent but it is not war.

The Russians now withdrew in good order and the Allies proceeded to invest the town. On 5 November the Russians made an attempt to break the siege by attacking the extreme right of the Allied lines with 55,000 men, using thick fog as a cover. The fog, however, made it impossible for the commanders on either side to control the battle, which degenerated into a series of confused bouts of concentrated hand-to-hand fighting. Not for nothing was Inkerman afterward called 'the Soldiers' Battle.' The Russians were repulsed, suffering 12,000 casualties to 4200 of the Allies. This was the last time they attempted a major relief effort, and the siege of Sevastapol continued unabated.

Winter set in and the administrative shortcomings of the British Army came home to roost. Lacking adequate winter clothing, short of both food and fuel, having only tents to protect them from the elements and hampered by totally inefficient transport, the troops began to succumb to sickness in droves. Even when evacuated to hospital many still died through the lack of medical facilities. Cholera was the main killer and one doctor, Surgeon Buzzard, recalled from his civilian practice in London that infected water was the main cause. Yet he could convince few of his fellow doctors of the importance of

drinking only boiled water, such was the general medical ignorance of the time. *The Times* correspondent in the Crimea, William Howard Russell, the first of the modern war correspondents, wrote continual accounts of the conditions in which the troops were trying to keep alive, and there was no censorship in those days to prevent him from telling the truth, as he saw it. The result was that, for the first time, the public expressed concern over the lot of their soldiers and this rose to such a clamour that the government of the day, under Lord Aberdeen, was forced to resign. As far as the troops in the Crimea were concerned, the first concrete result was the arrival of Florence Nightingale and a party of nurses, who set up a base hospital at Scutari. The unaccustomed care and attention the sick and wounded received was reflected in a soldiers' song of the time, *The Nightingale in the East*, which dubbed her 'one of

Above: The Thin Red Line. Colin Campbell's 93rd Highlanders at Balaklava.

Below: Sir James Scarlett, whose Heavy Brigade performed so brilliantly at Balaklava.

Right: General Sir James Simpson, who took over command of the British troops in the Crimea after Raglan's death in June 1855.

Far right: The Battle of Balaklava.

Below: The Heavy Brigade at Balaklava. The Scots Greys supported by the Inniskillings (now 5th Royal Inniskilling Dragoon Guards).

Bottom right: 'The Lady with the Lamp'. Florence Nightingale in her hospital at Scutari.

Heaven's best gifts.' Transportation was overhauled with the formation of the Land Transport Corps, which was kept in being after the peace in 1856 as the Military Train. Proper huts were provided for the winter of 1855-56 after the eventual fall of Sevastapol in September, and while the troops waited for the peace to be signed. Furthermore Alexis Soyer, the French *maître chef* of the Reform Club, was sent out to the Crimea to overhaul military cooking and insisted that the Army use properly trained soldier cooks. His name still lives on in the British Army in the Soyer stove, which has been in continuous use for well over 100 years. Finally there was a radical streamlining of the hitherto cumbersome higher direction of the Army. From now on there would just be two heads, the Secretary of State for War at the War Office responsible for the civil departments connected with the Army, and the Commander-in-Chief at Horse Guards for all military departments.

To say, as many historians do, that the British Army went to sleep after 1815 and was awoken with a rude shock in 1854 is an over-simplification. Admittedly the conservative influence of the Duke of Wellington, who lived on until 1852, was a restraint, but there were many reforms, as we have seen. The basic problem was that of reconciling defence of Empire with preparedness for a possible European war. This required two different armies, a dilemma the Army would continue to face for many years. In any case the politicians were finally responsible, for they had declared war on Russia with little regard for the imperfect instrument available to wage it.

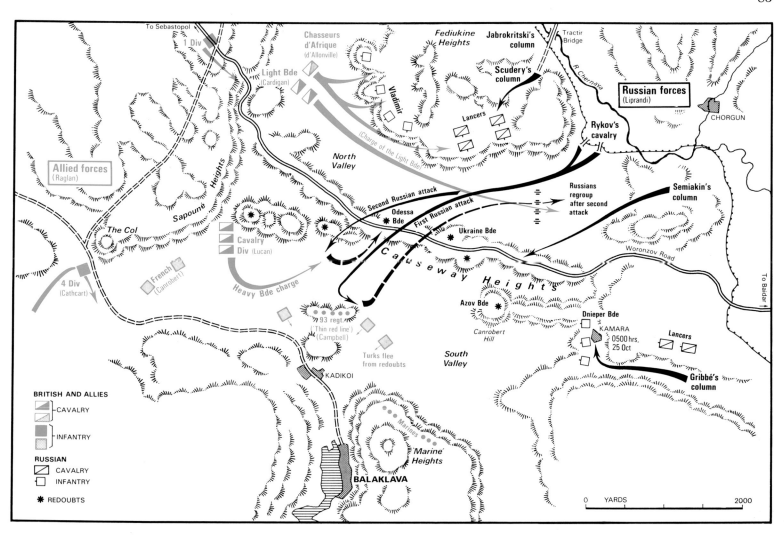

Allied forces
(Raglan)

Russian forces
(Liprandi)

To Sebastopol
1 Div
Chasseurs
d'Afrique
(d'Allonville)
Light Bde
(Cardigan)
Fediukine
Heights
Jabrokritski's
column
Tractir
Bridge
R. Chernaya
Scudery's
column
Vladimir
Lancers
CHORGUN
(Charge of the Light Bde)
Rykov's
cavalry
North
Valley
Russians
regroup
after second
attack
Semiakin's
column
Sapoune Heights
Second Russian attack
First Russian attack
The Col
Odessa
Bde
Cavalry
Ukraine Bde
Div (Lucan)
Causeway Heights
Woronzov Road
To Baidar
4 Div
(Cathcart)
French
(Canrobert)
Heavy Bde charge
Azov Bde
93 regt.
(Thin red line)
(Campbell)
Dnieper Bde
KAMARA
0500 hrs,
25 Oct
Lancers
Canrobert
Hill
Turks flee
from redoubts
KADIKOI
South
Valley
Gribbé's
column
Marines
'Marine'
Heights
BALAKLAVA

BRITISH AND ALLIES
CAVALRY
INFANTRY
RUSSIAN
CAVALRY
INFANTRY
REDOUBTS

0   YARDS   2000

DEFENDING THE EMPIRE 1857-1914

86

Previous page: Highlanders inspect the Sphinx after their victory at Tel-el-Kebir in 1882.

With the return of the army from the Crimea there was, amid all the recriminations, one happy event when Queen Victoria held an investiture on Horse Guards Parade. This was to award a new decoration to officers, soldiers and sailors who had performed particular acts of gallantry in the Crimea. Each Victoria Cross was cast from the metal of guns captured at Sevastapol, the supply of which ran out only in 1942, and was the second British award for gallantry, the first being the Distinguished Conduct Medal instituted for NCOs and men in 1854. The Victoria Cross remains the highest award in the land, taking precedence over all other orders and decorations. It was the Sovereign's own personal way of recognising the hardships her soldiers and sailors had been through and the fortitude with which they had faced them. For the Army, however, there was to be little time to savour the joys of peace.

No sooner had the Crimean War ended than there was another rift with Persia, when the latter occupied Herat once more. Seven thousand men were sent to Bushire on the Persian Gulf and after a short sharp campaign the Persians agreed to remove their presence from Herat. More serious trouble was brewing in India, however. The

East India Company had been tightening its grip in rather a heavy-handed way. This was especially resented in the Bengal Army, many of whose soldiers were of high caste, and there was particular discontent at the seemingly casual way in which the Company appeared to treat the native rulers and its apparent lack of regard for the religions of the country. Matters came to a head towards the end of 1856, when the Enfield rifle, which had now finally replaced the Brown Bess, began to be introduced. The cartridges for the rifle had to be torn with the firer's teeth before use, and the rumour spread among the sepoys that they were covered with beef or pork fat, though it was against the Hindu religion to eat beef and pork was forbidden to Moslems. At the time there were only 38,000 European troops in India and 200,000 sepoys, and the former were poorly deployed to cope with the Mutiny when it broke out at Barrackpore near Calcutta in January 1857. Trouble spread rapidly as the sepoys turned on their British officers and their families and massacred them before moving off to Delhi, where Bahadur Shah, the last of the ancient Mogul rulers, was restored to his throne. In some garrisons, however, small parties of Europeans managed to hold out, especially at Lucknow,

Below: The Indian Mutiny. Storming the Delhi Gate.

where a garrison of less than 2000 men, including some loyal sepoys, was besieged until November by 60,000 mutineers. Delhi, however, was the key and throughout the hot summer of 1857 a British force invested the city, but was not strong enough to take it. Meanwhile numerous reinforcements were sent out from Britain, and Delhi finally fell into British hands in September. Columns then harried the remaining rebels and by the spring of 1858 British authority had been restored, although the last rebels were not run to earth for another year.

The Indian Mutiny had come as a nasty shock, especially since British rule in India had appeared so secure. In order to prevent such an outbreak again, the authority for governing British India was removed from John Company and placed in the hands of the Crown. Queen Victoria became Empress of India, and her personal representative in the country was to be the Viceroy, who replaced the Governor-General, the administration of India being controlled by the India Office in London. The British Army presence in the country, as opposed to what was now called the Indian Army, was increased to 65,000 men, and as a general principle every garrison was now to contain at least one British regiment.

Left: Generals Sir Colin Campbell (right) and William Mansfield during the Indian Mutiny.

Below: The Indian Mutiny. Sir Henry Havelock relieves Lucknow.

At home, in 1856, the Duke of Cambridge, who had commanded a division in the Crimea and was a cousin of the Queen, was appointed Commander-in-Chief, a position he would occupy for the next 40 years. One of his first acts was to address the problem of staff training for officers, and in 1858 he established the Staff College in the grounds of Sandhurst, where it still resides. The British Army would finally have professionally trained staff officers, something which Continental armies had had for some time. It was, however, to be a few years yet before the importance of Camberley, as the Staff College is often called, would be recognised by the Army as a whole, and a feeling lingered on that those who aspired to become students there were 'deserting' their regiments.

In 1859 a scare gripped the country that the French, fresh from victory over the Austrians in northern Italy, might invade Britain. This brought about the formation of a new Volunteer force, a successor to that which had operated, along with the Militia, during the Napoleonic invasion scare. By the summer of 1860, 160,000 men had been enrolled. They had to provide their own uniforms and paid for the privilege of being Volunteers through the entrance fees and subscriptions, the Government merely providing rifles. Because they were virtually 'private armies', the War Office had little control over them, and their military prowess, like that of their forebears, was often of doubtful quality. Nevertheless the country was taking much more interest in military matters than hitherto, and this helped the Regular Army achieve a higher standing with the British people than ever before.

The old concept of small scattered garrisons about the country now disappeared and regiments were grouped together in large camps such as Aldershot, Colchester and later Salisbury Plain, with large manoeuvre areas nearby. Uniforms changed, and it is interesting to note that armies have often adopted the style of dress of their main potential enemy. Thus for a time the British adopted the French *képi* and long jacket, as did the US Army. After the Franco-Prussian War of 1870-71, which saw France vanquished, the fashion changed, the German *pickelhaube* being worn. There were also radical improvements in weapons. In 1860 the first rifled field gun made its appearance, and in 1867 came the breech-loading rifle, the Sneider, which was followed in 1871 by the Martini-Henry hammerless rifle, with an effective range of 1200 yards. The US Gatling gun was introduced in the same year, as the British Army's first machine gun. Few of the technological advances in weaponry at this time were of British origin, and new weapons were adopted only after they had been proved in other armies.

In 1869 a furore was created in military circles by the publication of Lieutenant Colonel Garnet Wolseley's *The Soldier's Pocket Book*. Wolseley was highly experienced, having seen active service in Burma, the Crimea and the Indian Mutiny, and was regarded as one of the most promising of the younger officers. Rather than just being a manual of tactics and drill, his book espoused a new military philosophy. His main thesis was that the long-established gulf between

officer and soldier was artificial, and did little for the fighting efficiency of the Army. He accused many officers of spending their time:

'...without discovering that the military career has any higher aim than that of moving men on parade by a most complicated process called drill, and that of keeping order amongst them by a rigid system of espionage, which is believed to be discipline. There is but little real sympathy between them and their men. Forgetting that the feudal system has passed away, as long as they do their duty by their soldiers, they expect to find them always ready to obey their nod, and to stand by them in all moments of peril.'

Instead, soldiers were to be treated as individuals and with respect, and officers should make much more effort to get to know their soldiers. While this was much the same message that Coote Manningham had been preaching to his officers 70 years before, it had been largely ignored in the Army as a whole, and was viewed as heretical by many conservative-minded officers, including the Duke of Cambridge. One, however, who was

Above: General Outram leads the first of the relieving force into the residency at Lucknow.

Opposite, above: The penalty for mutiny. Captured mutineers are tied to the guns of the Bengal Horse Artillery.

Opposite, below: The bitter fighting for the Kashmir Gate at Delhi.

Left: Viscount Cardwell, the military reformer.

Right: By the 1880s organised sport was being actively encouraged in the Army. Here the 59th Foot (now Queen's Lancashire Regiment) play rugby while at Khelat-i-Gilzai during the Second Afghan War.

Below: Assaulting a redoubt during the Second Maori War.

interested in what Wolseley had to say was Edward Cardwell, who had been appointed Secretary of State for War in 1868 and was bent on major reforms. At Cardwell's insistence Wolseley was placed on the staff of the Commander-in-Chief in a position where he could advise Cardwell on future reforms.

Cardwell's first objective was to do away with purchase, and his moment came after a Royal Commission had been appointed to investigate the perennial problem of over-regulation payments. When Cardwell introduced his Army Regulation Bill in the House of Commons in 1871 there was a vociferous outcry, and even the Queen commented that: 'She must honestly own to Mr Cardwell that she sees with deep regret the destruction of the system which has worked for so long, and under which the British Army established its reputation.' Nevertheless Cardwell eventually got his bill through, and the only concession made was that officers could still arrange exchanges between themselves with the approval of the Commander-in-Chief, a practice which continued until 1939. To overcome the problem of promotion blockages, which had been experienced for so long in the Royal Artillery and Royal Engineers, compulsory retirement was introduced, captains having to leave after 20 years' service, majors after 27 and generals when aged 70. Furthermore, regimental command was limited to a maximum of five years. There was, however, a prolonged debate over how officers should be selected for promotion. A Royal Commission which sat in 1876 recommended that it should be by 'seniority tempered by rejection', but in practice the Duke of Cambridge based it on seniority alone, so that too many incompetent officers were still promoted to ranks higher than they deserved.

Cardwell's next step was to tackle the terms of enlistment. The 12-year term introduced in 1847 had not been successful on two counts. It did not attract a significant increase in numbers because potential recruits feared that after 12 years they would be at the wrong age to fit back easily into civilian life. The long enlistment also did not include any reserve liability, and the Regular Army could call upon little more than 5000 reservists in the event of another war in Europe. This increasingly worried the authorities as they watched Prussia defeat Denmark (1864), Austria (1866) and France (1870) in a series of short wars. In 1866 Prussia had been able to field an army of 400,000 men, a mixture of short-term conscripts and reservists. While conscription was totally unacceptable to the British, a shorter term of service, with a reserve commitment afterward, would solve the problem. The result was the 1870 Army Enlistment Act, which retained the 12-year term, but those serving in Britain went on to the reserve after three years with the colours, while in India the term was six years. It also authorised the discharge of men of bad character.

Cardwell also reorganised the administrative structure of the Army at home, so that it could better support the imperial demands on troops. Since 1825 regiments had been organised into service and depot companies, the latter feeding the former. Many regiments, however, were only of a single battalion, and if this was under strength, as it often was, manpower commitments could not be fulfilled. Cardwell's answer was to divide the country into 66 districts, each the responsibility of an administrative brigade headquarters. Each district had a depot, two Regular battalions, one or both often away, two Militia battalions and the Volunteers. Besides bringing all three elements 'under one roof', it also aided recruitment in creating a much closer association between them. The final stage occurred in 1881, after Cardwell's time, when the old

Above: General 'Bobs' Roberts at the time of the Second Afghan War.

system of numbering regiments of the line was superseded. Each regiment was given two Regular battalions and a territorial title, normally reflecting the county in which it was based; it had its own depot in that county and recruited locally. Apart from the amalgamations of regiments at various times since, the system in essence remains the same today.

Cardwell carried out a further reorganisation in the higher direction of the Army by making the Commander-in-Chief, at least on paper, subordinate to the Secretary of State and merged Horse Guards with the War Office. The Duke of Cambridge, however, with the Queen behind him, resisted this as he had all Cardwell's other reforms, and in practice there was little change.

While wars raged on the Continent of Europe Britain managed to remain on the sidelines, but her army overseas was involved on active service almost continuously. In 1860 an Anglo-French force was sent to China to enforce trade agreements, and after bombarding the Taku forts moved on Peking and burnt the Summer Palace there. Several regiments still possess silver acquired from the looting that took place. During 1867-68 the Abyssinian Expedition occurred, a British force from India marching 300 miles through uncharted country to defeat King Theodore at Magdala in response to the way in which he had treated British envoys. There were three campaigns against the Maoris in New Zealand in the 1860s, and in 1870 a punitive column under Wolseley travelled 1200 miles from Toronto to put down unrest among the settlers of Manitoba, who objected to their territory around the Red River being transferred from the sovereignty of the Hudson's Bay Company to that of the newly formed Dominion of Canada. The ringleader, Louis Van Riel, escaped, however, to cause further trouble and have another expedition sent against him in 1885. It was Wolseley, too, who led a further expedition in West Africa against the

Left: The march to King Coffee's stronghold, Ashanti Expedition of 1873-4.

Below: Garnet Wolseley c1875. A popular expression of the day was 'all Sir Garnet' meaning 'everything in order.' Wolseley was also the original 'Model of a modern Major General' of the Gilbert and Sullivan operetta.

Ashanti King Coffee during 1873-74, after the king had been terrorising tribes under British protection. The 34 officers Wolseley selected to accompany him to organise native troops for the campaign were all supporters of his philosophy and became known as the 'Ashanti Ring.'

Wolseley was not the only officer in the limelight during this period. He had a rival, Frederick Roberts, 'Bobs Bahadur', who became the darling of the Indian Army. Indeed, while those who believed in radical change supported Wolseley, the more conservative elements fell in behind Roberts, whom they regarded as their champion. He had fought in the Mutiny, winning the Victoria Cross, and took part in the Abys-

sinian Expedition, as well as in a number of punitive expeditions in India, but his moment really came with the outbreak of the Second Afghan War in 1878.

The British decision to invade Afghanistan for a second time came about because the Russians had been allowed to establish a mission there, whereas when the British attempted to do the same it was turned back at the border. The planned invasion was to be made by three separate forces. In the north a force under General Sam Browne – inventor of the officers' leather belt of that name – was to occupy the Khyber Pass, which it did with no fighting. Likewise in the south a second force advanced from Quetta to

Kandahar, again without fighting. In the centre Roberts, with 6500 men and 18 guns, advanced up the Kurram Valley. Meeting opposition at the Peiwar Kotal Pass, he carried out a brilliant out-flanking move by night and overcame it at little cost to his force. These moves caused the Afghan ruler Sher Ali to flee to Russia, a British mission was installed at Kabul and all British forces were withdrawn except for Roberts' which remained in the Kurram Valley. The Afghans then revolted and overcame the mission, which had a small escort from the crack Regiment of Guides. Roberts set forth, beat a superior Afghan army and re-established the British presence in Kabul in October 1879. His force, however, was too small to be able to impose British rule on the unruly Afghans, and by the end of the year he was under siege in his camp outside Kabul. In May 1880 General Stewart arrived with re-inforcements and, being senior to Roberts, as-sumed command. The British now decided to evacuate the northern part of the country, but at the end of July the Afghans began to threaten Kandahar. A force sent out to foil them was sur-rounded and badly cut up at Maiwand, and the Afghans besieged Kandahar. It was now that Roberts carried out his epic march from Kabul to Kandahar covering the 320 miles over very rough terrain and in temperatures as high as 44 degrees C (110 F) in the shade in 24 days. Having arrived he proceeded to destroy the Afghan army again, outflanking the enemy to create surprise. The army was now able, unlike in the First Afghan War, to withdraw in good order and by April 1881 the last British soldier was safely across the border, and Roberts a national hero.

In South Africa there was also further fighting at this time. During 1877-78 the Kaffirs were finally brought to heel in the last of nine wars against them since Napoleonic days, but one major native threat, the Zulus, still remained. The Boers in the Transvaal were unable to de-fend themselves against the depredations of these warriors under their king, Cetewayo, so their country was annexed in 1878. The next year Lord Chelmsford, the local British com-mander, embarked on an advance to the Zulu capital of Ulundi using three separate columns. Early disaster struck when the Zulus overran the base camp of the central column at Isandlwhana, and a Zulu invasion of Natal was thwarted only by the gallant defence of the mission station at Rorke's Drift by B Company of the 24th Foot (South Wales Borderers), seven of whose mem-bers won the VC. It was an apt revenge for the loss of the remainder of the battalion at Isandl-whana. After a four-month pause Chelmsford once again advanced and shattered the Zulu power on the outskirts of Ulundi. The Gatling guns with the force were especially effective. The indefatigable Wolseley now arrived to carry out the mopping up, capturing Cetewayo himself.

The Zulu threat to them now removed, the Transvaal Boers revolted against British rule, investing the small and scattered British gar-risons in the state. A small force was sent from Natal in January 1881 to relieve them, but was blocked by the Boers at Laings Nek, which mark-ed the last recorded occasion when a British regiment, the 58th Foot (2nd Battalion North-amptonshire Regiment), carried its colours in

battle. Part of the same force tried to dislodge the Boers at Majuba Hill a month later, but was overwhelmed. Roberts was now sent to take charge, but the British Government came to an agreement with the Boers that they could govern the Transvaal in all respects save foreign policy. It was, however, a warning that the Boers, with their fine marksmanship and ability as horse-men, could not be treated in the same way as the native tribes.

Attention now switched to Egypt. In 1869 the Suez Canal had been opened, radically speeding up communications between Britain and India, as well as the other British territories in the Far East; Britain was a major shareholder in the

Above: The last stand of the 66th (now the Duke of Edinburgh's Royal Regiment) at Maiwand in 1880.

Below: The Duke of Cambridge, Commander-in-Chief of the Army 1856-95.

Above: 3rd London Rifle Volunteers (now 6th/7th (Volunteer) Battalion, the Queen's Regiment), with Gatling gun, 1893.

Below: Playing on despite his wounds, Piper Findlater, Gordon Highlanders, winning his Victoria Cross during the storming of the heights of Dargai during the Tirah Expedition against the Pathans, 1897.

Canal. Egypt at this time was still nominally under Turkish rule, but in 1882 an Egyptian nationalist, Arabi Pasha, raised the standard of revolt. A number of Europeans were murdered and the Canal seemed threatened. The Royal Navy bombarded Alexandria, and Wolseley, with an expeditionary force sent from England, landed and defeated the rebels at Tel-el-Kebir.

Trouble now brewed to the south in Sudan, where a religious fanatic, Mohammed Ahmed, declared himself the Mahdi and set forth with the aim of converting the whole region to Islam. Sudan was supposedly under the control of Egypt, but this was soon lost, especially after a Turco-Egyptian Army under Hicks Pasha was defeated near El Obeid in October 1883. (The Egyptian Army was trained on British lines and led by British officers, who adopted Turkish ranks, on secondment from the British Army.) Other Egyptian garrisons were destroyed, and the Egyptian Government asked for the services of General 'Chinese' Gordon, another controversial Victorian soldier who had got his nickname when leading a Chinese army during the Taiping revolt of 1863-65. Gordon arrived in Sudan in early 1884, and promptly got himself shut up in

Khartoum. The British Government was not keen to become involved, and Gladstone, the Prime Minister, suspected that Gordon had gone to Khartoum to provoke the sending of a British expeditionary force. Not until August did he relent, and Wolseley was appointed once more to take charge. He was faced with innumerable difficulties, however, especially over transport, and when after many vicissitudes the relief force finally arrived at Khartoum at the end of January 1885, it found that Gordon had been killed two days earlier. Gladstone, who until then had been known as 'GOM' (Grand Old Man), now became 'MOG' (Murderer of Gordon). Apart from the occupation of Suakin, this was the end of the campaign, since the Government decided not to pursue the Mahdi, and the troops retired to the Nile Valley.

It was to be 11 years before the British again ventured into Sudan, and this time the primary reason was not so much to defeat the Mahdi, whose mantle had now fallen on the Khalifa Abdullah, Mohammed Ahmed having died, as to help a European ally. The Italians in an attempt to carve themselves a colonial empire had been decisively defeated by the Abyssinians at Adowa in 1896, and could ill afford to have the Khalifa at their backs. This time the operations were under

the control of Herbert Kitchener the Sirdar or Commander-in-Chief of the Egyptian Army and another of the leading military lights of the time. Using the River Nile and a railway, which he built as he went, Kitchener advanced with 15,000 troops, mostly Egyptian, which eventually rose to 26,000. Gradually he pacified the country, finally reaching Khartoum at the beginning of September 1898. The Khalifa, in a last desperate throw, attacked him with 60,000 men in the Battle of Omdurman, but they were annihilated, with a third killed. Noteworthy was a charge made by the 21st Lancers, in which a youthful subaltern of the 4th Hussars, Winston Churchill, took part.

During this time the army in India had also been kept fully occupied. During 1885-87 there had been another campaign in Burma, which resulted in the whole of Upper Burma coming under British control, and the next few years there saw numerous operations to quell the activities of the local bandits or dacoits, as they were called. There were also constant campaigns on the North-West Frontier against the fierce, proud and wily Pathans. They were not under British rule, but constantly made forays onto the plains of northern India. Indeed, during the period 1847-1913 no less than 66 punitive ex-

peditions were mounted in this area, carried out by forces varying from a few hundred to many thousands, and few British regiments serving in India did not take part in at least one of these. The 1890s was an especially turbulent period, as the bars of the 1895 India Medal indicate – 'Defence of Chitral 1895', 'Relief of Chitral 1895', 'Punjab Frontier 1897-98', 'Malakand 1897', 'Samana 1897', 'Tirah 1897-98'. This frontier fighting provided, if nothing else, very good

Above: Saving the guns at Colenso, 15 December 1899, during the Black Week. Lord Roberts' son won a posthumous VC in this action.

Below: The charge of the 21st Lancers (now 17th/21st) at Omdurman in 1898.

practical experience of soldiering. Generally a punitive expedition took the form of a column which advanced into the troubled area. The key, in view of the Pathans' tactic of trying to ambush the column from the high ground which inevitably dominated the route, was the cry 'picquet the heights', which meant that detachments had to be sent up to cover this high ground before the column advanced. The detachments then leap-frogged forward in parallel with the column. Every night a fortified camp was made, and this was a favourite time for the Pathans to fire on the troops and also, if possible, to sneak into the camp to steal weapons, which they were expert at doing despite the numerous sentries. Every man usually slept with his weapon strapped to him. Once the column arrived at its objective it was the task of the political officers to parley with the village headmen and extract a fine from them for their misdemeanours. Once this had been achieved the column retired. One aspect of this style of warfare is still remembered by the British Army in the annual Khud Race in Hong Kong. Very much Gurkha inspired, it is a race up and down a very steep hill in the New Territories, a reminder that the picquets had to move fast to get up and off the heights to prevent the Pathans arriving first.

The British Army's efforts to defend the Empire or, as it was later called, imperial policing, did not go unrecognised by the public at home. The introduction of the telegraph meant that correspondents accompanying these expeditions were able to get their reports back to their newspapers in a comparatively short time, so that people were far better informed as to what was going on in the Empire than ever before. There was also an extraordinary national feeling that the British were superior to all other nations and had the largest empire the world had ever seen to prove it. This attitude was called Jingoism, and took its name from a popular song of the late 1870s, when Russia was again at war with Turkey and there was a possibility that Britain might come in on the Turkish side once more.

'We don't want to fight, but by jingo if we do,
We've got the ships, we've got the men, and got the money too.'

The Army also had two unofficial publicists in Rudyard Kipling and Sir Henry Newbolt. Kipling became the spokesman for the largely in-articulate soldier, especially the soldier serving in India.

'We aren't no thin red 'eroes, nor we aren't no black-guards too.
But single men in barracks, most remarkable like you;
And if sometimes our conduck isn't all your fancy paints,
Why, single men in barracks don't grow into plaster saints.'

Newbolt, on the other hand, looked to the young officers, the vast majority of them educated in the public schools, numbers of which had sprung up in Britain during the second half of the nineteenth century. Indeed, he summed up the public school ethic:

'To set the cause above renown,
To love the game beyond the prize,
To honour, while you strike him down,
The foe that comes with fearless eyes;
To count the life of battle good,
And dear the land that gave you birth,
And dearer yet the brotherhood,
That binds the brave of all the earth....'

It was also during this period that the first Military Tattoo was seen, with the establishment of the Royal Tournament in 1880. Originally the aim was to encourage military skill-at-arms, but it quickly grew into a pageant as well. Held every summer at Earl's Court in London, it continues to attract large audiences from all over the world.

During the 1890s trouble had been brewing once more in South Africa. The root was the discovery of gold in the Transvaal in 1886, which resulted in an invasion of fortune seekers, many of them British. The Boers, understandably, resented these new arrivals or *Uitlanders*, as they called them, especially since their standards of behaviour offended the Boer's strict Calvinist outlook. In retaliation they severely restricted the rights of the *Uitlanders* in terms of franchise and taxes. In 1896 an attempt supported by the *Uitlanders* was made to topple the Transvaal government, but this so-called Jameson Raid ended in disaster, provoking even tougher Boer reaction. In November 1898 an English Uit-lander was killed by a Boer policeman in circum-

Below: British infantry on the march during the Boer War.

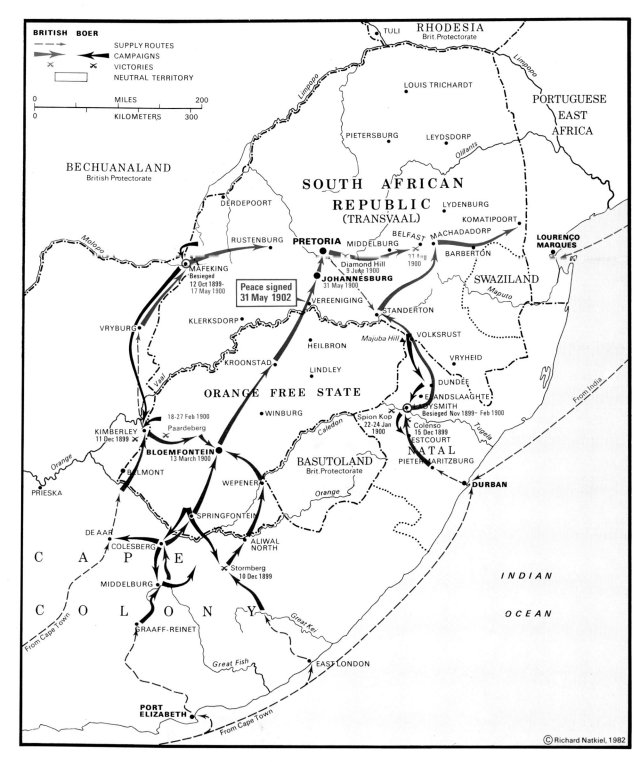

Above: Kitchener in his uniform of Sirdar of the Egyptian Army.

Left: Battles and campaigns of the Boer War.

stances which smacked of murder. The policeman, however, was not only acquitted but commended by the judge, and over 20,000 *Uitlanders* now petitioned the Queen to resume full sovereignty over the Transvaal. In May 1899 the British Government accepted the petition and instructed the High Commissioner for South Africa, Sir Alfred Milner, to approach the Transvaal government. From then matters went from bad to worse and on 11 October 1899 the Boers declared war.

In 1899 the British Army had some 8000 men in South Africa out of a total strength of 100,000, excluding India, where there were 150,000 men in the British and Indian armies. The conservatism of the Duke of Cambridge, who had been succeeded by Wolseley as Commander-in-Chief in 1895, had percolated through much of the Army. The troops at home carried out only 20

days of field training during the year, and large-scale manoeuvres were still the exception. The soldier fired only 50 rounds annually on the open range with the new Lee Enfield magazine rifle which had been introduced in 1895. Much of the training was still concentrated on close order drill; camouflage and entrenching were not covered, although the traditional red coat had now given way, at least overseas, to the more practical khaki – first used during the 1882 Egyptian campaign. The Maxim gun had taken over from the Gatling, but there was a 25 per cent shortfall in establishment, and only junior officers were trained in its use. The artillery was made up of 8-pounders, 12-pounders and 5-inch howitzers, but ammunition reserves were critically short, only 200 rounds per gun. There were serious deficiencies in the holdings of reserve war stocks, the worst of which was that there was

Above: Boers ambushing a supply convoy. They will quickly melt away into the veldt.

Below: A mounted Pom Pom section in South Africa. The Pom Pom was an automatic weapon firing 1-inch shells, and the name came from its distinctive sound.

literally no field hospital equipment. While a Royal Commission under Lord Harrington had recommended in 1890 that a Naval and Military Council be set up to oversee imperial defence and that the post of Commander-in-Chief be abolished in favour of setting up a proper General Staff on Continental lines, these suggestions had not been followed through, and too much strain was imposed on the Commander-in-Chief, who was now feeling the strain of his advancing years, and on the commanders in the field.

The Boers had no regular forces apart from the Staat Artillery, officered by Dutch and Germans, and their police. The backbone of their military organisation was the mounted Commando, of which there were 40 in the Transvaal and Orange Free State at the outbreak of war. They were equipped with modern Mauser rifles and could muster some 50,000 men, with possibly another 40,000 if there was an insurrection in Cape Colony. Expert shots, fast-moving, requiring only the minimum of logistic support (their main diet was dried meat and coffee), well versed in camouflage and fieldcraft, the Boers provided a stark contrast to the British.

The war started with a Boer invasion of Bechuanaland and Cape Province, Kimberley,

Mafeking and Ladysmith quickly being put under siege. The British, however, had early successes at Dundee and Elandslaagte, but efforts to prevent the siege of Ladysmith were unsuccessful, one small British force surrendering to the Boers. In November reinforcements arrived from England in the shape of a 47,000-man army corps under General Buller. He split his force into three for an advance into the Orange Free State, but two weeks before Christmas disaster struck during the so-called Black Week. Each of the three groups was defeated, at Stormberg, Magersfontein and Colenso. In the last-named battle, Lord Roberts' son won a posthumous Victoria Cross for saving some artillery guns, and one British general said: 'I didn't see a Boer all day.'

Black Week came as a sharp shock to the British public, accustomed as they were to the easy victories of other recent colonial wars. The Government's first step was to send out two of the greatest heroes of the age, Roberts to take charge, and Kitchener, as his Chief-of-Staff. The desperate need for more men was solved by sending out Militia companies and also by allowing the Volunteers, until then precluded by act of parliament from serving overseas, to go out to South Africa. The first Volunteer regiment to go was the City of Westminster Volunteers, which was given an emotional farewell by the people of London. The Government, for reasons of parsimony, would not feed, pay and transport the militia, yeomanry and volunteers until they arrived in South Africa, so that only 40,000 went during the first six months. Further sources of manpower were the Dominions, and Australia, Canada and New Zealand all sent contingents. Some British regiments were also sent across from India, but the Government decreed that native troops were not to be used against the Boers and was also fearful of weakening the army in India too much.

Roberts and Kitchener arrived in South Africa in January 1900. Roberts saw his first task as building up his strength and was prepared to remain on the defensive until he was ready. He also had a large number of deficiencies to make

DAILY

RELIEF OF MAFEKING.

THE BESIEGERS' CORDON BROKEN BY THE FLYING COLUMN.

HEAVY BOMBARDMENT AND FLIGHT OF THE BOERS.

THE UNKNOWN BRITISH FORCE TRIUMPHANTLY ENTERS THE TOWN.

UNPARALLELED SCENES OF REJOICING.

Mafeking is relieved; after a siege last-
i_ 216 days. The southern relief force
and after hard fight-

which have fallen to the lot of few garrisons
in the whole annals of warfare, and they
steeled their hearts to hold out till help
came.

he story of the last and desperate Boer

REJOICINGS ABROAD

HOW THE NEWS WAS RECEIV IN AMERICA.

AUSTRALIAN ENTHUSIASM

(From Our Own Correspondent.)
NEW YORK, Friday, May 1
The announcement of the relief of M.
king was bulletined here late in the af
noon. It soon attracted big crowds aro
the bulletin boards in the vicinity of
newspaper offices, and at up-town po
where the information was displayed
cheering of the crowds was almost conti
ous, as new arrivals were constantly com
to take the places of those who had fe
their eyes on the good news and pass
In City Hall Park, where
crowd gathered despite the drizzli
several British flags were unfurled
British sympathiser procured the so
several bands as soon as possible,
spent the early part of the evening a
ous points playing "God Save the Q
and other English patriotic tunes, a
and then the "Star-Spangled Banne
The excitement has been stirred
past two days by alternate announce
of the relief and surrender of Mafekin
the confirmation of the report of its
caused great enthusiasm.
The newspapers will generally ex
to-morrow morning over the rel
brave garrison, which has triumn
valorously with
exp

good. First of all there was a grave lack of mounted troops, and it was essential to have the same mobility as the Boers. Roberts therefore converted some of his infantry into mounted infantry and formed a number of 'irregular' horsed units from Dominion volunteers and locally enlisted British South Africans. The supply system was in tatters and he began an extensive railway building programme, set up a system of supply parks and collected a vast number of oxen, mules and wagons, giving each regiment its own train. He overhauled the intelligence organisation and imposed strict security regarding his future plans. Finally he urgently requested better medical facilities from Britain, and set about trying to raise the personal hygiene standards of the troops, many of whom were succumbing to dysentery. The mental attitude deeply ingrained in the British Army's close-order approach also had to be changed. The British soldier had to be

made to overcome the problem of dealing with an enemy who shot at him but was seldom seen. This was not easy, especially when even Kitchener commented:

'The Boers are not like the Sudanese who stood up in a fair fight. They are always running away on their little ponies. . . . There are a good many foreigners among the Boers, but they are easily shot, as they do not slink about like the Boers themselves.'

Nevertheless, within a month Roberts considered himself ready to take the offensive. After defeating Cronje in the 10-day Battle of Paardeberg, Roberts pushed on and in early March 1900 seized the capital of the Orange Free State, Bloemfontein. He now paused, since his sick list was reaching alarming proportions and his lines of communication had become overstretched. Two Boer raids on his communications were a portent of things to come. In April Roberts moved on again, and on 17 May Mafeking, which had been held by Robert Baden-Powell, father of the Scout movement, was relieved. When the news reached Britain a new verb entered the English language, 'to maffick', which the dictionary defines as to 'exult riotously', which was what the people of London did. The other garrisons were relieved and Johannesburg and Pretoria captured. On 10 September Roberts annexed the Transvaal and declared that, apart from minor guerrilla skirmishes, the war was effectively over. He then returned to England to become Commander-in-Chief and Kitchener took over, but not until May 1902 did the war finally come to an end.

The last 18 months of the war were very much what is now called a counter-insurgency campaign, something the British Army would become very used to in later years. Boer commandos carried out raids, while the British tried to trap them into surrender. Much of the reason that this last phase went on for so long was that Kitchener was suffering from a shortage of mounted troops. The belief that the war was to all

Above left: General John French, who commanded the cavalry in South Africa and would lead the British Armies in France 1914-15.

Above: How the news of the relief of Mafeking broke in London.

intents and purposes over by autumn 1900 had resulted in most of the Yeomanry and colonial mounted regiments returning home and the purchase of horses being restricted. Kitchener eventually managed to get more mounted troops, and indeed the total troop strength in South Africa rose to 260,000 men against less than 20,000 Boers still in the field. Endless columns moved about the veldt trying to track the commandos down. A blockhouse system was set up in order to pen the Boers in, and eventually over 10,000 were built, covering 5000 square miles of country, each manned by a section or more of men. There were what were called 'New Model Drives', in which thousands of men advanced, soldiers being placed 12 yards apart in a continuous line, with the idea of driving the Boers against a line of blockhouses. Boer farms were burnt to deny the commandos supplies and, even more controversially, Kitchener began to intern Boer Families in 'Concentration Camps.' Bad siting and poor medical facilities resulted in a mortality rate of up to 60 per cent in one or two camps and produced an outcry both at home and abroad. Gradually the commandos were worn down and their leaders eventually made peace at Vereeniging at the end of May 1902.

As after the Crimean War, there was a wide-ranging investigation of the Army's shortcomings at the end of the Boer War, and even more dramatic reforms resulted. These were introduced by three Secretaries of State in the immediate post-war era, Broderick, Arnold-Foster and Haldane. At the very top the Committee for Imperial Defence was set up, its main task being to 'survey as a whole the strategical needs of the Empire.' It was to be headed by the Prime Minister, with, among others, the naval and military ministers, the professional heads of the two services, and the heads of naval and military intelligence on the committee. In 1904 the post of Commander-in-Chief was finally removed, Roberts having been the last incumbent. In its place was substituted that of Chief of the Imperial General Staff (CIGS), who would have under him three principal staff officers, the Adjutant-General, responsible for the administration of the troops, known as 'A' matters, the Quartermaster-General covering supply ('Q'

Below: The last part of the South African War was one of intense tedium. The garrison of No 29 Blockhouse comes from the 1st Coldstream Guards. The natives were locally recruited as scouts.

matters) and the Master-General of the Ordnance, who retained his traditional responsibility for weapons procurement. Directly under the CIGS came the four operational branches ('G' matters) – Directorate of Military Operations (DMO), Directorate of Military Training (DMT), Directorate of Staff Duties (DSD), responsible for organisation and the deployment of troops, and the Directorate of Military Intelligence (DMI). The Army Council was also established to provide a single collective body to decide questions of policy, on much the same lines on which the Admiralty operated. There was also a positive policy to delegate routine administration down to districts, which were set up for this very purpose, and leave the field formations more time to concentrate on operational training.

As the 1900s went on it became clear that war in Europe involving Britain was increasingly possible. In 1904 Britain and France become allies as a result of the Entente Cordiale set up by Edward VII and Germany was seen as the most likely enemy. Staff talks were begun and it was eventually agreed that on the outbreak of hostilities on the Continent Britain would send across an expeditionary force of one cavalry and six infantry divisions within 15 days. Given the organisation of the army at home at the time and the likelihood that the war might be drawn out and reinforcements required, it was impossible to do this without major changes. The 12-year engagement had already been altered to nine with the Colours and three on the Reserve because of the demands overseas. There were also five 'paper' corps and one, I Corps at Aldershot, which was real. Lord Haldane now built on I Corps to create his expeditionary force, and this eventually consisted of three corps each of two divisions. There was, however, the thorny question of home defence, and the danger that the country would be singularly ill-equipped to defend itself once the expeditionary force had departed. Haldane tackled this by dissolving the Militia and Volunteers and forming the Territorial Force which, so that it would be 'ready in all respects for mobilisation immediately on the outbreak of a great war', was organised into 14 infantry divisions, complete with integral supporting arms and services, and 14 cavalry brigades. Some 70 Militia battalions were amalgamated with regular regimental depots in order that they might provide an immediate alternative reserve for the regiments to draw on besides their own time-served men. This was called the Special Reserve.

In terms of professionalism and training, the Army went through a dramatic change. Large-scale manoeuvres now became commonplace. There was much emphasis on musketry training, those qualifying as marksmen being granted extra pay; fieldcraft too was given much attention. The formation of the General Staff dramatically increased the importance of Camberley, which every aspiring officer now wished to attend. The syllabus at Sandhurst and Woolwich was revised to make it more applicable to modern warfare. Finally, and not least important, official manuals laying down in detail staff responsibilities and procedures, *Field Service Regulations*, were introduced.

While the army at home was undergoing these

dramatic changes, the small wars overseas had continued. In 1900 the Boxer Rebellion occurred, when the Chinese Boxer fanatics besieged the foreign legations in Peking, and an 8000-man force was sent from India to join other detachments of troops from Japan, Germany, France, Russia, the USA, Austria and Italy. There were constant campaigns in Somaliland against the Mad Mullah, and further campaigns in West Africa. In 1904 there was an expedition to Tibet and there were constant rumblings on the North-West Frontier. Often the main burden of waging these small wars rested on forces recruited from the indigenous peoples of the area, with British officers and Non-Commissioned Officers (NCOs) to lead and train them. Corps such as the Royal West African Frontier Forces, the King's African Rifles, the Burma Rifles and the Somaliland Camel Corps were formed.

In March 1914, however, an event much nearer home rocked the nation. In 1912 the Liberal Government had introduced yet another Home Rule Bill for Ireland. By 1914 it seemed as though this might become law. The Ulster Protestants had long resisted Home Rule, and in 1912 had formed a paramilitary force, the Ulster Volunteer Force, which vowed to 'fight rather than unite.' If Home Rule was to be forced on Ulster it seemed possible that the army in Ireland might be used to do it. Many officers in the army were Protestant Irishmen who were discomforted by the thought that they might have to fight their kith and kin. General Sir Arthur Paget, the Commander-in-Chief in Ireland, went across to seek clarification from the Secretary of State, JEB Seely, who said that any officer who came from Ulster would be allowed to 'disappear', but any others disobeying in the event of an order being given to move into Ulster would be dismissed. Paget returned to Ireland and asked the officers of the 3rd Cavalry Brigade

what they intended to do. The commander, Brigadier General Hubert Gough, and 58 out of his 70 officers declared that they would prefer to be dismissed from the service. They received backing from General Sir Douglas Haig, who was in command at Aldershot and stated that his corps would not move to Ulster if ordered. The Government then backed down and assured the officers concerned that there was no intention of using the Army against Ulster, although at the same time it declared that in future no officer would be allowed to question the intentions of his subordinates should a particular order be given, and that 'an officer or soldier is forbidden in future to ask for assurances as to orders which he may be required to obey.' The Curragh Mutiny, as it was called, since this is where the 3rd Cavalry Brigade was based, was an unusual incident, but the fault must lie with the Government for not making the situation clear and, perhaps more importantly, for not recognising that the Army might have some sensitivities. In any event Seely was forced to resign, but neither he nor the other principal actors came badly out of it. He himself was to command the Canadian Cavalry Brigade in France with much distinction, Gough would become an army commander and Haig would lead the British armies in France for most of the First World War.

During that long hot summer of 1914 it was Ireland rather than Europe which held the attention of British soldier and civilian alike. The murder of the Archduke Franz Ferdinand of Austria-Hungary and his wife in the little town of Sarajevo in Bosnia on 28 June was recognised only by a few for what it portended. Yet, as ultimatum followed ultimatum and the armies of Continental Europe began to mobilise, it began to dawn that the war clouds were sweeping over the English Channel and were about to engulf Britain.

Above: London welcomes back the City Imperial Volunteers, wearing their distinctive slouch hats, from South Africa at the end of 1900.

THE MONSTROUS ANGER OF THE GUNS 1914-18

Previous page: 8-inch howitzers in action in the Fricourt-Mametz sector of the Somme, August 1916.

On 1 August 1914 Germany and Austria declared war on Russia and the same night German troops entered Luxembourg, in contravention of treaty, and demanded free passage through Belgium, which was rejected. France, which had been subjected to a German demand on 31 July to stay neutral and surrender her fortresses of Toul and Verdun, refused to do so, and Germany declared war against her on 3 August. German troops entered Belgium, and Britain sent an ultimatum to Germany stating that if her troops did not withdraw from Belgium a state of war would exist between the two countries from midnight 4/5 August. No such undertaking was forthcoming and Britain was embroiled in a major European conflict for the first time since 1815.

The introduction of the magazine rifle, the machine-gun and quick-firing artillery, together with smokeless powder had weighted the scales in favour of the defence, and an indication of this had been the trench warfare of the Russo-Japanese War of 1904-5, to which all the European armies had sent observers. The German and Franco-British plans at the outbreak of war did not reflect this, however. The German strategy, known as the Schlieffen Plan after its originator, called for a massive wheel through the Low Countries which would pass west of Paris, with the intention of defeating the French with their backs to their own frontier defences. The French

Below: Answering Kitchener's call. The London Recruiting Office in Whitehall, 1914.

Plan XVII also envisaged an offensive, and was based on the premise that the Germans would not have the strength both to mount an attack through Belgium and carry out an effective defence of Lorraine. The French therefore resolved to attack in Lorraine.

The pre-1914 Anglo-French staff talks had evolved a plan whereby the small British Expeditionary Force (BEF) would cross to France and deploy on the left of the French line. Mobilisation was begun on 3 August, not the most convenient time since it was a public holiday and many Territorial Force (TF) units were just moving to their annual two weeks' summer camp. Orders were immediately sent to cancel the camps, and the TF returned to its depots. Meanwhile telegrams were sent to all regular officers and soldiers on leave, as well as to the reservists. On their arrival at their depots they drew their weapons and equipment, which had been held in store for them. Only a very minute fraction of reservists failed to answer the call, and there were numerous cases of men previously posted as deserters or absentees reporting to their regimental depots. The operation went remarkably well. One battalion, which had required almost 600 reservists to make it up to war establishment:

'On the evening of the third day of mobilisation, ie the 7th August, the whole Battalion, at full war strength, paraded at 5 pm, complete with mobilised transport. It was a marvellous sight, and a truly wonderful piece of organisation accomplished in three days.'

It was a triumph of thorough and accurate staff work, and illustrated just how much more efficient the British Army had become during the previous decade.

The Government decided that the BEF should

initially consist of four infantry and one cavalry divisions, together with an independent infantry brigade. For the time being the other two earmarked divisions would remain in Ireland, in case there was trouble there, and in England, until the mobilisation of the TF was complete. Selected to command the BEF was General Sir John French, a cavalryman who had distinguished himself in South Africa. Under him was I Corps, commanded by Lieutenant General Sir Douglas Haig, another cavalryman, and consisting of the 1st and 2nd Divisions, and II Corps, commanded by Lieutenant General Sir James Grierson, who died of a heart attack shortly after arriving in France and was replaced by General Sir Horace Smith-Dorrien. This corps consisted of the 3rd and 5th Divisions. Each division was

Above: The Grenadier Guards pass Buckingham Palace on their way to France.

Below: Recruits for a London rifle regiment drill in Hyde Park. It will be some days before all receive uniform.

made up of three brigades, each of four battalions. The battalion itself was at this time undergoing a transition from an eight- to a four-company structure. The four companies were each broken down into four platoons, each of four sections. There was also a machine-gun section with two Maxims, along with signallers, transport, cooks and storemen. The battalion had a total establishment of 30 officers and 977 other ranks, the former being armed with sword and pistol and the latter with the new short Lee Enfield magazine rifle.

Each infantry division also had a cavalry squadron, four batteries of Royal Field Artillery, equipped with the 18-pounder quick-firing gun, and a battery of 60-pounders of the Royal Garrison Artillery (RGA). It also had two Royal Engineers field companies. The Cavalry Division, commanded by Major General Edmund Allenby, had five brigades, each of three regiments. A cavalry regiment had three squadrons, each broken down into four troops, together with a two-gun machine-gun section. A regiment's total establishment was 25 officers and 526 other ranks. Lancers were equipped with the lance, while the remainder – dragoons, dragoon guards and hussars – had sabres. All carried the Lee Enfield cavalry carbine. The Cavalry Division also had five Royal Horse Artillery (RHA) batteries, each with six 13-pounder guns.

The basic tactical concept for the attack saw two phases. The first was the winning of the fire fight, which was carried out by the scouts reinforced by the firing line and if necessary by the supports. Once the enemy had been worn down, the general reserve would attack one of his flanks. A force would be kept in the same two parts for defence, and the emphasis here lay on the counter-attack. This was called active defence, and the other main form, passive defence, whose object was 'to beat off an attack without hope of being able to turn the tables on the enemy by assuming the offensive at some stage of the fight,' was only to be adopted as a last resort. This was very much an infantryman's battle, although he relied to a large extent on artillery to help him win the fire fight. Cavalry still occupied its traditional roles of screening, flank protection and the pursuit.

The BEF began to cross the Channel on 12 August, strengthened by a message from King George V saying: 'I have implicit confidence in you my soldiers. Duty is your watchword, and I know your duty will be nobly done.' The troops were warmly greeted by the French when they landed, although, as one young officer recorded, '. . . it seemed very strange walking about in uniform on French streets'. There was, however, little time to pause, and they were placed in trains to take them up to their deployment area, experiencing for the first time the cattle trucks which had chalked on them 'Hommes 40, Chevaux 8', meaning that each could take 40 men (a platoon) or eight horses. They got off the trains at railheads in the Maubeuge area, and then marched northwards to take up positions on the Mons-Condé Canal just inside Belgium. It was now that the reservists began to suffer on the cobbled French roads since their feet were not sufficiently hardened to boots, and many fell out, although they caught up at halts. The first troops

into action were C Squadron, 4th Dragoon Guards, who clashed with a German cyclist/cavalry patrol in the village of Soignies on 21 August, and Corporal Thomas of that squadron is credited with firing the first British shot of the war. There were also other cavalry brushes during the next 24 hours.

Two days earlier another historic event had taken place, when aircraft of the Royal Flying Corps made their first reconnaissance flights in support of the ground troops. Blériot's historic first flight over the English Channel in 1909 had awoken military interest in the aircraft as a potential weapon of war, and privately owned flying machines had taken part in the Army manoeuvres of the following year. In 1911 all military aeronautical activities had been put under the umbrella of the Air Battalion Royal Engineers, but in May 1912 the Royal Flying Corps had been formed, and 63 aircraft had flown to France with the BEF.

Above: Somewhere in France British troops snatch a quick meal.

Top left: A very neatly-constructed trench of a Lancashire regiment, photographed in November 1914.

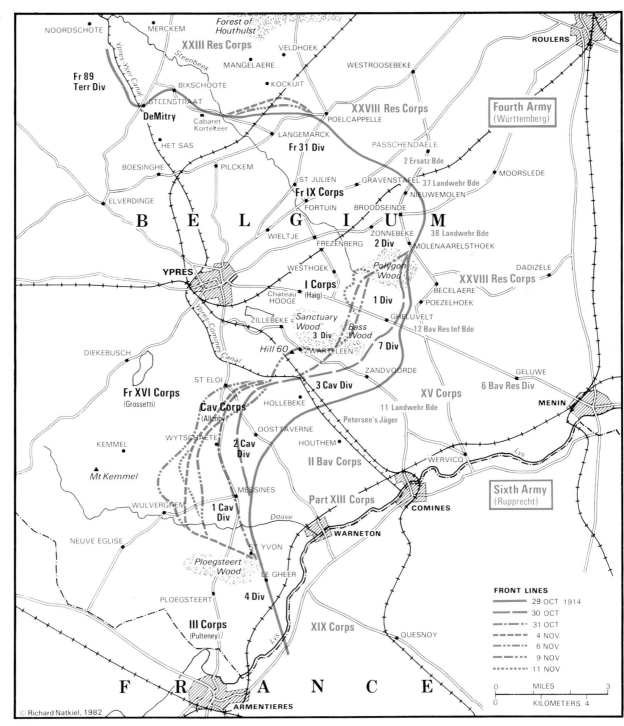

Left: The 16th Lancers (now 16th/5th) pass French cavalry, September 1914.

Right: The First Battle of Ypres.

Above: Trench warfare, winter 1914-15.

Right: Sir John French. His handling of the Battle of Loos in September 1915 brought about his removal from command.

By this stage the German advance had moved through Belgium and was entering France, while the French Plan XVII had proved disastrous, 300,000 men being killed, wounded or captured during the ten-day Battle of the Frontiers. On 23 August the Germans came up against the main British position, not expecting to find them there. They advanced in mass formation, and it was now that prewar musketry training showed its benefits. A corporal in the Royal Irish Rifles:

'Our rapid fire was appalling even to us, and the worst marksman could not miss, as he only had to fire into the "brown" of the masses of the unfortunate enemy, who on the fronts of our two companies were continually and uselessly reinforced at the short range of three hundred yards.'

Indeed, the Germans thought that the British infantry battalion was equipped with nothing but machine-guns, instead of merely the two that they had. By the afternoon, though, the Germans had brought up their artillery and the British experienced for the first time the effects of a modern bombardment. Nevertheless the British infantry held, and the Germans considered they had been defeated. Unfortunately the French on the British right had decided to withdraw, and the BEF had no option but to conform though the troops could not understand why they had to withdraw after giving the enemy such a 'bloody nose.' Day after day the retreat went on under the hot August sun. On the 26th, against orders, Smith-Dorrien, now reinforced with the 4th Division, albeit without its transport, medical services and Royal Engineers, turned at bay at Le Cateau and forced the Germans to pause. Then the retreat went on. More and more men fell out from exhaustion, though most rejoined later. At every halt it became harder and harder to get on the march again. 'We were reeling about like drunken men ourselves, past hoping for rest, but knowing we had to go on', one officer recalled. In the meantime General Gallieni, the Governor of Paris, was organising another army to come up on the left of the hard-pressed BEF, and much of it was moved to the front using Paris taxicabs. Combined with a move by Lanrezac's French Fifth Army on the British right which caught the enemy on his exposed left flank, this forced the Germans to halt.

On 6 September the retreat finally came to an end, south-east of Paris and just to the north of the River Seine. In 14 days the BEF had covered nearly 150 miles as the crow flies, and must actually have marched at least twice this distance. Over-extended, the Germans were now driven back, in what was dubbed the Miracle of the Marne, to the River Aisne. Here the Germans established strong positions on the high ground to the north of the river and the Allies could get no further. Both sides now dug in and the next two weeks saw the beginning of trench warfare, which was to mark the fighting on the Western Front for the next four years.

By this time the casualties for the BEF were mounting considerably. Individual replacements were sent out to France, and the 6th Division arrived from Ireland, the BEF now being reorganised into three corps of two divisions. The 8th Division, and the Indian Corps of one cavalry and two infantry divisions, were on their way from India. There was also the 7th Division made up of regular battalions from the United Kingdom and colonial garrisons. To the new Secretary of State for War, Lord Kitchener, it was certain that the war would last at least three years, and would not be 'over by Christmas' as popular opinion had it. It was therefore essential that a mass army be raised, but Asquith's Liberal Government refused to countenance the idea of conscription. There was of course Haldane's Territorial Force, but Kitchener viewed this with contempt, even though many of its members had volunteered for service overseas. Instead he disorganised the carefully built-up Territorial divisions by sending many individual battalions to India, Egypt and other places to take over from the Regular Battalions being moved to France. A few Territorial battalions were also sent to France to guard the lines of communication.

To provide his mass army Kitchener decided to capitalise on the mass patriotic fervour which had swept the country on the outbreak of war. He initially called for 100,000 volunteers, using what has become perhaps the most famous British advertising poster of all time. Men flooded the recruiting offices, and Kitchener dropped the 100,000 limit. By the end of 1914 no less than 1,186,337 men had responded to his call. Kitchener did not form new regiments but expanded the existing ones, and by the end of the war some had over 40 battalions, the record being held by the Northumberland Fusiliers who fielded no less than 52 battalions. Many of these new battalions were raised from men with a common interest or profession or who came from the same town or city district. There were Sportsmen's battalions, a complete brigade of Royal Fusiliers

Above: Lieutenant Colonel Philip Robertson, a cousin of the author, who commanded 17th Northern Division during the latter half of the war, inspecting his battalion's (1st Cameronians) trenches at Bois Grenier, January 1915.

Left: King George V inspects the 29th Division, prior to its departure for the Dardanelles.

Public School Battalions, the Tyneside Scottish (a battalion of the Northumberland Fusiliers), the Bradford Pals (from the West Yorkshire Regiment) and many others. Indeed these units became known as Pals Battalions, although their official designation was Service Battalions. All volunteers had to meet the Regular Army's minimum physical requirements of a height of 5 feet 3 inches and 34-inch chest, but there was an outcry from those below the minimum height who considered themselves perfectly fit to be soldiers, and Kitchener allowed the formation of Bantam Battalions specifically for them; there were instances of volunteers as small as 4 feet 9 inches being accepted. The Canadian Army adopted a similar system.

The main problem with the New Armies was equipping, clothing and training them. There were only a handful of Regular officers left in Britain, and they were quickly grabbed, together with Indian Army officers on long leave. Many retired officers, some even wearing the medal ribbons of the Crimea, offered their services, which were gratefully accepted, even though militarily these 'dug-outs' were hopelessly out of date. The bulk of the officers for the new formations were selected in an almost arbitrary fashion, and many came with just the experience of their public school's Officer Training Corps (OTC), another Haldane innovation, behind them. Cadet battalions were later set up, using Oxford and Cambridge colleges, but many of the early volunteer officers, who were given temporary commissions and were known by Regulars rather disparagingly as 'temporary gentlemen', had to learn on the job.

No uniforms were initially available, apart from those for the officers, who were given an allowance to purchase them, and tailors throughout the country had never made so much money. The other ranks had to make do at first with their civilian clothes, although they received a finan-

cial allowance to cover wear and tear. Eventually they were kitted out with old scarlet and blue uniforms. Meanwhile manufacturers were working overtime to produce proper khaki uniforms and finally the New Armies were able to feel like proper soldiers. Rifles also posed a problem. For some weeks the men had to make do with broomsticks before a consignment of Japanese rifles arrived. Not until the beginning of 1915 were supplies of Lee Enfields issued in significant quantities. For the artillery of the New Armies the situation was even worse, dummy field guns and old 12- and 15-pounders having to be used. Accommodation was also very short. In the early days the old system of billeting troops on civilians had to be adopted, although the civilians were generally only too glad to help out. The battalions were then moved into vast tented camps near major training areas such as Aldershot and Salisbury Plain, and many endured the bleak winter of 1914-15 in the most spartan conditions. Yet the spirit of the men never wavered.

The New Armies were formed into divisions numbered 9-41. (The Territorial Divisions numbered 42-56) and here another major problem arose. Camberley had been closed at the outbreak of war, and trained staff officers were desperately needed in France and the other theatres of war. Consequently the New Army divisions had to struggle on with inexperienced staffs who had to do their best to learn as they went along.

Meanwhile in France the BEF was grappling with the new style of warfare. It quickly learnt, for example, to site trenches not on forward slopes, where they were easy prey for the enemy's artillery observers, but on reverse slopes. There was also a worry that a new passive mentality was developing. A British general lecturing officers of the 8th Division in October before they left for France said:

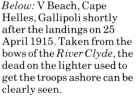

Below: V Beach, Cape Helles, Gallipoli shortly after the landings on 25 April 1915. Taken from the bows of the *River Clyde*, the dead on the lighter used to get the troops ashore can be clearly seen.

'You must do something to save your infantry from this nerve-racking work in the trenches and at the same time be preparing for your forward movement. You must not remain absolutely on the passive defensive. . . . I think our tendency has been rather too much digging into these trenches and being satisfied to stay there. There has not been enough effort to move ahead and look forward to the time when we have got to push on.'

It was just at this time, though, that the war became more mobile again. The Germans began a series of moves northwards, called the Race for the Sea, in an attempt to outflank the Allies, and by the middle of October the BEF found itself centred on the ancient Belgian cloth town of Ypres. The first reaction of the troops was that it was almost unpronounceable, and very quickly it was dubbed Wipers. It was soon to become a symbol for the British Army.

The Germans decided to try to punch a hole through the Allied lines in this area and from the middle of October until mid November made repeated attacks against the BEF. It was a desperate battle, the British troops knowing there were no reserves behind them and that if the Germans broke through they would capture the Channel ports and thus cut the BEF's communications with Britain. Time and again positions were taken and retaken in counterattacks. Cooks, clerks, dismounted cavalry and Royal Engineers were sent up to fight as infantry. At one stage the Germans sent barely trained students into the attack. Advancing in massed ranks because they had not been taught to do anything else, they were mown down in droves, and it became known as the *Kindermord bei Ypern* – The Massacre of the Children at Ypres. Somehow the British soldiers held, exhibiting what the author C S Forester called 'those qualities of unflinching courage and dogged self-sacrifice in which they were pre-eminent.' By 1 November, of 84 infantry battalions present in the Ypres area 18 had fewer than 100 men, 31 less than 200 and 26 under 300. The old British Army died in the First Battle of Ypres, and died gloriously, and the survivors have ever since been known as the Old Contemptibles after an

order given by the Kaiser to the commander of the First German Army on 19 August to 'walk over General French's contemptible little army.'

Both sides now stopped to lick their wounds, digging deeper and deeper where they were able, though much of the British sector was in low-lying waterlogged ground where this was difficult, and trying to rebuild their shattered strength. More Special Reservists and old Militia men arrived to bring the British battalions back up to strength, but as one NCO survivor of First Ypres recalled, they 'had not the smartness of the Regulars, and I could not take them rapidly to my heart. Their habits were unsoldierly, and repellent to me.' Yet these in their turn would quickly become veterans to be looked up to by those who joined later. For most it was the first chance they had had to have any rest since the outbreak of

Above: 'Over the top', Gallipoli, summer 1915. Another local attack gets underway.

Below: Early gas masks, here worn by the 2nd Argylls, Bois Grenier sector May 1915.

war, and then came 'the astonishing news that leave to England is granted', and some veterans were able to spend Christmas at home, seven days being allowed. For those who remained in the front line Christmas Day 1914 saw an unusual truce with the Germans. Groups of soldiers got out of their respective trenches and met in the middle of no man's land, exchanging gifts, souvenirs and addresses. Then at midnight the war restarted.

Although the Western Front was, from the British point of view, the main theatre of war, there was fighting involving British troops elsewhere. The 2nd South Wales Borderers, along with the 36th Sikhs, helped the Japanese force the German garrison of the port of Tsingtao in China to surrender. Imperial troops were driving the Germans out of their colonies in South-West Africa and the same was happening in East Africa, although this campaign continued until the war's end. A force from India had been landed at Basra on the Red Sea to begin the long and arduous Mesopotamian Campaign against the Turks, and Australian and New Zealand troops were capturing German Pacific islands. Indeed the Empire was responding wholeheartedly. Over 30,000 Canadian troops were in England by the end of October, and it would not be long before they were in France; the First Australian and New Zealand Army Corps, known as the Anzacs, were in Egypt by Christmas. The South Africans were virtually running the South-West Africa campaign, and in every colony, large and small, troops were being trained and offered up.

By the beginning of 1915 Kitchener and Churchill, who was First Lord of the Admiralty, had concluded that the possibility of an early breakthrough on the Western Front was slight. At the same time there was a plea from Russia for the Western Allies to take some of the Turkish pressure off her in the Caucasus. From these two factors was born the Dardanelles campaign, whose object was to take Constantinople, which might knock Turkey out of the war, and then threaten Germany's ally, Austria-Hungary. The French agreed to co-operate, and the eventual plan evolved was for the combined fleets to force the Dardanelles Straits and get into the Sea of Marmora, after which the British would land on the Gallipoli Peninsula and the French on the south side of the Straits. General Sir Ian Hamilton was appointed to command the British land forces, but was given only 40 days in which to build up a force. He managed to gather together the Anzac Corps, which was still in Egypt, and two divisions from home: the newly formed 29th Division, organised from regular troops who had been in overseas garrisons until relieved by Territorials and local units, and the Royal Naval Division. The latter had been the brainchild of Winston Churchill and had been created out of Royal Marine battalions and naval reservists for whom there were no ships immediately available; it had taken part in an abortive attempt to help the Belgians turn the Germans back from Antwerp.

For many who were to take part, nurtured as they were on a classical education, the operation had much romance about it. As a Royal Artillery officer who was to be awarded a posthumous VC on the day after the landings wrote in his last letter home: 'Well we are off in a day or two if the weather stays fine; just like the Greek fleet going to Troy....' The landings themselves took place on 25 April 1915, a full month after the ships had unsuccessfully bombarded the narrows. The Australians and New Zealanders landed at the aptly named Anzac Beach, but a mile further north than planned, and by the time they had struggled up the precipitous cliffs which confronted them, the Turks had had time to reinforce their positions. The 29th Division landings were at Cape Helles. The 1st Lancashire Fusiliers suffered 533 casualties getting ashore, but were awarded no less than six VCs for their gallant efforts on W Beach. V Beach was marked by the efforts to land 2000 men from an elderly merchant vessel the River Clyde, many being cut down by machine-guns before they could get ashore. At the other two beaches, X and Y, the troops landed with virtually no opposition, but owing to poor communications merely halted on their original objectives. No attempt was made to reinforce their success, and the campaign was condemned to a fruitless stalemate. The Turks were able to reinforce, and the hilly country was ideal defensive terrain.

Throughout the summer attempts were made to get forward, but the only result was ever-lengthening casualty lists. Otherwise the arduous tedium and dangers of trench warfare were endured in temperatures which often rose above 38 degrees C (100 F). A New Zealander:

'...our troubles in the trenches were if you laid down in the dust you got full of lice and annoyed by flies and men walking over you, when on duty getting blown to pieces by bombs or the Turks tunneling towards us and blowing in the trenches, mixed with a shower of dirt from machine-gun and rifle fire from overhead.'

Lice, flies and insanitary conditions caused much

Left: A typical Bairnsfather cartoon. The caption reads, 'The young and talkative one: "Who made that 'ole?" The fed-up one: "Mice".' Bairnsfather served with the Royal Warwicks in France during 1914-15. Apart from their value as a morale booster, his cartoons gave the people at home an accurate portrayal of trench warfare.

Right: "A very satisfactory first day." Realisation of the awesome casualties suffered on the first day of the Battle of the Somme was slow in dawning.

Below: Bazentin Ridge, the Somme, July 1916. British and German walking wounded en route to a field dressing station.

ADVANCE OF ALLIES IN THE WEST STILL CONTINUES

French Drive Germans Back in Disorder and Gain More Ground—Curlu Taken.

HAUL OF PRISONERS NOW AMOUNTS TO 7,000

Furious Fighting to North of the Somme—Night Counter-Blows Repulsed.

(FRENCH OFFICIAL.)

PARIS, Sunday.—The following communiqué was issued this afternoon:—

To the north of the Somme fighting was furious during the night. The Germans launched violent counter-attacks against our new positions on the outskirts of Heudicourt (Hardecourt?).

Our curtain fire and our rifle fire inflicted serious losses on the enemy, who had to fall back in disorder, leaving 200 prisoners in our hands, of whom six were officers.

Pursuing our advantage on the right bank of the river, we gained possession after a sharp fight of the village of Curlu, which we occupied completely.

South of the Somme we have maintained all the positions captured by us yesterday, and have made some progress in the course of the night between Herbecourt and Assewillers.

According to further information to hand, the total figure of unwounded German prisoners captured by the French troops yesterday exceeds 5,000.

Between the Oise and the Aisne we captured a German patrol which tried to approach our lines near Bailly.

Champagne Front.—In Champagne we made a number of reconnaissances along the enemy front, several of which penetrated the German trenches, and swept them clear with hand grenades. We brought back fifteen prisoners.

Verdun Front.—On the left bank of the Meuse a German attack delivered yesterday evening against our positions north-west of the Avocourt Wood, after succeeding in penetrating the advanced elements of our trenches, was completely thrown back by our counter-attack.

On the slopes of the Mort Homme we effected a successful coup de main. In the course of the fighting which took place in the ___ ___ fifty ___ ___ some twenty were mad ___ also left in our ___

Map showing Thiaumont Work.

"A VERY SATISFACTORY FIRST DAY."

Further Developments Can Be Awaited with Confidence.

ALLIES' LOSSES SLIGHT.

PARIS, Sunday.—A semi-official statement issued last night says:—

The chief fact of July 1 on the western front was the beginning of the Franco-British offensive.

By a very extended bombardment, the enemy was kept in ignorance as to the possible field of attack, and consequently had to divide his reserve effectives and to disperse his artillery

The attack began at half-past seven in the morning and was preceded for half an hour by an artillery preparation the violence of which has never yet been equalled.

At nine o'clock the advanced defences of the German lines had fallen into our power.

The enemy's retreat made us masters of the villages of Montauban and Mametz, in the English zone, Becquincourt, Bussu and Fay ___ French zone ___

DESPERATE BLOWS AT RUSSIANS REPULSED.

Retreating Germans Fired On by Own Artillery.

BALTIC SEA SCRAP.

(RUSSIAN OFFICIAL.)

PETROGRAD, Saturday (received yesterday).—The communiqué issued to-day says:—

Western Front.—In the region between the Stokhod and the Styr the enemy is maintaining violent artillery fire.

Desperate fighting has begun in the village of Zatourtsy, where, in spite of a bombardment by the enemy of extreme violence, our troops have already repulsed nine successive attacks with heavy losses for the enemy.

In our sector of this region the Germans who were falling back were fired upon by their own batteries and forced to return to the attack.

The whole ground in this district is covered with enemy corpses.

Yesterday afternoon the enemy artillery produced gusts of fire in the region of Koptchie, Ghelenovka and Zabary, south-west of Sokul.

An energetic infantry attack then followed, but was repulsed.

North-east of Kisseline, near the village of Trystenn, we observed enemy troops mustering. The fire of our artillery dispersed them and put them to flight.

MASSED ASSAULT STOPPED.

South-east of Kisseline our fire stopped an offensive by massed formations of the enemy in the ___ Somerinka ___ there was a

Right: 'Over the Top'. 1st Artists' Rifles (28th Londons), Marcoing, 30 December 1917 by John Nash.

Below: 'Gassed', a dressing station on the Doullens-Arras road, August 1918, by John Sargent.

sickness, dysentery and malaria being especially prevalent. Other divisions, both British and Indian, were sent to the Dardanelles, but this made little difference. At the end of October the weather suddenly changed. Icy rain and howling winds, followed by blizzards, resulted in 280 deaths and 16,000 cases of frostbite, but by this time the decision had been made to abort the operation. The evacuation of the Gallipoli Peninsula took place during the second half of December and first week of January 1916. It was the most successful part of the whole campaign, scarcely a man being lost. The troops were taken to Egypt, where some would shortly be fighting the Turks once more, while others would go to France.

On the Western Front the Germans were content to remain on the defensive while they sought a decision against Russia in the east. The French and British were determined to attack. While the French mounted offensives in Champagne and the Vosges Mountains, the British attacked at Neuve Chapelle in March. A severe lack of artillery ammunition limited both the scope of the operation and the length of the preparatory bombardment, which was restricted to 35 minutes. There was initial success, but the Germans were able to reinforce more quickly than their opponents, and the attack was called off after two days. The result was a gain of 1000 yards of ground on a frontage of 4000 yards at a

cost of 18,000 casualties, 14,000 casualties being suffered by the Germans. In April 1915 the Germans attacked at Ypres using a new weapon, gas. Two French divisions broke, but the situation was restored by the Canadian Division, which had arrived in France in February. The battle rumbled on into May, with a total of 100,000 casualties on both sides. By this time the

Above: 'The Ypres Salient at Night' by Paul Nash, 1918.

Above: A Mk 1 male tank, with 6-pounder guns, of C Company Heavy Section, Machine Gun Corps (now 3rd Royal Tank Regiment), Chimpanzee Valley, 15 September 1916, the day the tanks first went into action.

Below: Flers-Courcelette, September 1916. Men of the 15th Scottish Division march back to rest after capturing Martinpuich, helped by one tank.

Ypres Salient had been reduced from six to two miles' radius. Indeed there were no sound military reasons for retaining Ypres since it was now virtually a deathtrap, but it was an important symbol and this symbol, combined with British obstinacy, was to ensure that Ypres would never fall to the Germans. This Second Battle of Ypres was notable for the tunnelling operations of both sides designed to blow up each other's trench systems, especially around the notorious Hill 60. Tunnelling companies of the Royal Engineers were created specifically to wage this type of warfare.

The shortage of artillery and artillery ammunition was such that guns were often limited to two or three rounds per day, while it seemed to the troops in the front line that the Germans had endless supplies:

'. . . we were shelled without stop, day and night. . . . Our casualties became very heavy and to see pals you have known and worked with for years killed and wounded; it nearly broke our hearts – especially when the dead had to be buried in a quickly dug hole.'

On 21 May Lord Northcliffe launched an attack in his *Daily Mail* on Lord Kitchener for the 'shell scandal'. The Ministry of Munitions was hastily set up under the dynamic David Lloyd George, but it would be some months before the situation improved. In the meantime further British attacks at Aubers Ridge and Festubert in May produced few gains and many casualties.

By this time Territorial and New Army divisions were beginning to arrive in France, and the BEF, which had been divided into two armies from December 1914, had begun to take over more of the line from the French, gradually extending southwards from the Ypres area. The new formations were inducted into the mysteries of trench warfare by spending short periods in the trenches under the tuition of experienced battalions. They quickly discovered that army and corps headquarters were static, and divisions circulated around the corps areas of command. Each corps normally had three divisions under command, of which two would be in the trenches and one at rest. Likewise the divisions had two of their brigades forward and one in reserve. Within each brigade two battalions would be in the trenches, normally for 7-10 days. From the air the trenches had a castellated appearance, rather than running in straight lines, in order to prevent defilade fire. The front line itself was protected by barbed wire just outside grenade-throwing range, No Man's Land being on average some 250 yards wide. Leading back from the front line were the communications trenches, which ran through the support lines and back until movement above ground was safer.

In the trenches everyone stood to for an hour at dusk in case of an enemy attack, this time and dawn being the most likely. After this the work of

the night began. Trenches were repaired and improved, wiring was carried out and often parties would be involved in digging trenches forward into no man's land to prepare jump-off positions for an attack. Patrols would be sent out, either as listening posts to eavesdrop on enemy activities or as foot patrols, usually of an officer and two or three men, who would prowl around no man's land, often on their hands and knees. Sometimes a trench raid would be mounted to get into the German trenches and seize a prisoner. Rations, ammunition and other supplies would be brought up, those 'at rest' immediately behind the line often being used as carrying parties. As dawn began to break these activities would cease and stand-to would be followed by breakfast, washing, shaving and sleep. Since a good proportion always had to be on watch and since there

were constant interruptions from shellfire, mortars and snipers, it was a lucky man who got more than four hours sleep a day.

Apart from providing working parties at night, those at rest immediately behind the lines concentrated on training. Although long moves might be made partly by train or even truck, the infantryman still relied mainly on his feet to get him about, but these became soft in the trenches and route marches were needed to keep them tough. Within the battalion trench warfare was breeding more and more specialities, the rifle playing virtually a secondary role. Indeed it was very noticeable during the more open warfare of 1918 that musketry skills had deteriorated alarmingly. A number of new weapons were now being introduced. The more efficient Vickers machine gun had taken over from the Maxim,

Above: Royal Garrison Artillery 12-inch railway gun in action on the Somme, August 1916.

Below: Awaiting the breakthrough. The Queen's Bays (now Queen's Dragoon Guards), Hardecourt Wood, September 1916.

Above: Easter Rising, Dublin, 1916. Escorting Republican prisoners.

Below: Trench scene. Men of the Border Regiment near Thiepval Wood, on the Somme front, August 1916.

were organised into brigade batteries manned by troops seconded from the brigade's infantry battalions. Heavier mortars were controlled by the Royal Artillery. Grenades, too, were a dominant weapon. In the early days they were hand-made from tin cans, but then came the Mills bomb, still used by the British Army as the No 36 Grenade. Each battalion appointed a Bombing Officer, responsible for training the men in grenade throwing. The rifle grenade was also developed. In order to retain an automatic fire weapon in the battalion, the Lewis Gun, named after its inventor Colonel Lewis of the US Army, was adopted as a section light machine gun. There were too a number of marksmen especially selected to become the battalion snipers and scouts. All this meant that the size of the section was inevitably reduced, sometimes to as few as five or six men, and the problem of providing specialists while retaining a reasonable strength of rifle and bayonet men worried battalion commanders throughout the war.

and machine guns were now concentrated in brigade companies of 16 guns and were the responsibility of a new corps, the Machine Gun Corps. Eventually this would consist of divisional machine gun battalions. There were also Motor Machine Gun Batteries of the Motor Machine Gun Service, which were amalgamated with the Machine Gun Corps and were equipped with machine guns mounted on motor-cycle side-cars. Trench mortars, with their ability to lob high-trajectory bombs into the opposing trenches, were also coming to the fore. The majority were the 3-inch Stokes mortar, and

Artillery too was undergoing changes and was already widely recognised as the dominant weapon on the battlefield. The prewar emphasis on shrapnel, effective against men in the open but not when they were entrenched, quickly gave way to high-explosive shells. The 18-pounder still remained the basic artillery support weapon, but heavier and larger calibre guns were added to the armoury – 8-inch, 9.2-inch and 15-inch howitzers joining the early 60-pounders.

Left: Loading a 9.45-inch trench mortar, a picture taken in the Gommecourt area in March 1917. Heavier calibres of mortar, like this type, were manned by the Royal Artillery.

Below: Westminster Dragoon (now Royal Yeomanry), Palestine 1917. It was in this theatre that cavalry came into their own.

Gunnery techniques were also becoming more sophisticated. In March 1915 the concept of using aircraft to spot for the guns by means of wireless communications had been introduced, and the 'heavies' of the Royal Garrison Artillery began slowly to develop the art of firing accurately by the map, rather than having to rely on forward observers.

The British soldier's diet changed little if at all during the war. His staples were bully-beef, tinned vegetable stew with meat gravy (called Maconochie after the manufacturer) and sometimes meat and vegetable (M & V). For breakfast he might have a little bacon, and there were always ration biscuits and jam, almost invariably plum and apple, and known as 'pozzy'. There was also tea to wash it down, made with condensed milk and chlorinated water which might still retain the tang of petrol from the petrol cans in which it was often carried. If he was lucky he would receive parcels from home to supplement his diet, and when at rest he could go to the local *estaminet* to have his favourite plate of egg and chips and drink a glass or two of watery French beer or wine. He also had his rum ration in the trenches, which he usually took in his tea. The officers could afford to purchase additions to this rather monotonous diet and tended to mess by companies, as they had done during the Peninsular War. Most company messes in the line could at least offer whisky to visitors, and some kept port and wine as well. Indeed, the Commandant of the Senior Officers' School at Aldershot lecturing potential battalion commanders in April 1917 positively encouraged the running of a good mess in the line:

'If our Officers are insufficiently fed and are living

under depressing conditions, their health will certainly suffer, and with loss of health comes irritation, loss of temper, and weak Morale, and when this state of things prevails we all know that the men frequently suffer.'

The British soldier has invariably, at least since the introduction of universal education, been a copious letter writer. Censorship was imposed early on in the war, and this was a burden that fell heavily on the shoulders of the company officers. The fact that their officers read their personal letters was not resented by the men. Indeed, one is supposed to have written: 'The officers should known better how to treat us now, for they all get a read of our letters.' For the lazy or the overworked there was always the field postcard, where the writer merely had to cross out what was inapplicable – I am well/sick/wounded etc. As in any army, regular letters from home were a great morale booster for the British soldier, and the army mail system, run by the Royal Engineers, seldom failed him.

Apart from writing letters, training, sleeping and making good his clothing and equipment, efforts were constantly made to give the soldier at rest some light relief. The battalion would normally organise a sports meeting, and there were always footballs to kick, soccer being the favourite game. A battalion concert party, drawing on the light entertainment talents of its members, was always a standard item. Divisional concert parties were later organised on a permanent basis from those who had stage experience in civilian life.

Another highlight of being at rest was having a bath, the vats of disused breweries being the favourite venue. The soldier was also given a change of shirt and underclothing which helped keep down lice, that bane of trench warfare. One effect of lice was what was called trench fever or

Below: A sentry using a trench periscope. Snipers made it impossible to expose the head by day, while at night sentries stood breast high over the parapet.

'pyrexia of unknown origin', which had the symptoms of influenza and typhoid, although it was seldom fatal; not until 1918 was the cause established as the excreta of the louse. The other common trench ailment was trench foot, caused by exposing the feet too long to cold water. The feet turned blue and red and became a mass of chilblains, and in extreme cases gangrene could set in. The cure was constant attention to the feet, with frequent changes of socks and the use of grease or whale oil; foot inspections were a constant part of the platoon commander's life. One way of telling a good battalion was by its low incidence of this complaint, although it is interesting to note that the British troops in the Falklands in 1982 also had trouble from trench foot. For those wounded in battle, with penicillin not yet discovered, gangrene was the greatest enemy, and although there had been great advances in surgery during the previous 50 years, amputation of a limb was often the only way to prevent it and save life. Likewise plastic surgery was still very much in its infancy and the nearest to it was the development of lifelike painted masks by Captain Derwent Wood, a sculptor and member of the Royal Academy, which hid badly disfiguring face wounds. Every soldier longed to get a wound serious enough for him to be sent back to England, but not so grave as to disable him permanently, the so-called 'Blighty one.'

In 1916 the wound stripe was introduced as the equivalent of the American Purple Heart. It was a thin gold bar worn on the lower left sleeve, and one was awarded for each occasion a soldier had been wounded. Service chevrons were also introduced for time spent in an active theatre of war. That for 1914 service was red, and for the subsequent years of the war blue, and these were worn on the lower right sleeve. There were also a number of awards for gallantry. The Victoria Cross and the Distinguished Conduct Medal had been joined in 1886 by the Distinguished Service Order awarded to officers for distinguished services in wartime, usually in the face of the enemy; but until 1936, when the regulations were tightened up, not necessarily so. On 31 December 1914 King George V instituted the Military Cross for acts of gallantry by junior officers, and this was followed in March 1916 by the Military Medal for other ranks. Allied decorations, especially French and Belgian, were also awarded to officers and men.

There were few radical changes in uniform during the war. In 1916 the steel helmet was introduced, which undoubtedly helped to prevent casualties from shrapnel. The stiff cap of 1914 also became floppy and more shapeless, and therefore less of an obvious target for snipers, by removal of the stiffening wire inside. Highland regiments wore the kilt throughout, normally with a waterproof apron to protect it, and earned the nickname 'Ladies of Hell' from the Germans. They also wore the Highland bonnet, as did Lowland troops, or the glengarry, and the cutaway jacket. The high incidence of junior officer casualties during the first two years of the war gradually led to rank badges being transferred from the sleeve to the less-conspicuous shoulder strap, although some regiments disparagingly called this a 'wind up' jacket, and light-coloured riding breeches being discarded for more sombre

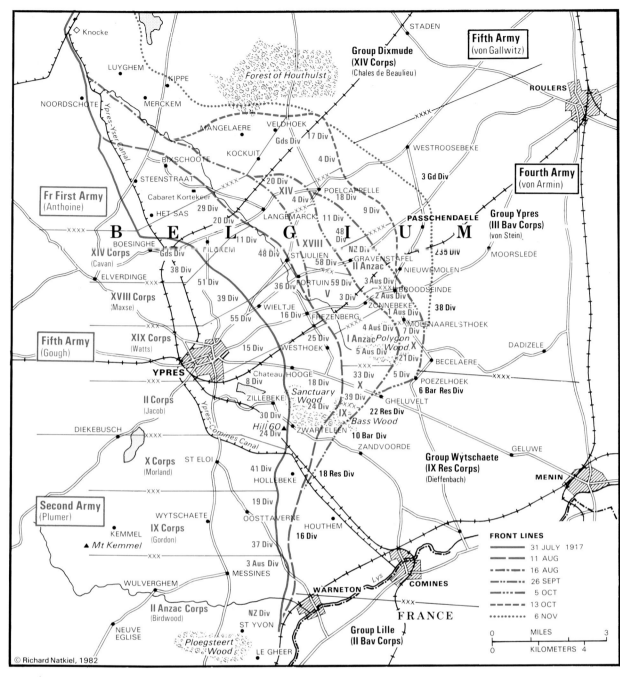

Map labels:

STADEN

Fifth Army (von Gallwitz)

Group Dixmude (XIV Corps) (Chales de Beaulieu)

◇ Knocke

LUYGHEM

KIPPE

Forest of Houthulst

ROULERS

NOORDSCHOTE

MERCKEM

VELDHOEK

Gds Div

17 Div

WESTROOSEBEKE

Fourth Army (von Armin)

BIXSCHOOTE

4 Div

3 Gd Div

STEENSTRAAT

20 Div

XIV

POELCAPPELLE

18 Div

Fr First Army (Anthoine)

Cabaret Kortekeer

4 Div

9 Div

PASSCHENDAELE

Group Ypres (III Bav Corps) (von Stein)

HET SAS

29 Div

LANGEMARCK

11 Div

BELGIUM

20 Div

11 Div

XVIII

48 Div

NZ Div

235 Div

MOORSLEDE

BOESINGHE

Gds Div

PILCKEM

48 Div

ST JULIEN

58 Div

GRAVENSTAFEL

II Anzac

NIEUWEMOLEN

XIV Corps (Cavan)

38 Div

ELVERDINGE

51 Div

36 Div

FORTUIN

59 Div

3 Aus Div

BROODSEINDE

XVIII Corps (Maxse)

39 Div

WIELTJE

16 Div

V

3 Div

2 Aus Div

38 Div

55 Div

FREZENBERG

1 Aus Div

ZONNEBEKE

25 Div

4 Aus Div

7 Div

MOLENAARELSTHOEK

XIX Corps (Watts)

15 Div

WESTHOEK

I Anzac

Polygon Wood

21 Div

DADIZELE

Fifth Army (Gough)

YPRES

Chateau HOOGE

18 Div

33 Div

5 Div

BECELAERE

8 Div

Sanctuary Wood

X

POEZELHOEK

6 Bar Res Div

II Corps (Jacob)

ZILLEBEKE

24 Div

39 Div

GHELUVELT

IX

22 Res Div

DIEKEBUSCH

30 Div

Hill 60

Bass Wood

ZWARTELEEN

24 Div

10 Bar Div

ZANDVOORDE

GELUWE

X Corps (Morland)

ST ELOI

41 Div

18 Res Div

Group Wytschaete (IX Res Corps) (Dieffenbach)

MENIN

HOLLEBEKE

19 Div

Second Army (Plumer)

WYTSCHAETE

OOSTTAVERNE

HOUTHEM

KEMMEL

IX Corps (Gordon)

▲ Mt Kemmel

37 Div

16 Div

FRONT LINES

— 31 JULY 1917

— 11 AUG

3 Aus Div

MESSINES

WULVERGHEM

NZ Div

ST YVON

FRANCE

II Anzac Corps (Birdwood)

NEUVE EGLISE

Ploegsteert Wood

LE GHEER

WARNETON

Lys

COMINES

Group Lille (II Bav Corps)

— 16 AUG

— 26 SEPT

— 5 OCT

— 13 OCT

6 NOV

0 MILES 3

0 KILOMETERS 4

© Richard Natkiel, 1982

Left: The Third Battle of Ypres.

Below: At rest. The infrequency of baths was a major cause of lice.

hues. In the attack, officers would often don the ordinary Tommy's jacket and equipment. Staff officers, of whatever rank, were distinguishable by the gorget patches worn on their lapels – red for General Staff, green for Intelligence Branch, purple for medical – and the same coloured band around their caps and gold braid round the peak of full dress hats, from which the term 'Brass hat' was derived. After the war, in an effort to bridge the gulf which had grown up between the staff and fighting troops, these trappings were removed except for full colonels and above. Apart from their regimental cap and collar badges officers and men also wore divisional patches on the right upper arm. Examples are the silver thistle on a dark blue background of the 9th Scottish Division and the red and white diamond of the 42nd East Lancashire Division.

The first real chance for the Territorial and New Army divisions to show their mettle was at the Battle of Loos in September 1915, the British contribution to the French attack in Champagne. It was also the first time that the British used gas, although its effect was patchy since in some places it blew back into the British front-line

Right: Vickers machine gun
section, Cambrai, November
1917. By this stage of the
war, machine guns were
organised in divisional
battalions of the Machine
Gun Corps.

Below right: General Sir
William Robertson by
Francis Dodd. Robertson was
Quartermaster General of
the BEF in 1914 and CIGS in
1915-18. He was sidelined by
Lloyd George in 1918.
Robertson's career was
particularly remarkable, in
that he originally joined the
army as an ordinary cavalry
trooper.

Below: 'Heavy Artillery' by
Colin Gill. The main subject
of the painting is a battery of
9.2-inch howitzers
camouflaged against
detection from the air.

trenches. Haig's First Army was charged with the attack and launched it with five divisions, the 1st and 7th, representing the old Regular Army, the 9th and 15th Scottish, the New Armies, and the 47th London, the Territorials. The 1st Division suffered from the blowback of the gas, but in the centre the 15th Scottish stormed through the German lines and advanced almost two miles to the dominant Hill 70, while the Londoners captured the village of Loos. Sadly things now began to go wrong as Sir John French had insisted on retaining control over Haig's reserve XI Corps and kept it too far back. That night, having agreed that Haig could use it, two New Army divisions which had only just arrived in France had to march all night to reach their attack positions, then went into the attack, losing over 8000 from 10,000 engaged in 3½ hours, mainly to German machine guns. When asked what had gone wrong the survivors said: 'We did not know

Above: 2nd West Yorkshires (now Prince of Wales's Own Regiment of Yorkshire), January 1918. The rockets were used as distress signals in the event of a sudden German attack or raid.

what it was like. We will do it all right next time.' There were now dangerous gaps in the British line, and the newly formed Guards Division was brought up to try to regain Hill 70, losing many men in the process. One observer described '...the most wonderful sight of my life, the Guards moving in open country under a curtain of fire. They marched, as if in Hyde Park, and I was very proud to think that some of them were friends of mine.' The battle dragged on until 4

November to maintain support for the French, but the issue had been decided in the first two days. It cost French his command and he was replaced by Douglas Haig.

The next year, 1916, was the year of Verdun and the Somme. During the first few months the Germans purposely drew division after French division into the cauldron of Verdun as they sought to wear the French down. Meanwhile the British began to prepare for their largest offensive yet, to take place on the rolling chalklands of the Somme, and besides trying for a breakthrough were also aiming to relieve pressure on the hard-pressed French. The BEF had now grown to five armies, and the initial attack was placed in the hands of Rawlinson's Fourth Army, now largely made up of New Army divisions, who saw the impending battle as the long-awaited culmination of the often frustrating months of training which they had undergone. As they marched along those dusty Picardy roads that June, moving ever nearer to the front:

All the hills and vales along
Earth is bursting into song,
And the singers are the chaps
Who are going to die perhaps.
O Sing, marching men,
Till the valleys ring again.
Give your gladness to earth's keeping,
So be glad, when you are sleeping.
(*Charles Sorley*)

On 24 June the preparatory bombardment opened and for the next six days the German positions were to be perpetually pulverised by no less than 1010 field guns, 427 heavies and 100 French guns. The day of the attack, 1 July, dawned bright. The gunfire rose to a final crescendo and at 0730 hours lifted into the German support trenches and all along the 25-mile front platoon commanders' whistles blew and the infantry of 14 British and three French divisions rose out of their trenches to brave no man's land. Disaster now struck. In spite of the prolonged bombardment, much of the German wire was found to be uncut and the Germans had constructed deep dug-outs which protected them from the artillery fire. As soon as the bombardment lifted they raced up to the surface and manned their machine guns. Advancing in extended lines, with the men at two- or three-yard intervals, and 100 yards between lines, the attackers were literally mown down. Only in the south was there any noticeable success. One officer 'quitted the field' at the end of the day 'on which such brilliant success had been expected that fine summer morning, leaving behind, dead or maimed, in that vast garden of scarlet wild poppies, some 90 per cent of the officers and about 60 per cent of the ranks of the 12 infantry battalions of my division.' In all no less than 57,470 casualties were suffered by the BEF that day, including 20,000 killed outright. It was a figure greater than the combined casualties of the Crimean, Boer and Korean wars, 32 battalions each suffering more than 500 casualties.

News of this disaster took time to percolate the various headquarters since communications were reliant on the field telephone and the runner. Cables were almost invariably broken by shellfire and runners often failed to get through.

It was a problem which would dog operations throughout the war. Further attacks were made and gradually the British inched forward, suffering casualties for every yard. Names such as Gommecourt, Fricourt, Montauban, High Wood, Delville Wood and Mametz became permanently carved in the memories of the survivors. Divisions were sent to the Somme, fought for a few weeks and then the battered remnants came out and were 'fattened up' for another appearance. The fighting went on through July and August and into September.

On 15 September 1916 an historic event in the history of warfare took place when the first tanks went into action. Their development was one of the best-kept secrets of the war. The British had employed armoured cars from very early on, but they had been manned by the Royal Navy, their original task being to protect Royal Naval Air Service advanced landing grounds in France and Belgium, during the early autumn of 1914.

Several squadrons of what became the Royal Naval Armoured Car Division were formed and fought on the Western Front, in the Dardanelles, the Middle East and South-West and East Africa. In early 1916, apart from a squadron serving in Russia and an experimental squadron which had much to do with the development of the tank the armoured cars were handed over to the Army and were grouped in Light Armoured Motor Batteries (LAMBs) under the Machine Gun Corps (Motors). The tank was developed, however, as a means of overcoming the problem of crossing trenches and wire under fire, the name 'tank' being a cover name to disguise its true purpose. By autumn 1915 a design had been arrived at and production orders placed. Haig had wanted to use them on 1 July 1916, but it was not until the end of August that 60 arrived in France. They were originally designated the Heavy Branch, Machine Gun Corps, and 49 went into action in an attack between Combles and Thiepval. Many broke

down, but others acquitted themselves well, one capturing the village of Flers, after which this battle takes its name. The German reaction was: 'The enemy . . . have employed new engines of war, as cruel as effective. No doubt they will adopt on an excessive scale these monstrous engines. . . .' It would, however, be another year before this prophecy came to fruition.

The Battle of the Somme rumbled on until November, when the autumn mud finally brought it to an end. By that time the Allies had had 630,000 casualties, mostly British, and the Germans slightly more. As Prince Rupprecht of Bavaria put it: 'What still remained of the old first-class peace-trained German infantry had been expended. . . .' For the British the Somme marked the grave of the New Armies and the loss of what has often been called 'the finest generation.'

During 1915 and 1916, apart from the Dardanelles campaign, the British Army's commitment had been rising in other theatres of war. During 1915 a force had been gradually advancing up the River Tigris in Mesopotamia, albeit dogged by ever-lengthening supply lines and poor administration. Not until October was it finally agreed that the commander, General Nixon, should try to seize Baghdad, but his necessarily slow advance, brought about by his logistical difficulties, gave the Turks time to prepare a good defensive position in his path at Ctesiphon. When the advance came up against this in November 1915, it was beaten back with heavy casualties, losing over a third of the force. There was no alternative but to withdraw to Kut el Amara, and the Turks invested this at the beginning of December. Two Indian divisions arrived from France at the beginning of January 1916 and were used to mount a relief operation, but this failed to break through the Turkish lines. At the end of April, with nothing left to eat, the garrison of Kut was forced to surrender and endured terrible privations during the subsequent forced march to the prison camps, many dying. Not until December 1916 was another attempt made to advance up the Tigris. The new commander, General Maude, had in the meantime overhauled the supply system, and during 1917 the Turks were slowly pushed back.

Above: Royal Field Artillery in action during the German drive of March 1918.

Opposite, top: Care of the feet was vital for the infantryman and officers were required to make regular inspections to help combat trench foot and other problems.

Opposite: British prisoners captured by the Germans in March 1918 are escorted to the rear.

In Egypt there was a halfhearted Turkish attempt to cross the Suez Canal in February 1915, which was easily beaten back, but most of the year was spent in running to earth bands of Senussi tribesmen, who were being incited by Turkish officers. The back of this trouble was broken by a brilliant cavalry charge by the Dorset Yeomanry at Agagiya at the end of February 1916, but a watchful eye had to be maintained on the Western Desert for the rest of the war, the task falling to the ubiquitous Light Car Patrols in their Ford cars, the forerunners of the Long Range Desert Group of World War II. With the withdrawal from Gallipoli and fresh troops sent from home, General Murray, commanding the troops in Egypt, was strong enough to cross the Suez Canal and take to the offensive, but had to contend with the desert of Sinai. He therefore constructed a railway and water pipeline as he advanced. This made his rate of progress slow, but having beaten off a Turkish counterstroke at Romani at the beginning of August 1916, he had crossed the desert by the end of the year, and passed into Palestine at the beginning of January 1917. Two attempts to break through at Gaza failed, and Murray was relieved by General Allenby, a cavalryman who had been commanding an army in France. He reorganised his forces, forming two infantry corps, largely made up of Territorial divisions, and the Desert Mounted Corps of Anzac, Indian, Regular and Yeomanry cavalry. Using his cavalry to outflank the Turks, he finally drove the Turks from Gaza and entered Jerusalem just before Christmas 1917.

While the Germans had been quickly forced to surrender in South-West Africa, the campaign in East Africa continued with little positive result, the wily von Lettow-Vorbeck keeping forces many times his size at bay. Another theatre had

Above: 'Travoys with Wounded Arriving at a Dressing-Station at Smol, Macedonia, September 1916' by Sir Stanley Spencer.

Above left: Sir Edmund Allenby, 'The Bull', who was victorious in Palestine, by James McBey.

Below left: Mk V tanks move forward during the Battle of the St Quentin Canal, September 1918. The 'cribs' are used for crossing trenches.

Below: The High Command, October 1918. (Left to right): Rawlinson (Fourth Army), Byng (Third), Haig, Horne (First), Lawrence (Chief of Staff, BEF), Birdwood (Fifth).

opened in October 1915, when Bulgaria had entered the war on the German side, and the two, along with Austrian troops, mounted an offensive against Serbia. In order to support the Serbs, an Anglo-French force was landed at Salonika, but because of political restraints did little during 1916 and 1917.

The ever-increasing manpower demands and the virtual drying up of Kitchener's volunteers by the second half of 1915 meant that the Army was beginning to face a manpower crisis, especially with persistent demands by the French that the British should shoulder more of the burden in the west. Conscription was the only answer and in January 1916 Lord Derby's Military Service Act called for all single men between the ages of 18 and 41 who were not in reserved occupations to register for call-up. Kitchener's volunteer scheme had attracted many men from the war industries, but these were having to be greatly expanded to meet the ever-growing demands of the war. Hence the manpower stocks from which

the Army could draw were contracting, and only 50,000 men came forward during the first six months of 1916. In May of that year universal conscription was brought in. Many of the jobs formerly done by men now passed into the hands of women, and this was also reflected in the Army. During the Boer War women of Queen Alexandra's Imperial Military Nursing Service had served in South Africa, and in the 1900s further voluntary military nursing organisations had been formed in the shape of the First Aid Nursing Yeomanry (FANY), whose founders envisaged themselves galloping on to the battlefield to save the wounded, and the Voluntary Aid Detachment (VAD), along with the Territorial Force Nursing Services. These were greatly expanded after the outbreak of war and were soon serving in all theatres. At the end of 1916 consideration was first given to using women to replace men in the base areas and on the lines of communication in France. Eventually, in July 1917, the Women's Army Auxiliary Corps (WAAC) was formed and freed many soldiers both in France and at home for front-line service.

The Anglo-French plan on the Western Front for 1917 was for a major French effort on the Aisne, with French and British subsidiary attacks north and south of the Somme. The British attack was to be at Arras, but the German withdrawal to the carefully-prepared defences of the Hindenburg Line, which they had been constructing during the winter, delayed the start, and it was finally launched on 9 April. The highlight was the Canadian capture of the dominant Vimy Ridge, but once again initial successes were not reinforced in time, and when the follow-up attacks went in they met strong German resistance and counter-attacks, which the Germans were notably quick to mount. To the south the French had a disaster, which was compounded by a mutiny in the French armies in its immediate aftermath, no less than 16 army corps being affected. While the mutineers were prepared to defend their positions they refused to take part in any more costly attacks. Meanwhile the Russian Revolution was also under way, which meant that Russia was virtually out of the war, although she would not be formally so for another year. The burden therefore seemed to rest on British shoulders alone, and Haig proposed an offensive in Flanders, which had seen little major fighting during the past year. Apart from taking pressure off the French, who needed time to reorganise, Flanders was the only place where the Germans could be outflanked, using the coast as a lever.

On 7 June, in a brilliantly executed preliminary attack, Plumer's Second Army, which had gallantly defended the Ypres Salient for the previous two years, captured the Messines-Wytschaete Ridge, exploding 19 enormous mines, the sound of which was heard in England, under it. There was now a pause, since Haig had entrusted the main attack to his youngest and most thrusting commander, Hubert Gough, of Curragh Mutiny fame, who commanded the Fifth Army. After a 15-day preliminary bombardment by 2299 guns on a 7-mile front, Gough attacked east of Ypres on 31 July 1917. The first objectives were quickly captured, but then the plan began to go awry. Much of the problem lay with the

Above: Moving up to the line during Third Ypres, 1917.

Above right: The Jewish community in Jerusalem receives Allenby, May 1918.

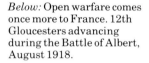

Below: Open warfare comes once more to France. 12th Gloucesters advancing during the Battle of Albert, August 1918.

disappointing performance of the tanks. The bombardment had upset the delicate drainage system and had reduced much of the ground to mud, bogging many of the tanks. In the afternoon of the first day it began to rain, and this continued for the next four days. By the end of August it was clear that Gough was not going to achieve a breakthrough, and the battle passed over to Plumer. He conducted a series of operations, all highly successful but limited in their scope, since he considered that the key to operations was never to allow his forward troops to get beyond the effective range of their supporting artillery, which, given the nature of the terrain, could not be moved forward quickly during an attack. These operations brought him to the foot of the Passchendaele ridge by early October. Haig was loath to allow his troops to remain in positions dominated by this during the winter, and decided on a last effort to capture it. The rains came down again and, by mid November, having captured the village of Passchendaele, the offensive was literally bogged down and halted.

Third Ypres, or Passchendaele, as it is often mistakenly called, marked the nadir in the morale of the British Army. Indeed, as the eminent war correspondent Sir Philip Gibbs wrote: 'For the first time the British Army lost its spirit of optimism.' The combination of conscription and the awful conditions led to a general lowering of spirit, and the burden of the last part of the battle fell very much on the Canadians and Australians, who both retained a volunteer force throughout. In September there was a serious disturbance at the infantry base depot at Etaples, and two battalions had to be withdrawn from the line to quell it. It was caused largely by the treatment the draftees for France received. Confinement to camp and being put through a rigorous course of training under instructors who had often not seen front-line service was especially resented, particularly by the veterans returning after recovering from their wounds.

Another ominous sign was a marked rise in what were termed 'shell-shock' cases. It had been recognised long before the war that a man in

close proximity to a bursting shell could be mentally injured, even if he were not physically so. As the war continued the incidence of nervous disorders increased, and it was gradually recognised that a man subjected to too much fighting could suffer from neurosis, and special shell shock hospitals were set up. Often this neurosis would manifest itself in a going absent during a battle, which according to British military law, along with a number of other offences, was punishable by death. During World War I no less than 3080 British officers and men were sentenced to death after trial by court-martial, and 346 were actually shot, including three officers. Over three-quarters of the executions were for desertion in the face of the enemy. There was, however, increasing concern among some politicians that the sentences were unjust and that the victims might be genuine medical cases. The problem was that in theatres of war the accused had to rely on a regimental officer to defend him who, like those officers detailed to try him, often had very little legal experience. That there were miscarriages of justice there is no doubt. (Eventually, in 1930, the death sentence was abolished for strictly military offences.) Lesser punishments could range from imprisonment with hard labour for serious crimes through restrictions of privileges, which meant being confined to camp and extra fatigues, down to stoppages of pay. There was, however, one relic of the old days in Field Punishment No. 1, in which the victim was tied by his wrists and ankles to a wagon wheel for an hour each morning and evening in full view of his comrades to humiliate him. This had, however, virtually died out by the end of the war.

In the autumn of 1917 the Italians, who had come in on the Allied side in 1915, suffered a disastrous defeat at Caporetto and it looked as though they might break. British troops were therefore quickly rushed from France to shore them up, and remained in Italy until the end of the war. In France itself, immediately after the closing down of Third Ypres, another battle occurred which suggested a way in which the deadlock of trench warfare might be broken.

On 20 November 1917, 378 tanks of the Tank Corps (so titled in July 1917), personally led by its commander, General Hugh Elles, rumbled out of the mist to attack the German lines in the Cambrai area. Overhead 289 aircraft of the Royal Flying Corps strafed the German positions, while six divisions of infantry followed and the Cavalry Corps stood by. By nightfall an advance of up to 5 miles on a 7-mile front had been recorded, with 8000 prisoners and 100 guns captured. Such was the excitement when the news reached England that the church bells were rung for the first time since the outbreak of war. The poor passage of information, however, prevented the cavalry from exploiting this victory, and mechanical failures, together with the exhaustion of the tank crews, meant that the advance now slowed down, especially as the Germans quickly brought up reserves. No further British reserves were forthcoming because of the commitment to Italy and the exhaustion of the divisions which had been fighting at Third Ypres, and the attackers found themselves over-extended by the end of the month.

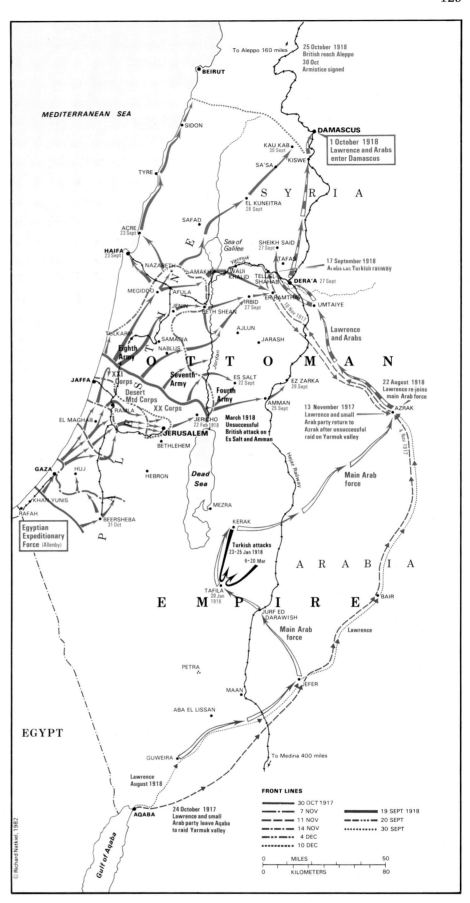

Above: The Palestine campaign 1917-18.

The Germans now counter-attacked and drove them back almost to their original start line. Nevertheless Cambrai showed how victory could be achieved, and ever since the Royal Tank Regiment has marked Cambrai Day, 20 November, as its regimental day.

The active fighting now closed down for the winter, and growing differences between the generals and the government at home came to a head. Lloyd George, who had become Prime

Minister at the end of 1916, had become increasingly discomforted by the high casualties in France and Flanders. He would dearly have liked to remove Haig from command, but there appeared to be no one better and such a step might lower morale among troops and civilians. Instead he put a brake on the reinforcement of the armies in France, and justified it by falsely stating that the strength in January 1918 was already higher than 12 months previously. This was not so, and in any event Haig had just been forced by the French to take over another 25 miles of front, which meant that the British line now stretched from Ypres down to south of the River Oise, a total frontage of some 180 miles. With few of his battalions having more than 500 men, half that of their establishment, Haig was forced to reduce each brigade in his 60 divisions, apart from the Australians and Canadians, to three battalions, and Gough's thinly spread Fifth Army now occupied the new southern part of the British line.

The Germans, with Russia now out of the war, decided to turn all their attention to the west and determined to attack before the growing US Army in France could make its presence felt. They had developed new tactics, creating units of specially trained storm troops who would infiltrate through the Allied lines and not stop, leaving follow-up troops to reduce pockets of resistance which they had bypassed. They struck their first blow on 21 March 1918 against the British Fifth Army and the Third Army to its north. The object was to separate the British from the French. In the course of a week the attack drove Gough's men back across the old Somme battlefields. It almost looked like a rout, but gallant rearguard actions and hastily flung together local reserves gradually slowed the Germans down. French troops came up from the south and fresh British divisions from the north, and by the end of the month the attack had been halted. It had, however, given the Allies a nasty shock. Sadly, too, Gough, to the fury of his men who took it as a personal slight, was removed from his command, probably to enable Lloyd George to hide his guilt over forbidding reinforcements to Haig. In April the Germans struck again, this time in the north on the River Lys. Once again their success was spectacular as they broke through a Portuguese division and found tired British divisions recovering from the March fighting. Haig issued a personal message to the troops, the only time he did so during the war, which ended:

'With our backs to the wall and believing in the justice of our cause each one must fight on to the end. The safety of our homes and the freedom of mankind alike depend upon the conduct of each one of us at this critical moment.'

Once again, with French help, the Germans were halted.

By this time, in order to make good the heavy losses recently suffered, thousands of 18-year-olds, their basic training barely completed, were rushed out to France. Until then 19 was the minimum age for being sent to an active theatre, but so desperate was the situation that this had to be reduced. Yet these A4 Boys, as they were called, would bear the brunt for the remaining months of the war and do it well.

The Germans struck again at the Chemin des Dames at the end of May, hitting four French and three tired British divisions, who had been sent to what had been considered a quiet sector for a rest. The attackers got across the River Aisne but were stopped by quickly deployed reserves, in-

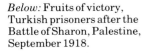

Below: Fruits of victory, Turkish prisoners after the Battle of Sharon, Palestine, September 1918.

Right: 57th Division liberates Lille, 18 October 1918.

cluding two American divisions. Two weeks later the Germans tried again, but the French, letting them come on and then counterattacking their flanks, halted this last drive within three days. The Germans had shot their bolt. Six weeks later the Allies began a counteroffensive.

In Italy, too, after an Austrian attack on the River Piave had been halted, the Allies went over to the offensive, and the British contingent under the Earl of Cavan played a leading part in the seizure of the Asiago plateau. British, French, Serbian and Greek troops drove back the Bulgarians in Macedonia. Attention in Mesopotamia was deflected by a threat to the vital oilfields in northern Persia, and a force was sent there, part going on to the port of Baku, which was held for a while in an uneasy alliance with Russian Bolshevik troops. The main offensive up the Tigris did not recommence until the closing weeks of the war, reaching as far north as Mosul before the Armistice came into effect. The decisive battle in Palestine was Megiddo in September. Allenby, helped by the operations of Colonel TE Lawrence and his Arab irregulars behind the Turkish lines, forced a hole in the Turkish defences north of Jaffa and, for the only time during the war, the cavalry had the opportunity to exploit, going as far as Damascus and further north, one cavalry division covering 550 miles in 38 days, including four major actions, and losing only one-fifth of its horses from all causes. Only in East Africa did von Lettow-Vorbeck refuse to give up, and he did not finally surrender until 23 November.

In France on 8 August 1918 the British Fourth Army launched an attack preceded by 324 heavy tanks. Such was the success of that day that Ludendorff, the leading German commander, called it 'the black day of the German army in the history of this war', and the German official history saw it as 'the greatest defeat which the German army had suffered since the beginning of the war'. The French and then the Americans also attacked. Once an attack looked like slowing down, and the Germans were still fighting as hard as ever, another attack would be launched. As the autumn wore on the Germans were forced farther and farther back until at 1100 hours on 11 November the Armistice came into effect.

It was perhaps poetic justice that the last British action of the war, like the first clash, should have involved the cavalry, especially in view of the frustrations of the four years in between. This time it was a squadron of the 7th Dragoon Guards which seized a bridge over the River Dendre at Lessines just before 1100 hours. It was made all the more appropriate when they amalgamated with the 4th Dragoon Guards, who had fired the first British shots of the war.

On that day a British officer who had seen the war on the Western Front from beginning to end, rising from platoon to brigade commander, wrote in his diary:

'Incidents flash through the memory: the battle of the first four months: the awful winters in waterlogged trenches, cold and miserable: the terrible trench-assaults and shell fire of the next three years: loss of friends, exhaustion and wounds: the stupendous victories of the last few months: our enemies all beaten to their knees.

Thank God! The end of a frightful four years, thirty-four months of them at the front with the infantry, whose company officers, rank and file, together with other front-line units, have suffered bravely, patiently and unselfishly, hardships and perils beyond even the imagination of those, including soldiers, who have not shared them.'

Above: The Victory Parade in London, 19 July 1919. Whippet tanks lead a section of the parade.

No more fitting tribute to the British soldier of the Great War could be paid.

British generalship and staff work during 1914-18 have been frequently lambasted, and a popular description of the British Army was of 'lions led by donkeys.' While there is no doubt of the leadership's sometimes grave limitations, many of them were caused by the unusual circumstances of the time. The style of warfare, especially on the Western Front, and the mass armies, many times larger than any previous British army, put almost intolerable strains on the system. No combatant country produced an outstanding commander on the scale of the Great Captains of history, but the British commanders fared better than many, as did the staff. During the last three months of the war in France and Flanders the British Army captured 188,700 prisoners and 2840 guns, while the remaining Allies – French, American, Belgian – took 196,700 prisoners and 3775 guns. On these figures alone it is easy to see which ally played the major part in the final victory. The cost, however, was high.

During the years 1914-18 a total of 4,971,000 enlisted in the British Army. Over 600,000 were killed or died, almost one in every seven. Just over two million were wounded, although this includes many who were wounded more than once, and over 190,000 were made prisoner. The graves of those who died lie scattered across the globe, but two-thirds are in France and Flanders.

There is no more fitting reminder of the gallant sacrifice made by the British Army during the First World War than a ceremony which has taken place at Ypres every night since 11 November 1929, apart from during the German occupation of the town during 1940-44. At eight o'clock in the evening two burghers of Ypres take up position beneath the Menin Gate, on the walls of which are inscribed the names by regiments of no less than 54,986 British soldiers who died in the Salient during 1914-18 and have no known grave. In a simple little ceremony the Last Post is sounded and echoes out over the fields that now look very different from the desolate landscape of 70 years ago.

Right: The Victory Parade. Standards, Guidons and Colours of the cavalry and infantry regiments pass the newly erected Cenotaph in Whitehall, a memorial to the nation's war dead.

THE STRUGGLE TO MODERNISE 1919-42

By the end of the 'war to end all wars', as the Great War was popularly believed to be, the British Army had swollen to an unprecedented strength of some 3,500,000 men, the vast majority of whom were enlisted merely for three years or the duration of the war and wanted desperately to get home and pick up the threads of their former civilian lives. The Ministry of Reconstruction had worked out a demobilisation scheme based on the assumption that the end of the war would result in large-scale unemployment. In order to get industry going again on a peacetime footing, priority was given to men who could positively contribute to this. Inevitably these men were often those who had joined the Army most recently, and this was resented by those who had served for longer. There was unrest in Army rest camps and depots, and alarm over talk of setting up 'soldiers' councils' on Bolshevik lines. Winston Churchill, now Secretary of State for War, acted quickly, changing the system and giving priority to those who had served the longest. In order to damp down any thoughts by agitators of stirring up revolution, as was happening in Germany and elsewhere, the Guards Division was brought back from Cologne and paraded through the streets of London.

The Army, however, could not immediately revert to its pre-1914 active strength since the end of the war had brought a number of additional commitments. For a start, as part of the peace terms with Germany, a garrison had to be maintained in the Cologne area on the Rhine, and this would not be finally withdrawn until 1929. In the Middle East a large British presence had to be maintained in Mesopotamia and Palestine, which had come under British mandate. For a short time, too, occupation forces were also required in Austria.

Across the other side of Europe, in Russia, there was another commitment. From the end of 1917 it had been Lloyd George's policy to give active support to Russians who were prepared to continue fighting the Germans, and arms, money and advisers had been sent to the northern ports of Murmansk and Archangel. This inevitably meant that the detachments of troops sent there were supporting the White Russians against the Bolsheviks, and in this way Britain became marginally involved in the civil war that was raging, as did her allies who had also sent contingents to the periphery of the country. In July 1918 a battalion of the Middlesex Regiment had joined American, Japanese and French troops in Vladivostok, and in early 1919 a British tank detachment was also sent to south Russia. The main British effort, however, continued to be in the north, but on all fronts British troops, along with Royal Air Force and naval elements, saw a good deal of action. The Allied contingents were too small and scattered to make any decisive impression, apart from the fact that the White commanders were generally too mercurial to be reliable, and although Churchill clamoured for a mass intervention, the British and other Allied contingents were almost all withdrawn by early 1920.

Ireland was another trouble spot. The Irish

Republican Army (IRA) was fighting not just for Home Rule for Ireland but the setting up of a republic. Its targets were the Royal Irish Constabulary (RIC) and the British Army, which had 40,000 troops stationed there. Much of the brunt was taken by ex-officers and soldiers, who had been recruited to strengthen the RIC, and the Auxiliaries and Black and Tans, as they were known, soon gained an infamous reputation as they rivalled IRA atrocities with counter-atrocities of their own. The pattern of ambushes, searches, raids and controlling riotous crowds was one that the British Army would find itself repeating 50 years later. The guerrilla campaign continued until the Irish Treaty of December 1921 set up the Irish Free State. The British Army now withdrew from the south of Ireland, which was immediately embroiled in civil war, as the IRA fought to overthrow the newly installed Free State government. Indeed, the Army handed over a number of artillery guns and other weapons to the Free State Army. It would, however continue to maintain a garrison in Ulster.

India, too, gave cause for concern. The fact that many Indians had been killed during the war fighting for the British helped add to agitation for greater autonomy. Unrest centred on the Punjab, and in April 1919 Brigadier General Dyer was sent with a force of Gurkhas to Amritsar. He was faced with an illegal assembly of several thousands who were being whipped up by agitators and, considering that his men were under threat and that the trouble should be nipped in the bud, he ordered his troops to open

fire after warnings had been given to the crowd; 379 Indians were killed and many more injured. To placate Indian opinion Dyer was removed from his command, but there were many who considered he had taken the correct course, and in a later libel action the judge ruled that it had been wrong to remove him. It was a problem of what constituted minimum force, one that the British Army would have to face increasingly when dealing with this type of situation.

Amritsar immediately triggered off trouble with Afghanistan. The newly crowned Amir Amanullah declared a holy war against Britain, partially in an attempt to secure his own tenuous position on the throne. A number of the frontier

Above: Demobilisation. Men receiving their last ration issue before re-entering civilian life. Note the wound stripes on the lower sleeves of the men in line.

Below: Guarding the Empire. Rolls-Royce armoured cars of the 3rd Armoured Car Company, Tank Corps, Egypt early 1920s. In 1923, the Corps was given the 'Royal' prefix and adopted the distinctive black beret.

Britain's leading theorists of armoured warfare, whose writings so influenced military thought and doctrine in Britain and elsewhere – Major General J F C Fuller (*right*, photograph taken in 1919) and Captain Basil Liddell Hart (*below*, 1953 photograph).

three months, and peace was finally restored by the end of the year, except in Waziristan, which continued to cause trouble.

In many ways peace was not immediately apparent to the British Army in the immediate postwar years, and the feelings of the troops were very aptly summed up in a cartoon by Captain Bruce Bairnsfather – who had made a name for himself early on in the war as the portrayer of Tommy humour on the Western Front – which appeared in the *Bystander* in September 1920. It showed a resigned British soldier wearing tin helmet and three wound stripes, with the following caption:

BILLY SMITH
'THE BRITISH SOLDIER'
Success! Success!
Played without a break in W Kaiser's Panto 1914-1920
OPEN ACCEPT OFFERS WARS!
This week . . . . Ireland
Next week . . . . Mesopotamia
WANTED! BETWEEN POLAND AND MEXICO
A FEW DATES ONLY
Sole Agent . . . . Winston Churchill Esq

British defence policy in the postwar era was bound by the Ten Year Rule, drawn up by Winston Churchill in 1919, which was based on the assumption that 'the British Empire will not be engaged in any great war during the next ten years and that no Expeditionary Force is required for this purpose.' It was to remain in force until 1932, when it would be reduced to five years. By 'major war' was meant war in Europe, and hence priority for defence reverted once more to the Empire and imperial policing. Together with severe financial restrictions, and the conservatism of many prewar soldiers, who regarded the late war as an aberration and longed to get back to what they called 'real soldiering', it was to put a severe brake on modernisation.

The Army was by 1923 reduced to a strength of 230,000 men and this would fall by another 24,000 by 1932. Many of the new corps raised during the war, notably the Machine Gun Corps and Labour Corps, were disbanded, and even the

tribes flocked to his banner. This caught the British at a bad time, with a number of their regiments waiting to go home after war service in India. Many too, perhaps thought of Kipling's lines:

When you're wounded and left on Afghanistan's plains,
An' the women come out to cut up your remains,
Just roll to your rifle an' blow out your brains,
An' go to your Gawd like a soldier.

Nevertheless a force was gathered and quickly drove the invaders back to Jellalabad. Significant support had been given by antique BE2C aircraft of the RAF, and it was this perhaps more than anything else which persuaded the Afghans to ask for terms. The main fighting finished after

Tank Corps held on only by the skin of its teeth in the face of opposition from cavalry generals who wanted to see it abolished. Nevertheless, in recognition that large numbers of cavalry were perhaps an expensive luxury, 16 cavalry regiments were merged with one another in 1921, forming eight new regiments whose new titles were generally an amalgam of the old titles – 14th/20th Hussars, 16th/5th Lancers. The following year, in recognition of the Irish Free State, five infantry regiments, who traditionally recruited from the South – Connaught Rangers, Prince of Wales's Leinster Regiment (Royal Canadians), Royal Dublin Fusiliers, Royal Irish Regiment, Royal Munster Regiment – were disbanded. This, however, did not stop Irishmen from enlisting in the British Army, especially during World War II, and a number continue to do so today. A further economy was the reduction of artillery batteries from six guns to four. The situation was not helped by a committee which sat under Sir Eric Geddes in early 1922, and recommended a sharp cutting back of public expenditure. The 'Geddes axe' put many officers and men, who wanted to stay on in the Army, on the streets. Among those left officers in particular suffered. Many who had been commanding brigades and battalions at the end of the war found themselves reverting to their substantive ranks, often two or three grades lower, and, such was the promotion blockage, that it would be many years before they reached their former ranks again. One bright spot, however, was that the Territorial Force, now called the Territorial Army, was kept in being on its Haldane divisional structure. The Special Reserve was abolished, and while the Militia was restored it existed only on paper and no appointments were made to it.

One policy, however, prevented the Army suffering from severe overstretch with its very much reduced strength. Lord Trenchard who commanded the young Royal Air Force was very conscious that in order to survive the jealousies of the two older armed services in peacetime he needed to find a worthwhile role relevant to the

priority of defence of the Empire. The effect of his aircraft on the Afghans gave him the clue, and he proposed that the RAF take over the responsibility for policing Iraq (formerly Mesopotamia), Transjordan and Aden. This was accepted by Winston Churchill, and the concept of 'air control' came into being. Using aircraft, and some armoured cars the RAF performed the task of keeping the peace very effectively.

Within this overall climate, it might be expected that military thought would stagnate as it had after previous wars, but, largely thanks to two individuals, this was not the case. Colonel JFC Fuller, known as 'Boney', was a prewar infantryman who had graduated from Camberley in 1914, and had eventually become the Chief of Staff of the Tank Corps in France. The plans for the Battle of Cambrai and for the attack on 8 August 1918 were widely recognised as being his work, and his Plan 1919 had been generally accepted by the Allies as a blueprint for the 1919 campaign should the war have gone on this long. This envisaged an Allied armoured force spearheading an offensive, but using tanks with much faster speeds than the models currently in use. From 1919 onwards Fuller used this as a basis to

Above: The evacuation of the Rhine garrisons, September 1929. 2nd Leicesters (now part of the Royal Anglian Regiment) leave their barracks at Konigstein.

Below: The shape of things to come. Royal Tank Corps Vickers Mediums on Salisbury Plain, 1928.

140

argue that wars of the future would be dependent on 'mechanical' rather than 'muscular' power. The pendulum would swing once more from defence to offence, but rather than using the traditional principle of defeating the enemy's army by applying a cudgel to it, he argued that fast-moving armoured columns could act like a rapier lunging at the enemy's heart, his command and control structure, which would result in defeat through paralysis. Captain Basil Liddell Hart had, like Fuller, an infantry background, but was a wartime Kitchener volunteer. While he wanted to stay in the Army after the war, he had been downgraded medically because of wounds, and found employment as a journalist. He was very taken by the 1918 German storm-troop tactics and developed the concept of the Expanding Torrent, which relied on infiltration to get into the enemy's rear areas. Both Fuller and Liddell Hart argued that a proper mechanised force be set up and attracted a number of disciples, many of whom transferred to the Tank Corps, which received the 'Royal' prefix in 1923 in recognition of the part it had played in the war.

Eventually, in 1927, an experimental mechanised force was set up for trials on Salisbury Plain. It comprised a tank battalion, a mixed armoured

car and machine-gun carrier battalion, a mechanised infantry battalion, with more machine guns, self-propelled artillery guns and engineers, and carried out exercises against the conventionally equipped 3rd Infantry Division. Fuller had been originally appointed to command the experimental force, but jibbed at the terms of reference, and the post went to a more stereotyped infantryman instead. The force dramatically displayed its potential but was broken up after a year, mainly for financial reasons but also because there was concern in high places that the more traditional arms might be swallowed up by the Royal Tank Corps, which was what Fuller now seemed to be suggesting. Indeed, this is where his path began to diverge from Liddell Hart's, since the latter argued that there was still an important role for conventional infantry. It could keep the enemy's attention while the armour attacked using what he called the Indirect Approach. Ramsay Macdonald's Labour Government, which came to power in 1929, embraced the pacifist idealism which influenced the country at the time, and regarded such thought as aggressive and more likely to provoke war than deter it. In 1928, however, two cavalry regiments, the 11th Hussars and 12th

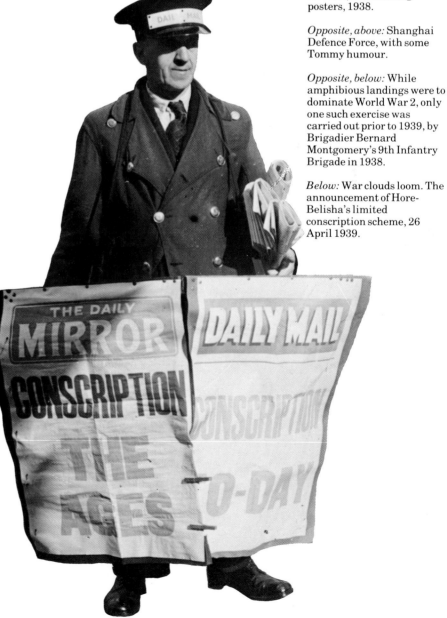

Above left: Recruiting posters, 1938.

Opposite, above: Shanghai Defence Force, with some Tommy humour.

Opposite, below: While amphibious landings were to dominate World War 2, only one such exercise was carried out prior to 1939, by Brigadier Bernard Montgomery's 9th Infantry Brigade in 1938.

Below: War clouds loom. The announcement of Hore-Belisha's limited conscription scheme, 26 April 1939.

Lancers, were converted to armoured cars, and the *Cavalry Journal* commented, while 'condoling' at the loss of their horses, that 'we feel that the future of the cavalry as a whole depends on the possibility of making them harder hitting and faster moving than they have ever been before.'

Further experimental mechanised forces were established on a temporary basis during 1930-32, and eventually, at the end of 1933, it was agreed that a permanent tank brigade be set up, and Brigadier Percy Hobart was appointed to command it. (The rank of Brigadier General was changed to Colonel Commandant shortly after the war, on the grounds that there were too many generals, but the new rank was thought cumbersome, and Brigadier was introduced in its place.) Hobart was a dynamic officer who had transferred to the Tank Corps from the Indian Army, and he quickly developed a tremendous spirit among all ranks of the 1st Tank Brigade. During the 1934 manoeuvres, however, every obstacle was put in the way of the tanks to prevent them being truly effective. As one young tank officer remembered:

'The infantry were allowed by the umpires to surround the area and lie on the road like the members of Gandhi's "disobedience campaign" in India. They were guided by officers' wives who had arrived by car earlier. As we closed in on them they would not move, and others attempted to climb on the tanks, while the artillery were allowed to bring up their field guns and block the roads at point blank range, in full view.'

Nevertheless the decision was taken that autumn to create Mobile Divisions made up of tanks and mechanised cavalry. Infantry transport was to be motorised and a tank battalion was made part of each infantry division.

Yet modernisation was still undertaken with great caution, as was indicated by the fact that the Army Estimates of 1935-36 allowed an increase of forage by £44,000 to £400,000, while petrol went up only by £12,000 to £121,000. By this stage the nation, faced by a resurgent Germany now under the rule of Hitler, was beginning to rearm. The problem was the widespread belief that, to use Prime Minister Baldwin's words, 'the bomber will always get

Below: First day on the drill square for Hore-Belisha's Militiamen.

through', and the main priority was being given to the RAF to build up a striking force to match that of Germany. The RAF's fixation with strategic bombing also resulted in little attention being given to close air support of the Army, which the advocates of armoured warfare were keen to develop. The Royal Navy also, as the traditional bulwark of Britain's defence, was given priority over the Army. A further dilemma was that an army geared to the imperial policing role required a different structure from that of modern European warfare. As Duff Cooper, the Secretary of State, said when introducing the Army Estimates for 1934-35:

'On Salisbury Plain or even on the fields of Flanders the tank is no doubt the most powerful weapon you can possibly use, but it is not necessarily the most powerful in the North-West Frontier, or the swamps and ditches that surround the suburbs of Shanghai.'

The Army continued to be busy about the Empire. During 1921-22 there was a revolt by the fanatical Muslim Moplahs on the Malabar coast which had to be put down. At the end of 1926 the various civil wars raging in China began to threaten the International Settlement at Shanghai, and a complete division, including two brigades from Britain and one from India, spent the whole of 1927 protecting it. During 1930-32 there was considerable unrest in Burma. There were also a number of calls for troops to help oversee the plebiscites conducted in various territories which had been under League of Nations mandate in the aftermath of the Treaty of Versailles. The last of these was the Saar, where 1500 British troops spent three months in 1934. The North-West Frontier continued to give trouble and there were two major frontier campaigns in the mid 1930s. Finally, increasing Arab resentment at the steady stream of Jewish immigrants into Palestine sparked off a revolt in 1936, and by 1938 two divisions had been deployed there, commanded by Dick O'Connor and Bernard Montgomery, both of whom would distinguish themselves in the world war to come.

In May 1937 a new Secretary of State, Leslie Hore-Belisha, was appointed. He came into office determined to bring the Army up to date and in a short time his efforts produced results. He increased pay and unblocked the officers' promotion blockage by laying down that a subaltern would automatically be promoted to captain after eight years (15 was the average until then) and to major after a further nine years. The result was that in August 1938 more than a quarter of the subalterns and captains found themselves promoted. He finally did away with the half-pay and built a number of new barracks to replace some of the old Victorian and First World War structures in which the Army at home lived. Many of these new barracks remain in use today. He raised Army cooking standards, and also introduced a new field uniform, Battle Dress, based on the ski suit, which the British army would wear throughout the war and into the mid 1960s.

More important, he tackled the problem of organising the Army to fight the European war which seemed increasingly likely. He called in Basil Liddell Hart, still working as a journalist, as his unofficial adviser, which made him very

Left: 'Somewhere in France,' 1939. Whatever other shortcomings the British Army had, its transport, unlike that of the German Army, was fully motorised by 1939.

unpopular with the military hierarchy, especially once it became known that Liddell Hart was advising on senior officers' appointments. It was this that caused the cartoonist David Low to introduce his famous character Colonel Blimp, the epitome of military conservatism. Liddell Hart had come to believe that in a major war it would be fatal to send a large expeditionary force made up of conventional infantry divisions, since they would have little effect on offensive operations. It would be better to restrict an expeditionary force to two armoured divisions, which would pack much more punch. Hore-Belisha was much taken with this argument, as were other ministers, who wanted to avoid any possibility of a mass army being sent to France and suffering the same losses as 20 years before. On Liddell Hart's recommendation the two Mobile Divisions agreed three years previously were now set up, one in Egypt and one in England. That in Egypt was initially commanded by Hobart, but his unconventional outlook, although it inspired those under him as it had in the 1st Tank Brigade, did not combine easily with the high command in Egypt, and he was replaced. Nevertheless he laid the foundations of what was to become one of the most famous of formations, the 7th Armoured Division, the Desert Rats. The creation of the Mobile Division in England went more slowly. Much of the problem lay in the extreme shortage of tanks, and the fact that funds had been diverted into setting up Anti-Aircraft Command, which encompassed five Territorial divisions. One positive step, however, which reflected the increasing mechanisation of the cavalry, was the formation of the Royal Armoured Corps, comprising the cavalry, less the Household Cavalry, and the Royal Tank Corps, which now became the Royal Tank Regiment.

As 1938 wore on and war seemed ever more imminent, staff talks were begun with the French, who were understandably not impressed with the offer of just two armoured divisions, as

the Mobile Divisions were redesignated, especially since neither was yet complete or trained. The opinion of the Government gradually changed and finally, in February 1939, it was agreed that four Regular infantry divisions and the UK-based armoured division should be equipped for the Continent, as would four Territorial divisions. At the end of March Hore-Belisha suddenly announced that the size of the Territorial Army was to be doubled. A few weeks later a form of conscription was introduced, all 20-year-olds being called up for six months service with the Regular Army, and then to go on to serve a further three and a half years in the newly created Territorial divisions. They were given the name of 'militiamen', thus reintroducing this ancient form of military service. At the same time military guarantees were given to Poland, Rumania and Greece. War was now inevitable and the Chiefs of Staff were horrified at the

Below: Gun drills with the 2-pounder anti-tank gun. It was as good an anti-tank weapon as any in 1939.

Above: Royal Fusiliers man an advanced post in France during the winter 1939-40. The Bren Gun (nearest the camera) had now taken over from the Lewis as the section's automatic weapon.

Below: Bewilderment. Troops on Namsos quay, Norway, await evacuation, May 1940.

timing of these commitments. The Army had been caught at the beginning of a major re-organisation for which there had been no chance to carry out any pre-planning. Twenty years of virtual neglect were coming home to roost.

At dawn on 1 September 1939 the German Army swept across the border into Poland. Two days later, their ultimatums rejected by Hitler, Britain and then France declared war on Germany. Unlike 1914, it took as long as five weeks for the first echelon of this new BEF to cross the Channel and take up, as before, position on the left of the French armies. In command was General Viscount Gort, a Guardsman with a First World War reputation as an officer of incomparable bravery, the holder of the VC,

three DSOs and the MC, who stepped across from being CIGS, a position now filled by a massively built artilleryman, 'Tiny' Ironside. Like Gort he had a reputation as a fine leader of men, but he lacked the intellect to grapple with the complexities of his new office. Under Gort were two corps, Sir John Dill's I Corps, with 1st and 2nd Divisions, and Alan Brooke's II Corps, with 3rd (commanded by Montgomery) and 4th Divisions. The much vaunted armoured division did not, however, put in an appearance. It was still far from complete, and would not be so for another nine months.

The Great War veteran would still find much that had not changed. There were differences in uniform and webbing, although senior officers continued to wear mounted service dress, albeit with the cross-strap of the Sam Browne removed, a meaningless order which was rescinded a year later. The tin helmet and the Lee Enfield rifle were the same, and the Vickers was still the medium machine gun. The Mills bomb was still the primary grenade, and officers continued to carry the Webley revolver. But there were new weapons. The cumbersome Stokes mortar had given way to the 2-inch mortar, a platoon weapon, and the heavier 3-inch mortar. The Lewis Gun had been largely replaced by the Bren Light Machine Gun, and the infantry's anti-tank weapon was the Boys anti-tank rifle, with an effective range against any known tank of 250 yards. The infantry was partially mounted in tracked Bren Gun carriers, and all its transport was now motorised, something which the German army, in spite of its emphasis on mechanisation, never came near to achieving. While the Royal Artillery, which had lost its Field and Garrison desig-

nations, still had many of the types of gun it had used in 1914-18, it now had the excellent and versatile 25-pounder gun/howitzer. It also had anti-tank regiments armed with the 2-pounder anti-tank gun, although the latter's effective range was only 500 yards. All guns were now towed by wheeled tractors.

British tanks at the outbreak of war were divided into three basic types. The divisional mechanised cavalry regiments were equipped with light tanks, the Mk VIbs, together with Bren Gun carriers. Their primary role was reconnaissance, and the tanks were armed with a machine gun only. There was also one 'army tank battalion', the 4th Royal Tank Regiment, which had the Mk 1 Infantry Tank, heavily armoured, but again having only a machine gun. As the designation implies, these tanks were used for infantry support. Later, in May 1940, a second army tank battalion, the 7th Royal Tank Regiment, would arrive which had the Infantry Tank Mk 2, fondly called the Matilda, with a 2-pounder gun. The main tank of the armoured divisions was the cruiser, lightly armoured, with a 2-pounder gun and fast moving, the two main types being the A10 and A13. These, however, would not appear in France until toward the end of May 1940. Finally, the BEF had one armoured car regiment, the 12th Lancers, in Morris armoured cars.

The higher Allied command organisation was cumbersome compared to 1914, when Generals French and Joffre had dealt directly with one another. In 1939 the BEF was firmly under command of the French, not the supreme commander, Gamelin, but a subordinate, Georges, who commanded the Armies of the North-East. Gort, however, had a right of appeal to the British Government if he felt that French orders were imperilling his army and he was also instructed to keep in close touch with the War Office.

By the end of September 1939 the Germans had overrun Poland and dismembered it with the Russians. The Western Allies now expected Hitler to turn on them, but the need to re-equip his forces and debates over the plan of attack delayed his strike for another seven months. This period, known as the Phoney War or Sitzkrieg,

was valuable for the BEF, which in Montgomery's words was at the outbreak of war 'totally unfit for a first-class war on the Continent of Europe.' Vital training needed to be carried out, which included brigades being sent down to the Maginot Line, the French border defences, to get battle experience, as well as the completion of the re-equipment programme. At the same time much effort was devoted to constructing field defences, and by May 1940 over 400 pill-boxes had been built and 40-miles of anti-tank

Above: The ever present air threat. Bofors gun team, Harstad harbour, Norway, May 1940.

Below: The British and French Commanders-in-Chief, Gamelin and Gort, France, January 1940.

obstacles created. The French, on the other hand, did little, and as one French officer remarked: 'We're no longer fighting the Germans, we're fighting *ennui* (boredom).' General Alan Brooke, watching a parade of French troops in November, was appalled by their slovenly turnout, but 'what shook me most, however, was the look in the men's faces, disgruntled and insubordinate looks.'

On the assumption that the Germans would come through Belgium, the Allies planned to support the Belgian Army by taking up positions on the River Dyle. The problem was that Belgium, still being neutral, would not allow any reconnaissance to take place or give details of her defences in this region.

The winter of 1939-40 was very cold. An infantry platoon commander:

'The men lived in barns and stables and slept on straw which was never more than two inches thick. They only received three blankets apiece, and as the buildings were full of holes, were swept by icy draughts. They had to wash in water drawn the night before in large tubs, with the result that there was never less than an inch, and sometimes two inches, of ice on it in the morning.'

Nevertheless there was little sickness, apart from some influenza, and morale remained high, especially since emphasis was placed on welfare, which included leave in Britain. As the months wore on further reinforcements were sent across. A Regular division arrived in December, three Territorial divisions in January and February, another two in April, together with three 'reserve' divisions, which had virtually untrained men and hardly any equipment.

At the end of November 1939 the Russians invaded Finland and the British and French had thoughts of sending a force to help the Finns, the British even raising a ski battalion, the 5th Scots Guards. The neutral Swedes, however, refused to allow men and supplies to pass through their territory, and the plan came to naught. At the beginning of April 1940 the Germans moved, not against the Low Countries but on Denmark and Norway. The former was quickly overrun and the Germans seized ports and airfields in southern Norway. An Anglo-French force was now sent to support the Norwegians. The British Army's contribution was 49th Division, a Regular brigade withdrawn from France, and 24th Guards Brigade. The expedition was, however, fated from the beginning. The Territorials of 49th Division were hopelessly under-trained, and there was little co-ordination since the force was split into three groups, the commander of each receiving his own instructions from the CIGS. Indeed the operation was run from London, each service receiving its own instructions from the Admiralty, War Office and Air Ministry respectively. The last troops were not evacuated from Norway until the beginning of June, having been hopelessly outfought by the better equipped and trained Germans, who had also had the advantage of overwhelming air superiority throughout. There was no time to digest the lessons of Norway because more momentous events had been taking place in France.

On 10 May 1940 the long-awaited German blow finally fell. Spearheaded by airborne land-

ings at key points, the Panzer columns moved swiftly into Belgium and Holland, which was forced to surrender after five days. The northern French armies and the BEF crossed the Belgian frontier at midday on the 10th and took up their positions on the Dyle as planned, although movement was severely hampered by refugees. The BEF had a frontage of 17 miles from Louvain to Wavre, held by three divisions. By 14 May they were in contact with the enemy and during the next two days successfully held off a number of attacks. Everything appeared to be going to plan, but to the south the Germans had produced a surprise. The French had long considered that the wooded terrain of the Ardennes was not suitable for tanks, but the Germans proved them wrong by thrusting through there, crossing the Meuse, breaking the French armies in front of them and then turning north-west toward the coast. The Allied left wing was now in danger of being cut off, and there was no alternative but to withdraw to the River Escaut. The British troops, who considered that they had given a good account of themselves, were bewildered, but nevertheless withdrew in comparatively good order, although mistakes in the transport arrangements meant some arduous forced marches, one brigade covering 40 miles in 27 hours. There were also over-hasty demolitions of bridges, which resulted in units being caught on the wrong bank.

By dawn on 19 May the BEF was firm on the River Escaut, but the German armour had already reached the Cambrai-St Quentin area, and was threatening the BEF's right flank. Gort, with most of his divisions in line, had only his ill-equipped and untrained reserve divisions to spare, and two of these, the 12th and 23rd, were deployed to the Canal du Nord, east of Arras. The Germans turned on them and quickly broke them up, although the war diary of the German XXXI Corps praised the 'outstanding bravery' of the British troops. Gort now received instructions from Ironside, who flew across from England, to advance southward towards Amiens and take up position on the left of the French once more, in order to restore some integrity to the Allied line. This was very much easier said than done. Pres-

Right: Dunkirk, May 1940.

Opposite, below: How the press viewed Dunkirk.

Below: Bren gun carrier moving up to the River Dyle line in Belgium, 10 May 1940.

sure was building on the Escaut line, and German armour was threatening Gort's line of communication to the coast. To advance southward would invite being cut off, and Gort sensibly ignored the order, limiting himself to a counter-attack at Arras. This was mounted on 21 May by 74 tanks of 4th and 7th Royal Tank Regiments, supported by elements of the 5th and 50th Divisions. Brigadier Douglas Pratt, commanding the tank brigade:

'We got about four miles forward before any infantry of ours appeared in sight. During this time we played merry hell with a lot of Boche motor transport and their kindred stuff. Tracer ammunition put a lot up in flames. His anti-tank gunners, after firing a bit, bolted and left their guns, even when fired on at ranges of 600 to 800 yards with machine-guns from Matildas. Some surrendered, and others feigned dead on the ground.'

By early evening, however, the infantry were exhausted, and the Germans were beginning to recover from their surprise. Both tank battalion commanders had been killed, and the operation was halted. Their enemy on this day had been 7th Panzer Division, commanded by Erwin Rommel, whom the British troops would come to know very well in the near future. He had believed that he was up against 'hundreds of tanks', and the Germans, fearing that their armour would be cut off from the infantry following behind, now moved very much more cautiously than they had intended, thereby buying valuable time for the BEF. Indeed the Arras counterattack, in spite of

the haphazard way in which it was mounted, with no reconnaissance and no detailed orders, was the only positive move the BEF was able to mount during the campaign.

By this time there was a serious breakdown in communications, and Gort found himself without any orders from his French superiors, as did the Belgians. German pressure was forcing him back from the Escaut line. The Germans had also reached Boulogne to which 20 Guards Brigade had been rushed from England. Calais was also under threat and another hastily assembled brigade, the motor brigade of 1st Armoured Division, was sent there, the rest of the division having begun to cross to France on 17 May. It was, however, still very under-equipped, as the history of the 9th Lancers recalls: 'The picture of C Squadron leader driving down the Southampton road in his private car handing out machine-guns, belt boxes and telescopes to his tanks was a grim reminder of our appalling lack of readiness.' After four days bitter fighting, Boulogne fell on the 25th, although the survivors of 20 Guards Brigade were evacuated. Calais was a different matter; 30 Infantry Brigade was ordered to defend it to the last. Attacked repeatedly on all sides, the defenders resisted until the 26th. When asked many years afterwards why his men had fought so well there, an officer of the 1st Battalion The Rifle Brigade replied: 'The Regiment had always fought well, and we were with our friends.' There is no more apt description of the British Army's regimental spirit.

By 26th May the BEF was surrounded in a pocket centred on Dunkirk. In Gort's view there was no option but evacuation if the BEF was not to be utterly destroyed. So began Operation Dynamo, the evacuation from Dunkirk. During 26 May–3 June 200,000 British, 100,000 French and 10,000 other Allied troops were taken off the beaches and transported back across the Channel in a masterpiece of improvisation. Those on the perimeter fought gallant rearguard actions to keep the Germans at bay, and the part French troops played should not be forgotten. Neither, too, should the contribution of the Royal Navy and the RAF. This left two British divisions still in France. The 51st Highland Division had been down in the Saar when the German offensive began and events had moved too quickly for it. Eventually it came under command of the French Tenth Army and was driven back to St Valéry on the coast. The Royal Navy was unable to evacuate the division and it was forced to surrender to Rommel. The 1st Armoured Division in its truncated form had several brushes with the enemy. After Dunkirk it was the intention to build up another BEF in Brittany, and 1st Canadian Division, which had recently landed in England, began to cross the Channel to join 1st Armoured Division. General Alan Brooke was sent over to take charge, but quickly saw the hopelessness of the situation and the remaining troops, including a number on the lines of communication, were taken back to England.

The BEF arrived back in England baffled but

Left: Some who got away. British troops about to sail home from a French port, May 1940.

Bottom: These didn't. British and French prisoners after the surrender of 51st Highland Division at St Valéry.

Right: Ready to face the Italians. A 1st Royal Tank Regiment A9 Cruiser, in the Western Desert, in May 1940.

Below: 11th Hussars (now Royal Hussars) Morris armoured car, Western Desert, July 1940.

unbowed. That they had been defeated and had left all their heavy equipment behind was obvious, and they were surprised at the warm welcome they received. Immediately an investigation was set up to establish what had gone wrong. General Bartholomew, in his report, concluded that too much time had been spent during the Phoney War in the preparation of fixed defences which had made the BEF too defensively minded, and 'the inculcation of a fiercer, aggressive spirit into their troops by all commanders' was a prime requirement. In truth, though, neither the British nor their allies were geared to operate at the speed required to blunt the German *blitzkrieg.*

While thought was being given to remodelling the British Army to defeat the enemy, a most pressing requirement was defence of the homeland against seemingly imminent invasion. Only some 500 guns and 200 tanks, many of them obsolete, were left in the country, but improvised armoured vehicles were quickly assembled to provide mobile reserves to counterattack the enemy should he get off the beaches. While conscription had been introduced on the first day of the war, with the same age range, 18-41, as in 1916, men were only gradually called up because of the shortage of equipment. In June, July and August 1940 there was a sudden influx of 275,000 men, the largest portion going to the infantry since it was this arm that had the most equipment available. Churchill also initiated a new volunteer movement for those over military age or in reserved occupations, the Local Defence Volunteers, the name shortly to be changed to the more evocative Home Guard. Initially armed with little more than pitchforks and shotguns, the Home Guard made up for its material deficiencies through the enthusiasm of its members, and a number of home-made weapon systems swelled its armoury. Eventually it got both uniforms and proper weapons and by March 1942 it had become a very efficient force. There was also a new women's service, the Auxiliary Territorial Service (ATS), the successor to the WAAC of World War I. They carried out many of the same jobs, but a large number of women served in Anti-Aircraft Command, where they did everything but actually squeeze the trigger of

Right: Infantry Tank Mark II, the Matilda, which proved a formidable weapon against the Italians in Libya.

Below: During the early stages of Operation Compass, Wavell's first Desert offensive. Some of the many Italian prisoners, 16 December 1940.

the gun. Her Majesty the Queen, then Princess Elizabeth, was to join the ATS in the later part of the war.

Beach defences were hastily thrown up around the coast and thousands of pillboxes dotted the country, many still existing to this day. Britain quickly became an armed camp and, inspired by Prime Minister Churchill's heroic speeches, acquired a sense of purpose lacking until then.

Churchill was determined that an offensive spirit be quickly developed on the lines of the Bartholomew Report recommendation, but he wanted to go further by immediately beginning to harry the enemy across the Channel. Out of this was quickly born the Commando concept and volunteers were called from all the Army commands to form 500-man units or Commandos, after the Boer units, 'to fight independently as an irregular and not as a formed military unit' as the original instruction put it. Eventually the

Independent Companies, 10 of which had been formed from second-line Territorial divisions to go to Norway to help guard the long coastline, were also integrated in the Commandos. Indeed it was volunteers from them, quickly formed into No 11 Independent Company, which carried out the first cross-Channel raid on the night of 24/25 June 1940 in the Boulogne area, and with No 3 Commando carried out another raid the following month on Guernsey. Both were abortive, and small raids were stopped by Churchill for the next year in favour of preparing for larger enterprises involving 5000-10,000 men. One Commando, No 2, was dedicated to parachuting. Shortly afterward, under a reorganisation, it became 11 Special Air Service Battalion and eventually the Parachute Regiment. Three Commandos, Nos 50-52, were also formed in the Middle East at this time, and it was to this theatre that attention now turned.

On 11 June 1940 the Italians had declared war on Britain and France and invaded the French Riviera. To the British this produced a threat not just to the Mediterranean but also Egypt and the Suez Canal, which lay within easy reach of the large Italian army in Libya. Another Italian army based in Abyssinia quickly overran British Somaliland and mounted two cautious probes into Eritrea and the Sudan. For the moment they made no move into Egypt, but General Wavell, commanding in Egypt and Palestine, was not content to wait and, though he had only 36,000 British and Dominion troops as against 200,000 Italian and native troops, launched a number of raids across the Egyptian frontier wire, known by the troops simply as the Wire. Eventually in mid September the Italians advanced 60 miles into Egypt, where they halted and set up a number of fortified camps. At about this time Wavell received from Britain the welcome reinforcement of an armoured brigade, together with anti-tank, anti-aircraft and field guns. He now decided to mount a raid on the Italian positions and preparations were made under great secrecy, only the higher commanders being told. The Western Desert Force under General Dick O'Connor, consisting of 7th Armoured and 4th Indian Divisions, was to carry it out. The attack was launched on 9 December 1940 and was an immediate success, the Italians being sent reeling back in confusion. Wavell now withdrew 4th Indian Division, sending it to East Africa, and gave O'Connor 6th Australian Division instead. At the beginning of January 1941, he launched the second part of Operation Compass, driving on into Libya. Bardia and then Tobruk fell, and O'Connor, even though he was short of fuel and his tanks were in desperate need of maintenance, launched an even more ambitious operation. While the Australians took the coast road round to Benghazi, the 7th Armoured Division struck across the rough terrain at the base of the Jebel Akhdar to cut off the Italian retreat. The leading elements arrived at the coast road at Beda Fomm, some 80 miles south of Benghazi, in the nick of time. The Italians tried repeatedly to break through the small force of 3000 men and tanks holding the blocking position, but it managed to hold, and in the end white flags started to appear, and more than 20,000 prisoners and 216 guns fell into British hands. As Anthony Eden, Churchill's Foreign Minister, said, suitably adapting Churchill's famous comment on the fighter pilots in the Battle of Britain: 'Never has so much been surrendered by so many to so few.'

The euphoria of this victory would not last long. The 7th Armoured Division was now withdrawn to Egypt to refit, and its place was taken by a brigade of the newly arrived 2nd Armoured Division, while the 6th Australian Division was replaced by the also raw 9th Australian Division. At the same time Hitler sent what was to become the Deutsches Afrika Korps, commanded by Erwin Rommel, to bolster up the Italians, and the British Army was shortly to feel his presence once more.

The Western Desert Force had been stripped to the bone immediately after Beda Fomm for two reasons. Firstly, Wavell had to clear the Italians out of East Africa. General Platt had advanced into Eritrea from the Sudan and had come up

Left: An Army Commando. His toggle rope and fighting knife, this model with knuckleduster handle, were part of his stock-in-trade.

against a strong defensive position at Keren. Reinforced by 5th Indian Division, he finally forced it in March after ten days' bitter fighting. Meanwhile General Alan Cunningham had seized Italian Somaliland and had moved into southern Abyssinia. Platt coming down from the north forced the final surrender of the Italians in Abyssinia at Amba Alagi in May, and he and Cunningham had now accounted for 350,000 Italians in four months.

Below: During the Commando raid on Vaagso, Norway, 27 December 1941. A wounded officer is helped back to the landing craft.

Above: A Yeomanry unit of the 1st Cavalry Division in Palestine, 1940. They did not lose their horses until late 1941.

Below: Commandos on return from the disastrous Dieppe operation, August 1942. Note the collapsible Goatley boat, which was much favoured by Commandos.

The second reason for weakening the Desert Force was Churchill's decision to send troops to help the Greeks who were faced with an Italian invasion through Albania. In March the New Zealand Division, commanded by General Bernard Freyberg VC, 6th Australian Division and a brigade from 2nd Armoured Division arrived in the country and took up positions with the Greek Army. On 7 April 1941 the Germans, with three corps, invaded Yugoslavia and Greece, and by the end of the month, in another *blitzkrieg* campaign, had driven the Allied troops out of the country. As at Dunkirk, all the heavy equipment had to be left behind, but the Royal Navy managed to evacuate 50,000 men. Many of them were sent direct to Crete, where a Regular British brigade had been deployed since the end of November 1940. Freyberg was appointed to command the now swollen garrison, but in view of the disorganised state of many of his troops was not optimistic over the chances of resisting a German attack. After six days' preliminary bombardment by the Luftwaffe, the Germans mounted a mass airborne attack on 20 May 1941. The German paratroops suffered heavy casualties but managed to seize the crucial airfield at Maleme. With an airhead now established, they were able to fly in reinforcements, and the tide of battle began to turn in their favour. The Royal Navy, too, was suffering severe losses from air attack, and the only reinforcements sent to Freyberg were two battalions of Commandos from the recently formed Layforce. By the end of the month Crete had been evacuated, almost all the Commandos, who had acted as the rearguard, being killed or captured. Evacuations by sea were becoming a way of life for the British and Dominion troops.

In North Africa the situation was equally grim. Rommel had wasted little time and at the end of March struck the weakened Western Desert Force in Cyrenaica and sent it reeling back. Benghazi quickly fell, and in what was afterwards called the 'Benghazi Handicap' the Western Desert Force was driven back across the Wire and into Egypt by the end of April. Only Tobruk held out. A halfhearted counterattack in mid May in the Sollum and Capuzzo area achiev-

Above right: David Stirling and one of his Special Air Service (SAS) patrols. The patrol's jeeps carry a typical armament of Vickers 'K' machine guns.

ed little, and both sides settled down to draw breath.

To compound Wavell's problems, he was now faced with a new threat, this time in his rear. There was a pro-Fascist revolt in Iraq in May, and the RAF's vital airfields at Habbaniyah were put under siege. The revolt was crushed by the end of the month, but by then it appeared that the Vichy French were prepared to allow the Germans the use of facilities in Syria, which the French still held, along with their territories in western North Africa. A week after the evacuation from Crete, General Wilson launched a three-pronged attack on the French in Syria. This included a Commando landing to seize a vital bridge over the Litani River, and the employment of the 1st Cavalry Division. Consisting of Regular cavalry and Yeomanry regiments it was still horsed and would not begin to convert to an armoured division (the 10th) until August 1941. The French were quickly beaten, and Wavell could now turn his attention once more to Rommel.

Churchill had been putting pressure on Wavell to drive the Axis troops back, and to encourage him had at great risk sent a convoy, code-named

Right: Portéed (truck-mounted) anti-tank guns in the Western Desert. This gave them more flexibility over the towed version. The guns are 47mm weapons captured from the Italians.

'Tiger', through the Mediterranean at the beginning of May. It carried 220 tanks, mainly Matildas and a new cruiser tank, the Crusader, and was sufficient to re-equip 7th Armoured Division. Now, bowing to Churchill's pleas, Wavell launched an attack on 15 June to relieve Tobruk. It failed, the German 88-mm anti-aircraft gun being used in the anti-tank role, inflicting heavy tank losses. Battleaxe, the code name for the attack, brought about Wavell's replacement by General Sir Claude Auchinleck. Wavell, during his time in command, had been constantly under the most enormous pressure, and in spite of the reverses his troops had suffered, it was remarkable what he had achieved with his thinly stretched forces. Much loved by his men, and a man of intellect, his failing was his inability to stand up to Churchill. The 'Auk', as his successor was known, was an Indian Army soldier, not well known outside India apart from a brief involvement in the ill-fated Norwegian campaign and in the defence of Britain immediately after Dunkirk, but nevertheless a man who radiated quiet confidence.

The experience of the last three months fighting in the Western Desert had shown that the Germans were still superior to the British in both tactics and equipment. German doctrine emphasised the all arms concept down to the lowest level. Tanks, infantry and anti-tank guns co-operated closely with one another. The British, on the other hand, still separated the tanks from their infantry, even in the armoured divisions. While they tried to draw the German tanks into tank versus tank actions, the Germans responded tempting the British armour on to their anti-tank guns with impressive results. While gun for gun the British tanks were not inferior, they were less mechanically reliable and also had only solid shot anti-tank ammunition, lacking the flexibility of the Panzers, which had HE rounds, suitable for engaging anti-tank guns as well. A further problem was that the widely different top

"My brother says he's on a lonely gunsite in Yorkshire — two miles from the nearest pub!"

Above: 'Jon's' Two Types, who were to the Eighth Army what Bairnsfather's Old Bill and Young Bert were to the BEF of 1914-18.

the Eighth Army, commanded by Cunningham of East Africa fame, had two corps, XIII with 4th Indian Division, the New Zealand Division and 1st Army Tank Brigade, and XXX Corps (7th Armoured Division, 1st South African Division and 22 Guards Brigade), with 2nd South African Division as Army reserve.

Throughout the long hot North African summer the two sides continued to glower at one another. Every night the tanks withdrew into close leaguers, where refuelling, 'bombing up' with ammunition and maintenance took place. Only when this had been done could the crews settle down under their blankets to get some sleep. An hour before dawn they stood to, and then motored out to take up their positions on the line of observation for the day. As the long hours passed, the main problem was to keep awake in the scorching heat, which made metal too hot to touch, but the crews had to be constantly alert for any sudden move the enemy might make. The tank commander's most vital piece of equipment was his binoculars, which he wore around his neck at all times. Navigation in the often featureless desert was by the sun compass, a very simple gadget which worked on the sundial principle and was remarkably accurate. A major move by a regiment or brigade would be controlled by a specially appointed navigator. The diet had changed little from 1914-18, with bully beef and hardtack biscuits still the staples, along with 'M & V', canned bacon, jam and tea. There were, however, also soya links, a canned sausage substitute, canned fruit and potatoes, and sometimes

speeds of the Matilda and Crusader meant that the two could not easily operate together.

Auchinleck refused to allow himself to become pressured into prematurely resuming the offensive to relieve Tobruk, which was largely being held by the Australians, who called themselves with great pride the Rats of Tobruk. Gradually he built up his forces until what was now called

Right: British artillery passes through a Greek village, spring 1941. The gun is a 3.7-inch howitzer.

fresh bread would be available, baked by the Royal Army Service Corps. Cooking was done by each vehicle crew, and many became very ingenious in the variety of dishes they managed to concoct from seemingly monotonous ingredients. Dress became more and more informal as the campaign went on. A shirt, shorts or slacks were the basic order, light desert boots taking over from the heavy ammunition boot. Scarves of varying hues were worn to protect the neck from sores. The nights could get very cold, and greatcoats, leather jerkins and sheepskin jackets abounded. In the early days troops were issued with pith helmets, but these quickly gave way to the ubiquitous beret; the Royal Tank Corps had been the first to wear it in 1923, as the most suitable headgear for the narrow confines of a tank. Regular leave to Cairo was available, except when a major operation was taking place, and many of those who had been wounded were sent to South Africa to convalesce.

By November 1941 Auchinleck was finally ready. In the meantime the hardpressed Australians in Tobruk had been relieved by a composite British formation, 70th Division, and a Polish brigade. Operation Crusader had as its aim the relief of Tobruk and the capture of the Cyrenaican airfields so that some pressure could be taken off Malta, now under virtual siege from repeated Axis air attacks, and the Mediterranean reopened for convoy traffic. On 18 November Eighth Army attacked. While XIII Corps moved on Tobruk, XXX Corps in the south was given the task of bringing the Axis armour to

Above: Operation Crusader, November 1941. Escorted by a Royal Tank Regiment trooper, members of the *Deutsches Afrika Korps* go 'into the bag.'

Left: 'The Auk.' General Sir Claude Auchinleck, Commander-in-Chief Middle East, 1941-42.

Left: Royal Tank Regiment Matildas. The pennants were used as identification symbols in the desert, their position on the radio antenna being changed each day.

Right: The fall of Hong Kong, Christmas Day 1941.

battle and destroying it. Cunningham had difficulty in locating the enemy tanks and his own armour became dispersed. Rommel was therefore able to defeat it in detail, a whole armoured brigade being destroyed on the airfield at Sidi Rizegh. Flushed with this success, Rommel led his armour in a dash for the Wire. Cunningham, on the other hand, faltered and wanted to call the operation off. Auchinleck stepped in and replaced him by his own Deputy Chief of Staff, Ritchie, and the thrust to free Tobruk continued. Rommel, having caused much confusion, ran short of fuel, and harried by the Desert Air Force was forced to pull back. Tobruk was finally relieved on 10 December 1941, and Rommel pulled back into Tripolitania to regather his strength. Crusader had been a battle of nerves and it was Rommel's which had given first.

The achievements of the Eighth Army at the end of 1941 were to be quickly overshadowed by events in the Far East. On 7 December 1941 came the surprise Japanese attack on Pearl Harbor. While finally bringing the USA into the war, it immediately caused further setbacks for British arms. Hong Kong, garrisoned by two British Regular battalions, two Indian and two recently arrived Canadian Militia battalions, was attack-

ed the next day, and by the 12th the Allied troops had been driven out of the New Territories and on to Hong Kong island itself, being forced to surrender, in spite of much gallantry, on Christmas Day. Simultaneously the Japanese turned their attention to Malaya and the great British naval base at Singapore.

The Malayan campaign is another example of prewar chickens coming home to roost. The defence of Singapore was originally seen as a naval responsibility, but then it was taken over by the RAF who believed that air power could forestall any invasion. Forward airfields had to be built in northern Malaya, which committed the Army to protecting them. There was, however, little co-ordination among the three services, and virtually nothing had been done to prepare the civil population for war. General Percival, the military commander, had the equivalent of one Australian division, two Indian divisions and two Malayan brigades, two-thirds of what he considered he needed, but commitments in other theatres meant that no more men could be spared. The quality of the troops in Malaya was not high, mainly because they lacked training, especially in jungle warfare which had been almost totally ignored on the

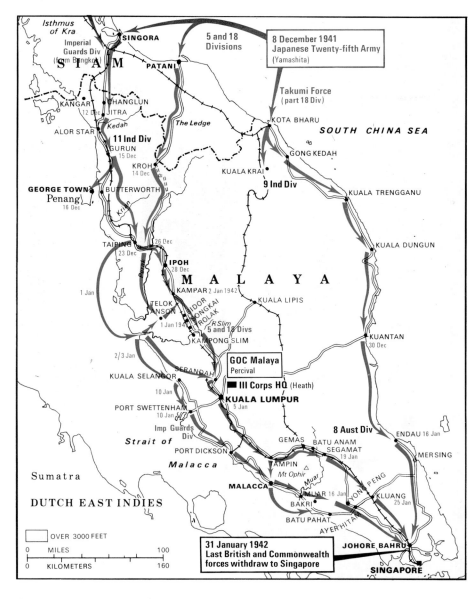

Above and above right: The fall of Malaya and Singapore.

assumption that the Japanese would use the roads. There was also a dangerous attitude of complacency in that the Japanese were not rated highly as soldiers. One British staff officer summed up the general attitude of the British high command: 'The Japanese Army is like a bubble waiting to be pricked.' Events were quickly to prove how wrong he was.

The Japanese invasion began on 8 December, four regiments landing on the east coast of the Malay peninsula just inside Siam, and another at Khota Bharu inside Malaya. Their first task was to capture the airfields, which was done with comparative ease. They quickly gained air superiority, and Allied morale suffered when, on the 10th, the capital ships *Prince of Wales* and *Repulse* were sunk by Japanese aircraft. At first the Japanese used the roads, with tanks leading the advance. If they came up against opposition they merely outflanked it by using the jungle and threatened it from behind. This seeming ability to appear from nowhere played havoc with morale. Positions were given up before they came under pressure, and co-ordination was lacking. By the end of the month the troops were exhaust-

Right: Where will the Japs strike next? Malaya, December 1941.

ed, and although Percival intended to hold on to the southern state of Johore, to which he had been forced back by the beginning of January 1942, Wavell, now appointed Commander-in-Chief of the Allied armies in the region, over-ruled him and ordered him to prepare to defend Singapore. By this time two divisions *en route* to the Middle East, 17th Indian and 18th British, had been diverted to Singapore, and Auchinleck also offered up the experienced 7 Armoured Brigade. The long retreat in Malaya continued, and nowhere was any positive counter put into effect, although individual battalions, Indian, Australian and British, often fought well. By 1 February Malaya had been evacuated and all troops were back across the Causeway which separated it from Singapore. The 18th Division had now arrived, 17th Indian and 7 Armoured Brigade having been diverted to Burma, but the rot had set in. On the 8th the Japanese attacked, infiltrated through the forward positions and forced the defenders back towards Singapore City. By now the civil government had virtually broken down, the streets of the city were throng-ed with deserters, always the sign of a beaten army, and there was clamour at the docks as people tried to get away before the Japanese took over. Defeat was inevitable and Percival, now responsible for a large civilian population as well, chose the only option available, and on 15 February 1942 the Japanese accepted his sur-render. Two days earlier General Sir Henry Pownall, Wavell's Chief of Staff, had written in his diary:

'It is a great disaster for British Arms, one of the worst in history, and a great blow to the honour and prestige of the Army. From the beginning to the end of this campaign we have been outmatched by better soldiers.'

For the survivors, now prisoners of the Japanese, there would be no smiling faces offering cups of tea, as there had been after Dunkirk, but only the appalling brutality of the Prisoner of War (POW) camps.

The third initial Japanese target was Burma, and here the story was much the same. The country was defended in the north by the Chinese, under the American General 'Vinegar Joe' Stilwell, Central Burma was covered by the British-officered 1st Burma Division, while to defend the south, which was where the Japanese would come, was 17th Indian Division, com-manded by Major General Jackie Smyth VC, with four brigades. The Japanese launched their attack on Burma on 20 January 1942. One Jap-

Above: Japanese General Yamashita accepts Lieutenant General A E Percival's surrender of Singapore.

Below: Japanese troops enter Rangoon, Burma, March 1942.

anese division crossed the frontier from Siam opposite Moulmein and came up against elements of 17th Indian Division on the River Salween, while a second landed from the sea, effectively outflanking the defences on the river. Smyth was forced to withdraw and was reliant on the single bridge over the Sittang river to get his troops back. The confusion created by the Japanese use of outflanking moves through the jungle had affected the staff of 17th Indian Division, and the result was that the bridge was blown with two-thirds of the division still on the wrong side. It cost Smyth his command, and has been held up ever since, along with the Remagen bridge over the River Rhine in March 1945, as a classic example of what can happen if arrangements to destroy a vital bridge go wrong.

The remnants of 17th Indian Division regrouped at Rangoon and were joined by 7 Armoured Brigade, and General Sir Harold Alexander was appointed to command the troops in Burma. The Japanese continued to thrust on Rangoon, which as Burma's major port was vital to the defence of Burma. As at Singapore public order broke down, and, aware of the dangers of being cut off, Alexander ordered a withdrawal and his troops got out just in time. Another officer, Lieutenant General Bill Slim, arrived to take command of the newly constituted Burcorps set up by Alexander to control the British and Imperial troops. Now began the toughest part of the whole campaign. It was approaching the hottest time of the year in Burma, water was short, morale was low and the route back no more than jungle tracks. Heat exhaustion, dysentery and malaria became widespread. Nevertheless by mid May the troops were back in Assam, although they had had to leave most of their equipment behind. While they had been consistently outfought by an enemy trained to fight in the jungle, there were the first glimmers of hope during the retreat, especially in the conduct of 7 Armoured Brigade and notably its two armoured regiments, the 7th Hussars and 2nd Royal Tank Regiment, in their American Stuart light tanks which the British called the Honey. They formed the rearguard until forced to abandon their tanks on reaching the River Chindwin, and time and again had turned on the Japanese, thus buying valuable time for the main body. There was, too, Slim's own bulldog personality which began to imprint itself on his troops.

Hong Kong, Malaya, Singapore and Burma had illustrated only too clearly, as had France in 1940, what could happen if a country failed to prepare itself adequately, and the commanders and their troops had suffered. For the survivors of these reverses there was much food for thought and an urgent need to apply their recent experiences to find means of breaking the seeming Japanese invincibility.

With the American entry into the war the decision had been made that the defeat of Germany should receive priority over that of Japan. Germany could be defeated only by an invasion of the continent of Europe, and the British Army in Britain, together with an increasing number of American troops being sent across the Atlantic, began to prepare for this. The training of the British troops came under GHQ Home Forces, and by the end of 1941 a new system had been set up, that of the 'battle schools.' Here troops underwent rigorous and tough field training, with maximum use of live ammunition, to instil in them the necessary offensive spirit. As yet, however, only specialist troops had the opportunity to close with the enemy. In March 1941 there had been a highly successful raid on the Lofoten Islands off northern Norway by the Commandos, and during the summer some small cross-Channel raids. A further raid on Norway, at Vaagso, was carried out in December. The embryo airborne force, 11th SAS Battalion, carried out its first operation against a viaduct in southern Italy in February 1941, and by the end of the year 1 Parachute Brigade had been formed. In February 1942 a company of this brigade carried out the highly successful attack on the German radar station at Bruneval in northern France. A further major Commando operation, in which much bravery was exhibited, was mounted at the end of March 1942 against the port of St Nazaire, and in May came the Madagascar landings, mounted by troops from Britain. This was the British Army's first major amphibious operation of the war, and was successful, although not until the beginning of November did Vichy French resistance on the island finally cease.

August 1942 saw the highly controversial and ill-fated attack at Dieppe. It was mounted as an experiment to investigate the problems of a cross-Channel invasion and resulted in the virtual destruction of 2nd Canadian Division, although the Commandos on the flanks of the attacks performed well. While there was much bitterness among the Canadians in the aftermath, the operation did provide vital lessons, the most important of which was that the Allies were not in a position to mount an invasion by the end of 1942 as the Americans had wanted.

While there was some understandable resentment among commanders in Britain that the spawning of 'private armies' such as the Commandos and paratroops merely served to cream off some of the best troops in their units, in the Middle East the situation was, if anything, worse. At the same time as the Middle East Commandos were formed a new unit, the Long Range Desert Group came into being. Its task was reconnaissance and it would operate deep in the desert throughout the campaign, and later in the Aegean, Balkans and Italy. A similar outfit was the Libyan Arab Force Commando, more commonly known as Popski's Private Army, after its commander Vladimir Peniakoff, a Russian émigré, which was made up of friendly Senussi tribesmen. In the late summer of 1941 David Stirling, a Commando officer, formed the Special Air Service (SAS) from the remnants of the Middle East Commandos and Layforce; its original primary function was to destroy Axis aircraft on their airfields. Other units also appeared and those who volunteered for these special forces did so mainly because they were frustrated by conventional soldiering and wanted to strike their own blow against the enemy.

Throughout 1942 the Middle East continued to hold the centre of the stage as far as the British Army was concerned. In January 1942, Rommel having been driven back out of Cyrenaica, the opportunity was taken to send several units back to the Delta to refit, which they badly needed

Left: Germans treating wounded British tank crewmen during Operation Crusader. A 'brewed up' British 'Honey' tank burns in the background.

Below: Freshly re-equipped with US tanks. An armoured regiment moves up with General Grants (37-mm turret gun, 75-mm sponson gun) and one Honey (General Stuart) with its 37-mm gun.

Above: The Eighth Army learned the value of recovering disabled tanks on the battlefield from the Germans. Here a Crusader is being winched aboard a low-loader.

Left: The crew of a Stuart tank keep a sharp lookout while awaiting night and the chance of rest in leaguer.

after Crusader. Rommel quickly spotted, through wireless intercepts, that the British were weak, and at the end of the month struck once more and drove Godwin-Austen's XIII Corps out of the Jebel Akhdar and back to the Gazala Line. There was now a four month pause while both sides made preparations to renew the offensive, but it was Rommel who moved first at the end of May. Ritchie, still commanding the Eighth Army, had made some fatal mistakes in his dispositions, creating a number of fortified 'boxes' of defence positions but these were too far apart to give one another mutual support, and he had also scattered his armour instead of keeping it concentrated. Rommel took full advantage and destroyed the armour piecemeal in the Gazala Line itself, in the areas known as the Cauldron and Knightsbridge. Ritchie, fearful that his forces would be cut off, pulled farther and farther back, in spite of orders from Auchinleck to hold west of Tobruk. Here the defenses had been allowed to deteriorate, and the port fell on 21 June. The Eighth Army looked in danger of disintegration as units rushed pellmell back into Egypt, and Auchinleck removed Ritchie and took personal command of the army himself. He tried to hold Rommel at Mersa Matruh, but did not have the time to organise an effective defence and withdrew to the last defensible terrain in front of the Delta, the el Alamein Line. While he intended to fight here, Auchinleck's primary in-

tention was to keep his army in being, and if he was forced to withdraw he would do so fighting, back into the Delta if necessary. Throughout the whole of July the two sides wrestled at el Alamein. Both were tired and Rommell had to contend with overstretched supply lines. Attack was followed by counterattack, but neither side could break through. While the British and Imperial troops managed to overcome their earlier bafflement, there were still problem areas. Staff work was often shoddy, communications constantly failed and combined arm tactics were still imperfectly understood. Yet in spite of the initial panic, which included the wholesale burning of papers at GHQ in Cairo, the Eighth Army held and forced Rommel on to the defensive. It lacked the means, however, to drive him back.

A few days later, on 3 August, Winston Churchill arrived in Cairo to see for himself. He decided that the Middle East Land Forces needed an injection of new blood. Discussion was complicated by the death of 'Strafer' Gott, just nominated to take command of the Eighth Army, when the aircraft taking him from the front, where he had been commanding XIII Corps, was shot down. Eventually it was announced that Auchinleck would be relieved, as Commander-in-Chief Middle East, by Alexander and that Montgomery would take over the Eighth Army. A new era was about to begin.

THE ROAD TO
VICTORY 1942-45

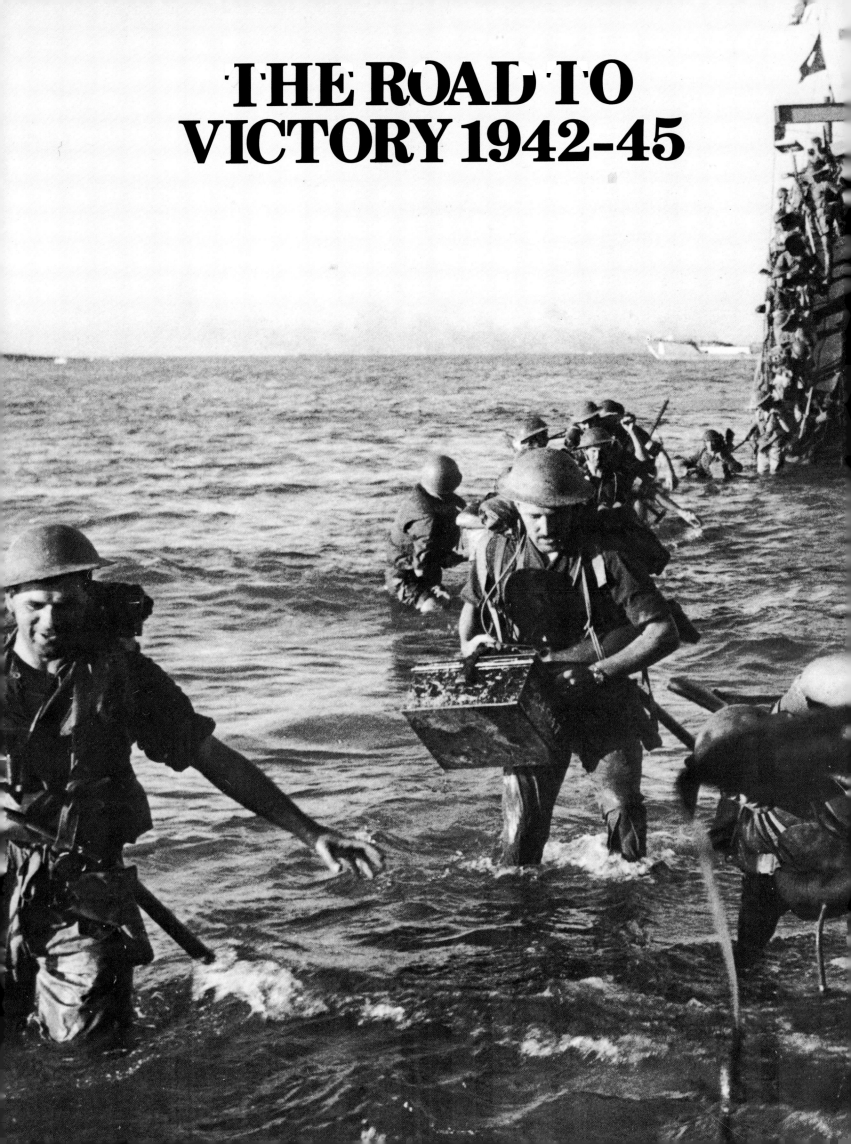

Montgomery's very first action on taking over command of the Eighth Army was to state that there would be no more withdrawals. The army would stay where it was on the el Alamein Line to repulse Rommel's next thrust, which he knew was imminent from deciphered intercepts of the German high level communications. He could then go on to the offensive, but only when he was ready. Montgomery's positive, extrovert personality, supreme self-confidence and the clear-cut way in which he explained his plans and intentions – which he insisted should be known, at least in outline, by the very lowest levels – had an immediate effect on the troops under his command. At last, they felt, there was a general who knew what he was doing and knew that he would succeed. He set about preparing his defences, deploying the three infantry divisions of XXX Corps (9th Australian, 1st South African and 50th Northumbrian) north of the Ruweisat Ridge. He expected Rommel to launch his main attack with his armour south of here, and disposed his two armoured divisions, 7th and 10th, in such a way that the Panzers would be steered on to the key terrain of the Alam Halfa Ridge, after which the battle would take its name. The New Zealand Division held the northern shoulder, and the newly arrived 44th Home Counties Division was placed in depth to the east of the Alam Halfa Ridge.

The previous eight months had seen some major equipment changes. There had been a large influx of US tanks, first the General Lee, with a 37-mm turret gun and a 75-mm rather unsatisfactorily mounted in a sponson, and then the Sherman, which was to become the most widely used Allied tank of the war. It had a turret-mounted 75-mm, good speed and reasonable armour, and its only drawback was a propensity to catch fire when hit, which gave it the nickname of the 'Ronson lighter'. An improved anti-tank gun, the 6-pounder, was beginning to appear, and while the 25-pounder continued to provide the main close support artillery weapon, the US 155-mm howitzer had come to join the 4.5-inch and 5.5-inch. Montgomery had also taken the step of locating his headquarters with

that of the Desert Air Force to make air support more responsive.

Rommel moved forward on the night of 30/31 August, harried as he did so by the Desert Air Force. He then pushed through the minefields in the south, but was delayed by 7th Armoured Division. Eventually he came up against the main position at Alam Halfa, and made two attacks, both of which were beaten off by Pip Roberts' 22 Armoured Brigade, which was under strict orders to stay put in defensive positions and not be tempted forward into an embroilment with the German tanks. With fuel now short, Rommel decided late on 1 September to withdraw, and an attempt to cut off his withdrawal failed. Nevertheless the Eighth Army had undoubtedly beaten Rommel and their tails were now up.

Much still had to be done before Montgomery felt confident of attacking, and for the next six weeks the Eighth Army carried out rigorous training. Having weighed up all the options, Montgomery concluded that only a frontal assault was feasible, and planned to put his main effort in the north, while some of his armour feinted in the south to keep the German armour tied down and make Rommel believe that this was the main attack. The Eighth Army had now built up a significant superiority in tanks, 1350 against 540, men, 164,000 compared with 100,000, and artillery. For the operation to be successful this was essential. Eighth Army was now organised into three corps: XXX Corps in the north, which would carry out the main break-in operation, had 9th Australian Division, the New Zealand Division, 1st South African Division, 4th Indian Division and the 51st Highland Division, which had been reconstituted after the St Valéry disaster in 1940, together with two armoured brigades. XIII Corps was responsible for the feint in the south, and had 7th Armoured, 44th and 50th Divisions, while X Corps had been formed as a *corps de chasse* to carry out the break-out and pursuit, with 1st and 10th Armoured Divisions and the headquarters of 8th Armoured Division, whose armoured brigades had been lent to XXX Corps.

At 2140 hours on the night of 23/24 October, almost 1000 guns opened fire, the intensity of the bombardment taking the Axis troops by surprise. Engineers and infantry moved forward to clear lanes in the minefields, the 51st Highland with pipers playing, as of old, to keep up spirits. In the extreme north the Australians had managed to get through by dawn, but farther south the Highlanders had had trouble from a number of strong-points. This meant that the armour could not yet move forward, in spite of Montgomery's urgings. He thus decided to continue the 'crumbling' attacks in the north, and succeeded in wearing down the enemy infantry and gradually destroying his armour, which became inevitably drawn into counterattacks. It was a wearisome business, and casualties were mounting, but Montgomery was convinced that Rommel would give way first, and by 1 November Rommel had had enough and began to withdraw. In spite of efforts by the *corps de chasse* to cut him off, he succeeded, with great skill, in extricating himself.

In Britain el Alamein was greeted as a great victory and, as at Cambrai 25 years before, the

church bells were rung throughout the land. For those who had taken part it had been an exhausting week's fighting, aptly summed up in a platoon commander's memories of 'the appalling din of guns firing and of shells bursting, the grim sights of mangled men and twisted corpses, the mental strain of sleeplessness and responsibility, the fear of breaking down in front of the men.' As Eighth Army now gathered itself to chase after Rommel, there was little elation among the veterans. The past two years had seen all too many pursuits and retreats; 'it was just another flog – up the blue'. Nevertheless el Alamein marked a major turning point. It was, like Stalingrad on the Eastern Front, the first of a relentless series of victories which would bring the Axis armies to their knees, and it was appropriate that it should be the last time that the British and Imperial troops waged a campaign on their own. From then on the operations in the Mediterranean and Europe would be conducted in concert with the American armies.

Only a few days after Rommel had pulled back from el Alamein in a retreat which would not stop until he entered Tunisia, the first of these Anglo-American enterprises was mounted, Operation Torch. The original idea for an attack on French

In order to fool Rommel, Montgomery had many of his tanks disguised as trucks during his preparations for the attack at el Alamein. *Above*, a Sherman gunner cleans the turret mounted Browning 0.50-inch machine gun, a picture taken inside the false canopy, while at *right* is a suitably disguised Crusader, seen from the exterior.

Above right: The Battle of El Alamein.

DAILY MIRROR, Thursday, November 5, 1942.

Daily Mirror

NOV 5

No. 12,136   ONE PENNY
Registered at the G.P.O. at a Newspaper.

★ He dished it out ★

Above: News of Montgomery's victory at el Alamein reaches Britain.

Below: Sherman tanks in action, November 1942. Note how the censor has removed the unit identification marks from the picture.

ROMMEL ROUTED HUNS FLEEING IN DISORDER

9,000 men captured
260 tanks destroyed
600 planes knocked out

ROMMEL'S desert army, blitzed as no German army has ever been blitzed before, is in full retreat with the Eighth Army in close pursuit of his "disordered" columns.

The dramatic story of General Montgomery's smashing victory was told in the following special joint communique from British Headquarters in Cairo last night:—

"The Axis forces in the Western Desert, after ...

...ny has been really ...stand up to the ...(above) and ...of this terri-... They are in

★ He couldn't take it ★

The Italians have asked for an armistice to enable them to bury their dead. The message does not state whether or not the request applies to all Italian forces on the Mediterranean Qattara front.

Left: Crusader and Sherman tanks in Mersa Matruh, 11 November 1942, as the advance after Alamein got under way.

North Africa had been mooted at the first of the great Anglo-American wartime conferences, Arcadia, held in December 1941. The American view had been, however, that this would merely detract from the primary objective of mounting an invasion of the continent of Europe, and it was not until July 1942, as Auchinleck stood with his back to Cairo, that Roosevelt decreed that it should go ahead. The object would be to seize Morocco, Algeria and Tunisia, and then turn on the Axis army in Libya. Landings were to take place at Casablanca, Oran and Algiers, the first two being carried out by US troops, and that at Algiers by an Anglo-American force. The British contingent was initially to be 78th Division, part of 6th Armoured Division, Nos 1 and 6 Commandos and 1st Parachute Brigade. Because it

was known that Vichy French feelings towards the British were still bitter, as a result of the Royal Navy's attack on the French fleet shortly after the surrender of France in 1940, it was decided that the British troops taking part should wear American helmets. It was hoped that the French would quickly capitulate.

The landings took place on 8 November 1942 and an armistice came into effect in the early hours of the 11th. The next task was Tunisia. For this the Eastern Task Force which had landed at Algiers was retitled the British First Army. Lieutenant General Kenneth Anderson was appointed to command it, and he had arrived at Algiers by the 9th. His strength was slender, the roads poor, information about the enemy scanty and his maps inaccurate. Nevertheless he knew he had to move fast, and the two infantry brigades of 78th Division were deployed, along with the 17/21st Lancers, the only British armoured regiment present, while elements of the 34th US Division were sent east on separate thrusts to Bizerta and Tunis. 1st Parachute Brigade was deployed ahead, one battalion capturing Bône airfield just before a German para-

Below: 25-pounder guns firing at night during the Alamein battle.

chute battalion tried to drop on it. The Germans, meanwhile, had reacted quickly. Firstly, aircraft had been deployed, and they soon began to make their presence felt. Indeed during the early part of the campaign the Germans enjoyed air superiority, operating from concrete runways, while the Allied aircraft had only grass airfields, which were quickly turned to mud by the winter rains, thus drastically restricting operations. German troops then landed. By the end of November there had been a series of meeting engagements, the hilly terrain very much favouring the defence. Try as they might, with their slender resources and lack of supplies, the British and Americans could not get through. German counterattacks increased in strength, as more reinforcements flowed in from Italy and Sicily, and the Allies were forced to give ground. It was noticeable, however, that while it was the first experience of combat for the British troops, as it was for the Americans, the last two years of training were paying off, in that there was no panic, and they gave as good as they got. Often it was merely lack of ammunition which forced them to pull back. Anderson made one more attempt at Christmas to get through to Tunis, but again failed, although there was some desperate fighting around a feature called Longstop Hill. The 2nd Coldstream Guards were heavily involved, and an account of theirs gives a good idea of the conditions:

'So heavy had the rain been that wheeled vehicles could not get within 5000 yards of the forward companies, tracked vehicles not nearer than 3000. Ammunition had to make the last stretch by hand, and casualties were manhandled down the hill the same way. On the summit the knee-high rosemary and coarse heather were sopping wet – painfully slow to get through. As night wore on, under heavy mortar fire, it was clear that in spite of the handful of reinforcements – a draft from England (hurried into battle as soon as they had dropped their heavy packs) and a company of French native troops – more troops, still more, would be needed if Longstop was to be held . . . .'

Eisenhower, in overall command, regretfully accepted that a further advance was not possible, and both sides settled down to pause for breath.

By the beginning of January the Allies in Tunisia had a somewhat complicated command structure. There were now three corps holding a front of 200 miles from Cap Serrat in the north to Gafsa in the south. The northern sector was held by the British V Corps, with 6th Armoured, 78th and the newly arrived 46th South Midland Division. Then came the French XIX Corps and finally II US Corps. Anderson was in overall command, and had 1 Guards Brigade and 25 Army Tank Brigade, equipped with the Churchill infantry tank which was soon to prove its agility in the hills, as his army reserve. HQ First Army was not organised to command such a disparate force, and Anderson himself perhaps lacked the tact to deal with his allies, especially the Americans. They tended to regard their British counterparts as 'pipe-smoking, blue-eyed bastards, with that elegant manner, and no manners at all', and resented their superior attitude born of having been at war for over two years longer than the Americans. The British, on the other hand, viewed the Americans as brash amateurs, who appeared to have limitless amounts of equipment

but very little idea of how to use it. Events in February were to reinforce this view.

On 23 January 1943, Montgomery's Eighth Army entered Tripoli, having pursued Rommel the 1000 miles from el Alamein. Here Montgomery halted to open up the port – vital if he was to shorten his by now severely stretched supply lines – and two weeks later Rommel crossed into Tunisia. He and von Arnim, commanding the Fifth Panzer Army in Tunisia, decided, after some argument to strike the First Army, and then Rommel could turn once more on the Eighth Army. After preliminary attacks at the end of January, the main blow was struck on 14 February against II US Corps, considered the weak link in the Allied line because of American inexperience. It took the Americans by surprise and they were thrown back in confusion, Rommel capturing the Kasserine Pass. Anderson, however, remained calm, sent a British armoured brigade and additional artillery down and the attack was halted. Rommel, conscious that Montgomery was once more on the move, turned east. While General George Patton came up from Morocco to relieve General Fredendall, to whom much of the blame for Kasserine must be allotted, in command of II US Corps, von Arnim struck at the British in the north and there was a week's fierce fighting all along the British front before the Germans decided that they had had enough.

In the meantime the Eighth Army had entered Tunisia on 16 February, spearheaded by 7th Armoured Division. The main obstacle facing them was the Mareth Line, defences constructed before the war by the French to protect against any possible Italian incursion from Libya. Montgomery, knowing from decoded messages that

Above: Orde Wingate (bearded), with Col Cochrane commanding the US No 1 Air Commando, which provided his air transport, watching his Chindits taking off for the second Chindit expedition, February 1944.

Opposite, top: Tank crews of First and Eighth Armies meet in Tunisia.

Opposite, bottom: The pursuit after Alamein was hindered by rain and mud. A Grant tank ploughs on regardless.

Rommel was intending to attack him, advanced cautiously so as not to lay his head on the block, and halted just beyond Medenine to prepare to receive him. When the attack finally came on 6 March 1943 Montgomery was ready and it was repulsed all along the line. Intelligent siting of the anti-tank guns was the decisive factor, and the highlight came from the anti-tank platoon of the 1st/7th Battalion, The Queen's Regiment, supported by a Royal Artillery anti-tank battery, which accounted for 27 tanks, over half those lost by the Germans on that day. Rommel wrote in his diary: 'A great gloom has settled over us all. The Eighth Army's attack was now imminent and we had to face it. For the Army Group to remain in Africa was now plain suicide.' He himself was ordered back to Germany on sick leave.

The Axis troops had now withdrawn to the Mareth Line, and General Alexander appointed as the Commander 18th Army Group, which covered the ground forces in Tunisia, saw that this must be forced before the campaign proceeded further. The Italian General Messe, who had now taken over from Rommel as the commander in Tunisia, had one German and four Italian divisions defending Mareth, and Montgomery planned on a break-in operation, sending a force round the Axis right flank to cut them off, while Alexander ordered Patton to carry out a diversionary attack at Gafsa. The 50th Northumbrian Division was to carry out the break-in, and attacked on the night of 20/21 March. Fighting was severe, and there were particular problems in getting tanks across the anti-tank ditch in front of the defences. A German counterattack then forced the attackers back on to the east bank. Montgomery now changed his plan and put

the main effort into his outflanking move, which was carried out by 1st Armoured Division and the New Zealanders. Having forced the Tebaga Gap, he then executed what was the first British *blitzkrieg* attack of the war, using waves of aircraft to attack with the tanks as they went forward, at el Hamma. Only the German anti-tank guns caused any problem, but this was sufficient to enable Messe to withdraw his forces through the Gabes Gap on 27 March. Alexander had now ordered Patton to link up with Montgomery, who was faced with another Axis defence line at Wadi Akarit. He broke through this during the first week of April, in another fierce battle in which the Gurkhas of 4th Indian Division especially distinguished themselves. A link-up was made with the Americans, and Alexander now ordered First Army to cut off von Arnim, but the Axis troops resisted strongly in the area of Fondouk, and were able to slip back to positions covering Tunis.

By now the Allied armies formed a continuous line hemming the Axis in with their backs to the sea. There was also a symbolic meeting between the First and Eighth Armies, and the contrasts between the two were stark. The Eighth came as veterans of almost three years continuous fighting culminating in a long advance. Their vehicles, battered and sand-coloured, and the casualness of their dress looked very different from the green-painted vehicles and more formally worn Battle Dress of the First Army, which had spent a tough, unglamorous winter in the hills and mountains of Tunisia, and there was some understandable initial mutual antagonism. There was rivalry, too, as to who should have the final honours.

Right: 4.2-inch mortars in action during the Italian campaign.

Montgomery tried to break through the next line of defences south of Tunis, but was rebuffed, the newly arrived 56th London Division, whose first battle it was, suffering heavy casualties. Alexander therefore switched the effort to First Army's front, reinforcing it with Montgomery's two veteran divisions, 4th Indian and 7th Armoured. Having painted their vehicles green, they moved into First Army's area and sampled the new Compo rations, with their much greater variety than ever the Eighth Army had known. (Compo still exists in essentially the same form as the British Army's food in the field even to this day.) As one veteran tank crewman remarked: 'First Army, no wonder they can't fight, they're too well fed.'

Operation Vulcan, the final attack, was launched on 4 May and on the 13th it was all over, with Bizerta in American hands, Tunis in British and a bag of over 200,000 German and Italian prisoners. Goebbels wrote in his diary: 'Our losses are enormous. We are indeed experiencing a sort of second Stalingrad.' Alexander signalled Churchill: 'Sir, it is my duty to report that the Tunisian campaign is over. All enemy resistance has ceased. We are masters of the North African shore.'

In the British Army's other active theatre of the time, the transformation of a beaten army into a victorious one was taking longer to achieve. In April 1942, while the British, Indian and Burmese troops were still struggling back into India, Wavell, as Commander-in-Chief of India, ordered planning for the reoccupation of Burma to begin. Before any practical steps could be carried out, the troops had to be trained not just in new methods to defeat the Japanese but also in how to live and survive in the jungle. Churchill, impatient as he often was, demanded that Wavell mount an advance into the Arakan to be followed by an amphibious operation designed to recapture Rangoon. Wavell was quite prepared to do this, but wanted to mount a diversionary attack in northern Burma at the same time. However, widespread internal unrest in India brought about by Gandhi's 'quit India' campaign, crises in North Africa and the need to send munitions to Russia, combined with a heavy monsoon, meant that Wavell lacked troops and materiel. Thus the plan was reduced to a single division clearing the Arakan coast and capturing Akyab island, important because of the Japanese air bases there dominating the Indian Ocean. Operation Anakim was launched in September 1942 and almost reached the coast north of Akyab by December, but Japanese reinforcements foiled any further advance. By now morale was suffering, with a high incidence of malaria, a cumbersome and creaking supply system and conflicting orders from higher commanders. In April 1943, the Japanese launched a counter-offensive and drove the division back to south of Chittagong. Once again the Japanese had shown themselves superior at jungle fighting and it was clear that the British and Indian troops still had a lot to learn.

There had, however, been a gleam of light in northern Burma. Brigadier Orde Wingate was an unusual man, very different from the normal stamp of British Regular officer, who had built up a sizeable practical experience of unconventional

warfare, first in Palestine before the war (the Israelis still regard him as a hero), then organising Abyssinian guerrillas during the 1941 campaign against the Italians. He proposed to Wavell the concept of using specially trained troops reliant on air resupply, to penetrate the Japanese lines and disrupt their communications. Wavell agreed, and in February 1943 Wingate crossed the River Chindwin with his 77 Brigade, which he called Chindits after the mythical Burmese beast, the *chinthe*. Its 3000 men were organised into seven columns and for the next two months Wingate harried Japanese communications, eventually drawing two out of the five divisions then in Burma towards him before withdrawing back into India. While he achieved nothing of strategic significance and lost a third of his men, Wingate did demonstrate that the Allied troops could live and work in the jungle just as well as their enemy, which led to a significant restoration of morale.

During the summer and early autumn of 1943 there were several changes in the command structure of the Allied forces in South-East Asia. In June Auchinleck took over from Wavell as Commander-in-Chief in India, and then in

Above: Carrying their sick and wounded with them, the Chindits withdraw back into Assam.

October Lord Louis Mountbatten arrived as commander of the new South-East Asia Allied Command (SEAC). One of his first steps was to reorganise the field army. He formed the 11th Army Group and under it created two corps, IV responsible for the central front around Imphal and XV for the Arakan, with the Chinese under Stilwell responsible for northern Burma. IV and XV Corps came under Fourteenth Army, which Bill Slim was appointed to command.

Slim had already been commanding in the Arakan from mid April 1943 and had begun his own reforms. Apart from the institution of jungle warfare schools set up the previous year, he concentrated especially on the health and morale of his troops. The incidence of malaria in the Arakan had reached such a stage that for every man wounded there were no less than 120 down with this disease. Dysentery and typhus were also rampant. The medical services were overhauled, the emphasis being on preventive research, which resulted among other innovations in the compulsory taking of daily mecaprine tablets, forward treatment of malarial cases and air evacuation for serious casualties. There was also a massive overhaul of the supply system,

roads and railways being built as close as possible to the front line. Above all Slim tackled the problem of morale. With the tide of victory now flowing in Europe, the men of the Fourteenth Army quickly began to feel that they were forgotten by their compatriots far away in Britain, and called themselves the 'Forgotten Army.' Slim, equally at home with British and Indian soldiers, pursued an active policy of making every man feel that he was important, however seemingly mundane his job. He instilled pride in belonging to the Fourteenth Army, setting up an Army newspaper, and insisted on first-class rest and training camps. He also made every soldier believe that he was better than the Japanese by laying down a policy of active patrolling so that the Fourteenth Army dominated no man's land like the BEF on the Western Front during 1914-18. The harvest of all this would be reaped from early 1944 onwards.

With the clearance of North Africa, the British and Americans now turned to Sicily as the next objective, an essential stepping stone for the invasion of the Italian mainland. The First Army, to the resentment of many of its members, was broken up, and its troops transferred to the

Top right: Monte Cassino, Italy, March 1944. New Zealand Vickers machine-gun crew, with Barr & Stroud rangefinder.

Below right: A group of Italian prisoners being escorted to the rear.

Below: The Italian campaign.

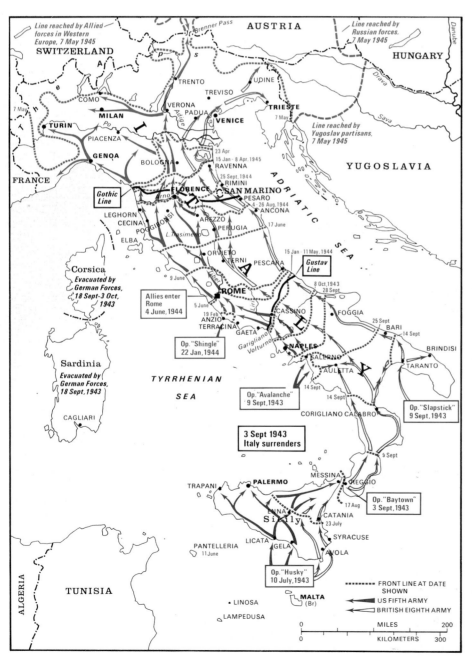

Eighth Army, which together with Patton's newly formed Seventh US Army would carry out the invasion of Sicily under the overall control of Alexander's 16th Army Group. Montgomery selected 5th, 50th, 51st and 1st Canadian Divisions for the operation, code name Husky, together with four independent brigades. Those Tunisian veterans 46th and 78th Divisions were earmarked as follow-up troops, and the newly created 1st Airborne Division would co-operate with the sea landings through parachute and glider operations. While the Americans landed in the south-west of the island, the British would cover the south-east. The troops hit the beaches in the early hours of 10 July 1943, the Commandos being first to land, as in all British amphibious operations from now on. All went smoothly except for the 1st Airborne Division operation, which was marred by inexperience with the gliders, and many men were drowned in the sea or landed at inaccessible places.

The first few days went according to plan, although the troops, who had had to leave most of their motor transport behind, found advancing on their feet in the hot Sicilian summer hard going. It was now that rivalry between Mont-

Above: 214 Field Company Royal Engineers improve an obstacle crossing, Italy, May 1944. Bailey bridge on the left and temporary cemetery on the right.

gomery and Patton, both prima donnas, came to the fore as they competed for the leading role in the overrunning of the island. Alexander compromised by allowing them both to advance northwards and it became a race to see who would reach Messina first. Patton undoubtedly showed more dash, but Montgomery faced the bulk of the German forces, who once again showed their skill in withdrawal, and try as he might his troops could not achieve a decisive breakthrough. The Germans were able to execute an evacuation across the Straits of Messina by 16 August, the day on which the Americans finally entered the town.

There was now a brief pause while the invasion plans for the Italian mainland were finalised. The first landings were made by the Eighth Army at Reggio in the toe of Italy on 3 September, but systematic German demolitions meant that the advance northward was slow. Six days

later two other landings took place. The 1st Airborne Division seized Taranto, and then captured Brindisi and Bari on the Adriatic coast, enabling 78th Division to be disembarked at the latter on 22 September. On the west coast, on 9 September, General Mark Clark's Fifth US Army landed at Salerno. Included in it was the British X Corps, with the 46th and 56th Divisions. The assaulting troops got ashore with little difficulty, but the Germans quickly concentrated four divisions and during the next week made repeated attempts to fling the invaders back into the sea. At times it was touch and go before the Germans finally drew off. The 7th Armoured Division was landed during the last few days of this dog fight and the Eighth Army finally linked up with the Fifth at Auletta on 20 September, Naples eventually falling on 1 October.

By now Italy had been knocked out of the war, but there were still sizeable German forces in the country. The Germans now set about preparing a number of defensive lines, the most significant of which was the Gustav Line, running along the Sangro river and then down through Monte Cassino to the west coast. Alexander's intention was for the Eighth Army to move up the east coast, break through the Gustav Line, capture Pescara to the north and then turn the German defences facing Mark Clark by advancing westwards. Progress was difficult, not just because of the defence lines themselves but also because to the troops on the ground there always seemed to be another dominating peak beyond the one they had captured. As the First Army in Tunisia had found, there were seldom enough troops, and the wintry Italian weather was a further burden to endure.

'There was a bitter, tearing wind from the east, which at times grew to such violence that movement was possible only on all fours .... To this were added hail and rain storms almost without pause, and the few trees which might have given the men some protection were torn to ribbons by shell and bullets. On the third day, as though every resource of man and nature was combining to complete their utter distress, there was a small earthquake.'

Eventually, by the end of November, the Eighth Army had struggled up to the now swollen Sangro and crossed it, but heavy resistance to the north and the worsening conditions caused Alexander to halt the advance still some way south of Pescara. In the west the story was much the same, the US Fifth Army finally reaching the Garigliano river, just south of the Gustav Line.

From the beginning Italy was viewed by the Allied planners as a secondary theatre in which to tie down as many German troops as possible so

that the primary operation, the invasion of France, would have the best possible chance of success. In this context three crack divisions, 7th Armoured, 50th Northumbrian and 51st Highland, had been withdrawn from Italy before the end of 1943 and sent back to England. As one veteran Desert Rat recorded:

'The big job was finished and another one would be starting soon. We had done well in Italy and had the valuable experience of operating in continental conditions. That was the reason we did not come home after Tunis, we had to be introduced to the conditions of the continent, so different from the desert. And we had done so. We had learned some new tricks and improved on the old ones and now we were going home.'

Above: General Sir Henry Maitland 'Jumbo' Wilson, Supreme Allied Commander, Mediterranean, with Oliver Leese, commanding Eighth Army, Italy, April 1944.

Left: A 5.5-inch gun crew of the Shropshire Yeomanry in action in Italy in September 1943. Between the two world wars many Yeomanry regiments were converted to the artillery or signals roles.

Above: Monastery Hill, Cassino, which saw some of the toughest fighting of the war.

Left: Bren gunner in the ruins of the monastery at Monte Cassino.

Right: Women of the Auxiliary Territorial Service played a vital role in the air defence of Great Britain. Here they are operating a Kine-Theodolite (above), which checks the predictor accuracy, while (below) they are using a rangefinder.

For some, who had been abroad since well before the outbreak of war, it was an emotional experience, as it was for Montgomery, who was also summoned back at the end of December 1943 to find himself a national hero.

By the beginning of 1944, much of the Army at home had been training for the return to France for well over three years, but during that time a number of changes had taken place in organisation, structure and equipment. Initially, after the experience of France in 1940, there had been a drive to create armoured divisions and no less than 13 had been formed, but subsequent experience revealed the need to get a better balance between armour and infantry and a number had been later disbanded. While the 1st and 6th Armoured Divisions remained in Italy, there were available for the North-West Europe campaign the Guards Armoured Division (formed by converting Guards battalions to the armour role) and the 7th and 11th Armoured. In addition there was a specialised division, 79th Armoured. By 1944, after a number of changes, the armoured division consisted of one armoured brigade of three armoured regiments (battalions) and a motorised infantry battalion, and a lorried infantry brigade with three truck-borne infantry battalions. There were also a divisional reconnaissance regiment with medium and light tanks, a field regiment Royal Artillery with towed 25-pounder guns, a self-propelled artillery regiment with 25-pounder guns mounted on a Sherman chassis, the Canadian-designed Sexton, an anti-tank regiment with 17-pounder guns, an anti-aircraft regiment with the 40-mm Bofors, and an engineer and a signals regiment,

together with supply, transport, repair and medical elements. In all the division had just under 15,000 men and 306 tanks, including 262 mediums, by now the Sherman and British Cromwell.

Although by mid 1942 there had been as many as 11 Army tank brigades, whose role was infantry support, they were gradually phased out in an effort to bring armour and infantry closer together. Five of them were absorbed into existing infantry divisions, which surrendered one of their three infantry brigades in the process, to form 'mixed' divisions, but it was subsequently found that this reduced the number of infantry by too much and the idea was abandoned. The armoured divisions in Italy, however, because of the nature of the terrain, each took on a second infantry brigade in the later part of 1944. The infantry division itself remained on the triangular structure of three brigades each of three battalions, but also had an armoured car regiment provided by the Reconnaissance Corps, a machine gun battalion, three field regiments Royal Artillery, an anti-tank and a light anti-aircraft regiment, together with engineers, signals and supporting services. The First World War Lee Enfield Mk 3 rifle had now given way to the Lee Enfield No 4, and the infantryman also had the Sten submachine gun and the Projector Infantry Anti-tank (PIAT), which fired a hollow charge bomb.

Apart from the Reconnaissance Corps and Parachute Regiment, a number of other new corps had come into being. With the need for

Above: General Sir Bernard Paget, C-in-C Home Forces 1941-3, inspecting 42nd Armoured Division on manoeuvres, September 1942.

liary Military Pioneer Corps in 1939, but the title was changed, also in 1940, to the Pioneer Corps, which has since received the 'Royal' prefix. To raise the standard of Army cookery a special corps was organised in 1941, the Army Catering Corps, and physical training became the responsibility of the Army Physical Training Corps.

The sudden expansion of the Army in 1939, combined with the increasing need for men with specialist, especially mechanical, skills resulted in very imperfect selection procedures for new enlistments, many finding themselves in the infantry when they would have been better employed in one of the more technical corps. It was therefore decided to form the General Service Corps. This came into being in 1942, and from then on every recruit initially joined it. His skills and aptitude were carefully screened, his own wishes also being taken into account, and he was then placed in a suitable arm or service, with which he did his basic and then special-to-arm training. The General Service Corps also provided a useful 'catch all' for other specialists, the requirement for which rapidly grew. Thus the Corps attracted people in an infinite variety of roles from Special Operations Executive (SOE) agents operating with resistance forces in enemy-occupied countries to the staffs of rest camps, movie makers and newspaper editors. Indeed there was great stress on welfare and tribute must be paid to the work of the Navy, Army and Air Force Institutes (NAAFI) who provided, as they still do, canteens and shops for the armed services, both in camps and in active theatres, as the old Expeditionary Force Canteens had during World War I, and the Entertainments National Service Association (ENSA), which laid on variety shows for troops and civilian war workers alike, often within the sound of the guns.

Officer selection quickly became very much more objective than during World War I. No longer was having the right sort of 'officer back-

more armour formations, a number of infantry battalions, apart from the Guards, were converted to the armoured role and were designated regiments of the Royal Armoured Corps (107th – 163rd Regiments RAC), wearing their original infantry cap badges on the Royal Tank Regiment's black beret. The vast amount of mechanised and motorised transport the Army now possessed needed considerable repair facilities and resources, and to this end the Royal Electrical & Mechanical Engineers (REME) was formed in 1942. Intelligence had always been a staff function until 1939. There was, however, a need for officers and men to carry out the day-to-day collection and collation of intelligence. Initially, at the outbreak of war, this was done by the Field Security Police, but in 1940 the Intelligence Corps was created. The Labour Corps of 1914-18 was resurrected in the form of the Auxi-

Right: One of Paget's Battle Schools, which gave realistic combat training to the troops at home. These men are under live fire.

Left: Somewhere in England, October 1942. A Churchill II crew work out their route.

ground' a passport to an instant commission. Except for those with previous officer service, all potential officers were required to do basic training in the ranks, and then would attend a War Office Selection Board. The candidates were subjected to three days of practical and written tests at these 'Wosbies', the examining board being made up of serving officers and a psychologist. The same system is still used in selection of the officers for today's Army, although without resident psychologists.

In September 1940 King George VI instituted two new gallantry awards. They were to recognise acts of heroism by both civilians and servicemen, not necessarily in the face of the enemy. The George Cross equates to the Victoria Cross, while the George Medal is awarded for lesser acts. Many of the early awards were made to members of the Royal Engineers Bomb Disposal teams, who were responsible for defusing bombs dropped by the Luftwaffe during the blitz.

By January 1944, plans for Overlord, the Allied landings in Normandy, were well developed, and much work was being carried out on

Below: Covenanters, which never saw action, on manoeuvres with infantry. The turret symbol on the nearest indicates 4 Troop of B Squadron.

techniques and special equipment for making landings under enemy fire easier. One of the keys was recognised by the spring of 1943 as being specialised armour. Various types were designed: kits to enable tanks to swim ashore from landing craft, Armoured Vehicles Royal Engineers (AVRE), mounting a Petard spigot mortar which fired a 40-pound 'flying dustbin' with 26 pounds of explosive for demolishing beach defences and strongpoints, flail tanks, known as Scorpions, for clearing paths in minefields, flamethrower tanks, bridgelayer tanks and many others. All these 'funnies', as they were affectionately called, came under the umbrella of 79th Armoured Division, commanded by Major General Percy Hobart, the original commander of the Mobile Division in Egypt. He had been retired at the beginning of the war and had become a corporal in the Home Guard until Churchill personally demanded his recall to the active list. He had then gone on to command and train 11th Armoured Division. While the Americans, to their cost, showed little interest in specialised armour, the British Army found 79th Armoured of inestimable value during the campaign in North-West Europe.

The eventual final plan for Overlord involved three British and two US corps landing on five beaches. In overall control would be Montgomery with the 21st Army Group. General Omar Bradley's First US Army would land on Omaha and Utah in the west, while General Dempsey's First British Army would tackle the three beaches in the east. The 3rd Infantry Division and 27 Armoured Brigade were to land on Sword in the extreme east and north of Caen; 3rd Canadian Division and 2 Canadian Armoured Brigade were to take on Juno, both beaches being the responsibility of Crocker's I Corps, while Bucknall's XXX Corps, with 50th Northumbrian Division and 8 Armoured Brigade actually carrying out the landings, would cover Gold. Two Commando brigades (known as Special Service, or, somewhat inappropriately, SS Brigades), each of four Commandos, would assist. The 6th Airborne Division had the task of landing before dawn, using gliders and parachutes, to seize the bridges over the River Orne on the eastern flank.

Space prohibits an account of the landings on 6 June in any detail. Suffice it to say that the troops managed to get ashore and capture their initial objectives, which made all those long years of

Below: The eve of D-Day. A Sherman Firefly, with 17-pounder gun, of the 13th/18th Hussars, who landed on D-Day.

training worthwhile. Neither the British nor the Americans were, however, prepared for the close nature of the Normandy countryside which, together with the resolute way in which the Germans recovered from their initial surprise and began fiercely to defend every inch of ground, caused the timetable increasingly to fall behind. The little fields with hedgerows on banks, the narrow twisting roads and the numerous little hills and ridges provided ideal defensive terrain. This produced a feeling of claustrophobia, greatly aggravated by the crump of unseen mortars, the bursts of machine gun fire, the crack of tank guns and the pounding of artillery. One infantry battalion commander noted that his casualties had been 23 officers and 350 other ranks in 14 days, and that 75 percent of his men were reacting 'adversely to enemy shelling and are "jumpy".' A tank troop leader writing of waiting for the order of advance:

'You wondered if you'd done the reconnaissance properly; if you'd again recognise those small landmarks, the isolated bush, the dip in the ground, which showed you where to cross the start-line. You wondered if in the smoke and murk of the half-light battle, with your forehead pressed to the periscope pad, you'd ever pick out the target. And all the while you saw in your imagination the muzzle of an eighty-eight behind each leaf.'

It was not just the towed 88-mm anti-aircraft gun to be feared, but also the Tiger and Panther tanks. The only British tank which could take them on was the Sherman Firefly, mounting a 17-pounder, but there was only one of these in every troop of four tanks. The losses in tanks therefore mounted steeply, but while these could be replaced, and often the crews managed to bale out unharmed, infantry casualties were more of a problem. Indeed, in early July the Adjutant-General, General Sir Ronald Adam, visited Montgomery and warned him that if infantry casualties continued at the same rate it would not be possible to replace them all and units would have to be broken up. For this reason both

the Commandos and Paratroops had to remain in the line, guarding the eastern flank, instead of being relieved for other tasks. The truth was that after almost five years of war the British Army was coming to the end of the manpower barrel, to such a degree that RAF conscripts had to be transferred to the Army.

Eventually, by the end of July, the Germans had been worn down. Patton's Third US Army broke out from St Lô, the bulk of the German armour having been tied down on the British front, and the war became mobile once more. There now followed a heady period as the Allies dashed across France. The British and Canadians swept across the Seine and through northern France. Only the Channel ports of Boulogne, Calais and Dunkirk held out, having been decreed fortresses by Hitler, and had to be reduced.

Above: Paratroopers en route to the Dropping Zone.

Below: D-Day 6 June 1944. Commandos of 1 Special Service Brigade about to hit the shore at Ouistreham on Sword beach.

Left: Churchill Armoured Vehicle Royal Engineers (AVRE) with its spigot mortar for destroying strongpoints, in a Normandy village.

On 2 September General Brian Horrocks, freshly returned to the fold after recovering from wounds received in North Africa, was sent a message by Dempsey: 'Dear Jorrocks [*sic*], You will capture (a) Antwerp (b) Brussels.' The Guards Armoured Division liberated Brussels next day, and 11th Armoured Division Antwerp the day after. In every village and town the troops passed through crowds flocked to greet them as they rolled by:

'Bedecked like natives of Hawaii, gifts were thrown, kisses given, treasured bottles of liqueurs, kept from the dark days of 1940 for just this longed for moment, were thrust home into our hands. Small wonder that none who experienced it can forget or escape one single facet of that crystallised moment of glory.'

The troops now had to halt for three days to allow their supplies to catch up – all were still coming through the artificial Mulberry harbour at Arromanches, Normandy, or over the beaches since the Channel ports were not yet open. This enabled the Germans to regroup to an extent, and they were now strong enough temporarily to hold up the advance on the Meuse-Escaut Canal.

Montgomery was now about to launch a far more ambitious operation than anything else he had ever mounted. He had obtained Eisenhower's agreement that he could use the Allied Airborne Army of British, Polish and US airborne formations, which had since D-Day 6 June been sitting in England in mounting frustration as operations were planned but then cancelled, to seize crossings over the three major rivers which now faced 21st Army Group, the Maas, the Waal and the Lower Rhine. If he could seize these he could turn the German flank and perhaps the war would end by Christmas. While the US 101st Airborne Division dropped at Eindhoven, the 82nd Airborne would seize the bridge at Nijmegen. Arnhem, was to be the responsibility of the British 1st Airborne Division and the Independent Polish Parachute Brigade.

On 17 September Operation Market Garden was launched. While the Allied airborne forces dropped, Horrocks' XXX Corps advanced to link up with them on the ground. The objectives at

Eindhoven and Nijmegen were secured without too much difficulty, but the 1st Airborne Division was beset by problems. Its landing zone was at a distance from its objective, the bridge at Arnhem; two panzer divisions refitting in the area after the Normandy battles were quickly on the scene, and there were constant communication problems. XXX Corps was also finding the advance tough. The waterlogged ground restricted the movement of the tanks to roads which ran along the raised dykes, making them easy prey. The British and Polish paratroops fought with desperate courage, but by 25 September Horrocks realised he could not relieve them in time, and ordered the survivors back across the Rhine. Only 3000 out of 10,000 got back, and 1200 were killed. The spirit of Arnhem has, however, inspired the Parachute Regiment ever since.

The First Canadian Army had been gradually reducing the Channel ports, but for the Allied advance into Germany to be maintained it was crucial that the Scheldt be opened up so that the port of Antwerp could be used. The Canadians cleared the south bank of the river, but the key lay in the heavily fortified island of Walcheren at its mouth. This was captured after an amphibious assault and eight days' hard fighting, and the Commandos, both Army and Royal Marine, played the leading part. Gradually 21st Army Group fought its way through southern Holland to close up to the Rhine. Montgomery's attention was, however, diverted by the launching of the German counteroffensive against the Americans in the Ardennes in mid December. This took the Allies by surprise, and the Americans were driven back some distance. Montgomery took command of the northern flank of the salient, and deployed troops to cover Antwerp, the main German objective. Few, however, came into contact with the enemy, as the Americans first halted the enemy and then counterattacked.

The advance on Germany was now resumed, but the British and Canadian troops had to clear the Reichswald Forest before they could reach the Rhine. This proved to be some of the toughest fighting of the whole campaign, in miserable

Right: The headline says it all. The Channel Islands were not, however, reoccupied until after the end of the war – a spoof to deceive the Germans?

Below: Normandy, July 1944. Montgomery congratulating men of 50th Northumbrian Division. Note how the wartime censor has concealed unit badges.

Below right: British commanders in Normandy, L to R, Crocker (I Corps), Dempsey (Second Army), Bucknall (XXX Corps).

"BLACK & WHITE"
It's the Scotch

Black-out: 11.10 p.m. to 5.2 a.m. CODE LETTER FOR TO-NIGHT **A** Moon: 10.0 p.m. to 5.57 a.m.

Evening Despatch

6·30 CITY

No. 16,504. Straits: Sun after rain TUESDAY, 6 JUNE, 1944. Radio: Page 3. ONE PENNY.

INVASION GOING WELL: TANKS ASHORE

ALLIES HAVE FOOTHOLD: SLASHING INLAND

Churchill reveals ## ALL TO PLAN—AND WHAT A PLAN

11,000 planes and 4,000 ships engaged

Our invasion is "proceeding to plan—and what a plan." This is what a confident Mr. Churchill told the House of Commons to-day in a brief review of the landings in Northern France which began soon after dawn.

AN IMMENSE ARMADA OF "UPWARDS" OF 4,000 SHIPS, WITH SEVERAL THOUSAND SMALLER CRAFT, HAVE CROSSED THE CHANNEL, SUSTAINED BY ABOUT 11,000 FIRST-LINE AIRCRAFT, DISCLOSED THE PREMIER.

Massed airborne landings have been successfully effected behind the German lines, landings on the beaches are proceeding and the fire of shore batteries has been largely quelled.

"Obstacles which the Germans had constructed in the sea have not proved to be as difficult as was apprehended," concluded Mr. Churchill.

HITLER TAKES OVER

HITLER HAS TAKEN PERSONAL COMMAND OF ALL THE GERMAN ANTI-INVASION OPERATIONS. REUTER'S MILITARY CORRESPONDENT, WHO SAYS THIS NEWS REACHED LONDON FROM UNDERGROUND SOURCES, ADDS THAT HE IS SURROUNDED INCLUDING

DAWN FOR GREATEST EVER ARMADA

This is part of the greatest armada the world has ever known photographed by a "Black & White" photographer flying in a plane at the gigantic fleet of warships, transports, landing craft and supply ships waited the signal which has launched the assault for the liberation of Europe. The large transport in the forefront is crowded with assault troops, who within only a few hours were storming the enemy beaches. Assault craft which took part in the great Dunkirk in reverse stretch as far as camera can see.

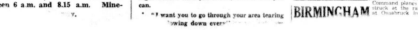

Landings on Guernsey, Jersey

The landings in Normandy, which were preceded by the heaviest attack ever by Bomber Command on German batteries along the French coast, was reported first by Berlin.

The biggest minesweeping operation in history, which paved the way for our landing craft, involved 70 miles of sweep wire and 10,000 officers and men.

S.H.A.E.F. states that more than 640 naval guns, from 16in. to 4in., are bombarding the beaches and enemy strong points in support of the armies.

Allied landings, it is understood in London, were made in Normandy between 6 a.m. and 8.15 a.m. Mine-

—Robert Reuben. Reuter's special correspondent, was due to go into Europe in one of the leading planes in the airborne units.

He tells of last-minute scenes among the parachutists in a despatch sent from the field of departure Somewhere in England.

Vast numbers of paratroopers, airborne pilots, glider pilots, glider troops and other personnel have been sealed in this airborne area of England (he writes). They are completing last minute preparations. Everyone is now "briefed."

"You have given your commanding officer grey hairs trying to keep you out of the guardhouse," the C.O. told his troops, "but this is one night when I want you to raise all the hell you can.

"I want you to go through your area tearing 'owing down every

THE KING TO BROADCAST

THE King is to make an invasion broadcast at 9 o'clock to-night.

General de Gaulle, who has been in this country some days, is to broadcast a message to the people of France.

General de Gaulle is accompanied by Mr. Duff Cooper, General Béthouard, Chief of Staff, and the following members of his staff: Col. Billotte, M. Palewski, M. Sonsièle, M. Alphand and M. de Courcel.

BIRMINGHAM

Luftwaffe kept away

THE greatest air fleet ever to assemble for one operation and probably outnumbering the Luftwaffe by at least three to one, is covering the invasion says an air correspondent. During the night and since the landings were made Allied bombers and fighter-bombers have been pouring thousands of tons of bombs on the enemy positions.

More than 1,300 R.A.F. heavy bombers helped to clear the way for the landings by a tremendous six hours' pounding of German batteries between 11.30 last night and sunrise. This was the heaviest-ever attack on these batteries.

Ten attacks were made, each by 100 or more bombers. Throughout the night, too, formations of R.A.F. Second Tactical Air Force concentrated on road and rail communications. Other Bomber Command planes without let-up struck at the railway centre at Osnabruck in North-west

Allied fighter flew over all members of the United Nations, have formed an umbrella to protect the landing ships and troops from the Luftwaffe.

They have roped off the whole battle area, and the only ticket of admittance is the white star of the liberating armies.

Garth McGowan, representing the Combined British Press, reporting from an English airfield after watching the Second Front start from the air, said to-day.

The situation seems to be well.

weather conditions and against fierce German resistance. Casualties were high, but eventually XXX Corps forced its way through and by the beginning of March the Rhine had been reached. On 23 March, XII and XXX Corps crossed the Rhine on a 12-mile front north of Wesel, while 6th Airborne and 17th US Airborne Divisions dropped on high ground to the east of the river. There was one symbolic moment during the crossing. The 4th Royal Tank Regiment was manning Buffaloes, amphibious tracked vehicles, and took across the Rhine the very same Tank Corps flag which 17th Battalion the Tank Corps had carried as the first troops to cross the Rhine in 1918. There was some fierce fighting to begin with, but bridgeheads were quickly secured and a quick and successful link-up was achieved with the airborne troops.

A pause to consolidate, and then began the final phase of the campaign, what Montgomery called 'beating about the North German plain'. Nevertheless during the month of April 1945 there was still fanatical resistance, especially by SS troops, and crews of armoured vehicles quickly came to fear the cunningly hidden *Panzerfaust*, the German equivalent to the PIAT. On 1 May tanks of the Royal Scots Greys met the Russians at Wismar. The Baltic ports of Hamburg and Bremen surrendered, and on the evening of 4 May Montgomery took the surrender of all German forces in Holland, North-west Germany and Denmark. Next day at 0800 hours the fighting was over.

It had been a long hard road, for none more so than 7th Armoured Division, the immortal Desert Rats. In July they moved up to Berlin, and Winston Churchill came to visit them. As their historian wrote:

'What must have passed through the minds of the veterans as they saluted their great war leader! Of that first venture through the wire of the Egyptian frontier

and the overwhelming victory of Beda Fomm and Sidi Saleh; of Sidi Rizegh in November 1941; and the desperate fighting in that same area a few months later; Alam Halfa and Alamein; Tripoli and Tunis; the crossing of the Volturno; the bloody fighting in the Bocage and the Plains of Caen; the exhilarating scenes of "Liberation" on the long road to Ghent; the harsh winter battles and the last long advance into the heart of the enemy's country.'

Churchill called it 'a march unsurpassed through all the story of war' and addressed them as 'Dear Desert Rats.'

In Italy, too, hostilities had come to an end, but again only after another exhausting struggle. In order to try once again to turn the Germans out of the Gustav Line and capture Rome, Anglo-American troops landed at Anzio on 22 January 1944, but were soon in trouble as the Germans counterattacked the beachhead. Reinforcements had to be sent from the main front and not until the end of February did the Germans cease their attacks. In the meantime 5th and 56th Divisions had got across the Garigliano, but attempts to get over the Rapido failed. General Mark Clark now switched his effort further to the right, and the French and Americans drove the Germans back to the hills overlooking Monte Cassino. The fighting there was to dominate the 1944 Italian campaign as British, New Zealand, Canadian and Polish troops flung themselves against it. Indeed Cassino itself, defended by German paratroops, never fell to direct attack, and it was only attacks elsewhere on the Gustav Line by both the Eighth and Fifth Armies in May which forced the Germans to abandon both Cassino and the Gustav Line.

By this stage both armies consisted of troops from a variety of Allied nations, and indeed the Italian was perhaps the most cosmopolitan theatre of World War II. Clark's Fifth US Army had two American corps, with one, VI Corps, in

the Anzio beachhead with two British divisions under command, 1st and 5th Infantry, together with General Juin's French Expeditionary Corps of four divisions. Eighth Army had two British corps, X and XIII, the former including Freyberg's indomitable New Zealanders, and V Corps, which had two Indian divisions, I Canadian and II Polish Corps. The 6th South African Armoured Division was Army reserve.

The Germans now fell back on successive defence lines, and on 4 June 1944 Clark's men finally entered Rome. The Germans were driven back to the formidable defences of the Gothic Line, which covered the approaches to the Po Valley. At this stage the Allies lost six divisions, which were required for Dragoon, the landings in the south of France, which took place in August. Nevertheless Eighth Army succeeded in creating a breach in the Gothic Line in the extreme east and captured Rimimi on 20 September. The nature of the terrain and the speed of the German reaction, however, as many times in the past, prevented any exploitation. Fifth Army now attacked in the mountains to the west, but progress was slow and casualties were high. As the winter came down morale was lowered, especially since it was realised by all that Italy was not the main front. Alexander therefore closed the offensive down at the beginning of January 1945.

During 1944 there had been also increasing activity to help the partisans in the Balkans. The Commandos had spent the summer operating against the islands in the Adriatic in conjunction with Tito's Yugoslav Partisans. Special Forces

Left: General Sir Harold Alexander in 1944 when he commanded the Allied armies in Italy.

Below right: Mule transport was much used in Burma. The Dorsets move up to Mandalay, which has just been captured.

groups had been parachuted in to assist the Partisans in Yugoslavia, Albania and Greece. Other elements, notably the Special Boat Squadron and the Long Range Desert Group, had been operating in the Aegean, while the SAS had been active behind the lines in both Italy and France. There was often much difficulty in reconciling partisan groups of widely differing political hues. In Greece the Communist groups tried to take over the newly liberated country; civil war broke out, and two British divisions, 4th and 46th, had to be sent there from Italy.

The final offensive was launched in April 1945. Eighth Army attacked first across the Santero river and Lake Comacchio, drawing the bulk of the German forces on to it. A week later the fifth US Army advanced on and captured Bologna, and then stormed on to Genoa, while Eighth Army punched through the Argenta Gap. By the end of the month the Germans had had enough and they surrendered unconditionally on 2 May.

The Italian campaign had been marked by a

series of short dashes followed by long slow slogs. It had not been fought in the limelight like that in North-West Europe, and indeed its main object had merely been to keep as many German divisions tied down as possible. It says much for the fortitude and the perseverance of the troops that they were able to maintain an offensive spirit throughout.

If Italy had not been much in the public eye, Burma remained even less so. The Fourteenth Army's great test came early in 1944, when the Japanese launched two offensives. The first was in the Arakan, where two divisions, 5th Indian and 7th Indian, had been advancing south in order to clear this area for subsequent operations. On 4 February a Japanese division had suddenly hit Messervy's 7th Indian in its rear flank, and even overran the divisional headquarters. Slim swiftly stepped in and ordered no withdrawal; the division was to stay and fight where it was. This it did, and the Japanese were beaten off after 12 days' fighting, much of it savage close combat with bayonet, grenade and bullet. This, however, was a minor affair compared with the Imphal front, which came under Scoones' IV Corps.

Scoones' troops were holding the line of the Chindwin, but they were reliant for their supplies on a single road, which ran from the railhead at Dimapur through Kohima and Imphal. On 10 March the Japanese Fifteenth Army launched an offensive aimed at these two points. Scoones quickly withdrew his three divisions, 17th Indian, now refurbished after the 1942 disaster, 20th Indian and 23rd Indian, to the plain of Imphal, with a small garrison at Kohima. The withdrawal in itself marked the new spirit of the Fourteenth Army. It was no longer a scamper to the rear as during the great

Left: Bill Slim and his wife with, right, General Scoones (IV Corps), one of Slim's principal subordinates.

Right: Final checks for a Churchill of 51st Royal Tank Regiment in Italy in 1944. The Churchill was the main British infantry support tank in the second half of the war and also the basis of much of the specialised armour.

retreat of 1942, but was marked by fierce counterattacks throughout, which kept the Japanese at arm's length and enabled the retirement to be carried out in good order. Nevertheless by the beginning of April 1944 both Imphal and Kohima had been surrounded and the road cut. From now on the two garrisons would be entirely reliant on a massive airlift to maintain them. Throughout April and May the fighting raged as again and again the Japanese, with suicidal fanaticism, flung themselves against the defences. At Kohima some of the fiercest fighting took place over a tennis court, with the Japanese at one end and the British and Indians at the other. Slim, however, had quickly reinforced the Kohima garrison with three divisions, 2nd British and the 5th and 7th Indian from the Arakan. By mid May he was in a position to begin counterattacking and eventually, at the beginning of July, the exhausted Japanese were driven back, having been fought to beyond the limits of their endurance, and Slim could again begin planning his major offensive. The

Japanese made another attempt in the Arakan, which now had three fresh divisions, in June, but to little avail, especially since movement was brought rapidly to a halt with the onset of the monsoon season in the middle of the month.

Throughout this time another operation had been going on east of the Chindwin and well behind the Japanese front lines. The Chindits, now swollen to four brigades, including one from 81st West African Division, under the overall command of Wingate's 3rd Indian Division, were airlifted to the area south-west of Myitkyina during the latter part of March as a means of supporting Stilwell's Chinese offensive in the north. Wingate was killed in an air crash, but the operation continued on much the same lines as the 1943 Chindit operation. The main difference was that the Chindits established bases from which to operate but these drew Japanese attacks and most had to be abandoned. The monsoon made life increasingly difficult and casualties, from both battle and sickness, mounted. There were several minor successes, but they

Right: DUKWs bringing supplies across the River Chindwin, January 1945.

Below: Holland, February 1945. 17-pounder Archer self-propelled gun on Valentine tank chassis in Kleve.

Below right: The battle for Mandalay, March 1945. A 5.5-inch gun in action against the last Japanese stronghold of Fort Dufferin.

measure through harassment of the Japanese and as information gatherers. Force 136, controlled by SOE, was responsible for assisting and organising resistance groups in the Japanese-occupied areas. Minor amphibious raids and reconnaissance missions were carried out by the Small Operations Group (SOG), while from the end of 1943 there was a complete Commando brigade in the theatre.

With the Japanese beaten back at Imphal and Kohima, Slim would now take to the offensive, but he had to wait until the end of the monsoon season. His major objective was Rangoon, and he planned to achieve this by destroying the Japanese army between the Chindwin and Irrawaddy rivers. In November 1944 he sent two corps, XXXIII and IV, across the Chindwin. IV Corps in the north linked up with the British 36th Division, which had been fighting with the Chinese and Americans on the northern front, thus linking that front with the central front, while XXXIII Corps moved on Mandalay. In order to trap the Japanese, Slim now redeployed IV Corps to cross the Irrawaddy at Nyaungu and then advance on Meiktila to the south of Mandalay, while XXXIII Corps threatened Mandalay from the north. On 8 March 1945 the attack on Mandalay itself opened, but such was the fanaticism of the defence that it did not fall for 12 days, the fighting being especially intense around Fort Dufferin. In desperation the Japanese counterattacked at Meiktila, which had been captured by 17th Indian Division on 5 March, but finding themselves up against a 'brick wall' withdrew. By the beginning of May, when the monsoon once more began, Fourteenth Army was at Pegu, 50 miles from Rangoon.

In the Arakan, too, there had been success. XV

were counterbalanced by the losses and the enormous air effort required to keep the force supplied. Eventually the remnants were flown out to India in August, and Slim disbanded the Chindits. Yet in spite of the controversy which surrounds the concept to this day, there is no doubt that in terms of the personal qualities displayed by the Chindits themselves they were one of the British Army's outstanding fighting forces of World War II.

By this time other Special Forces were also operating in Burma. From the early days of the campaign V Force, made up of hillmen from Assam, had been contributing in no small

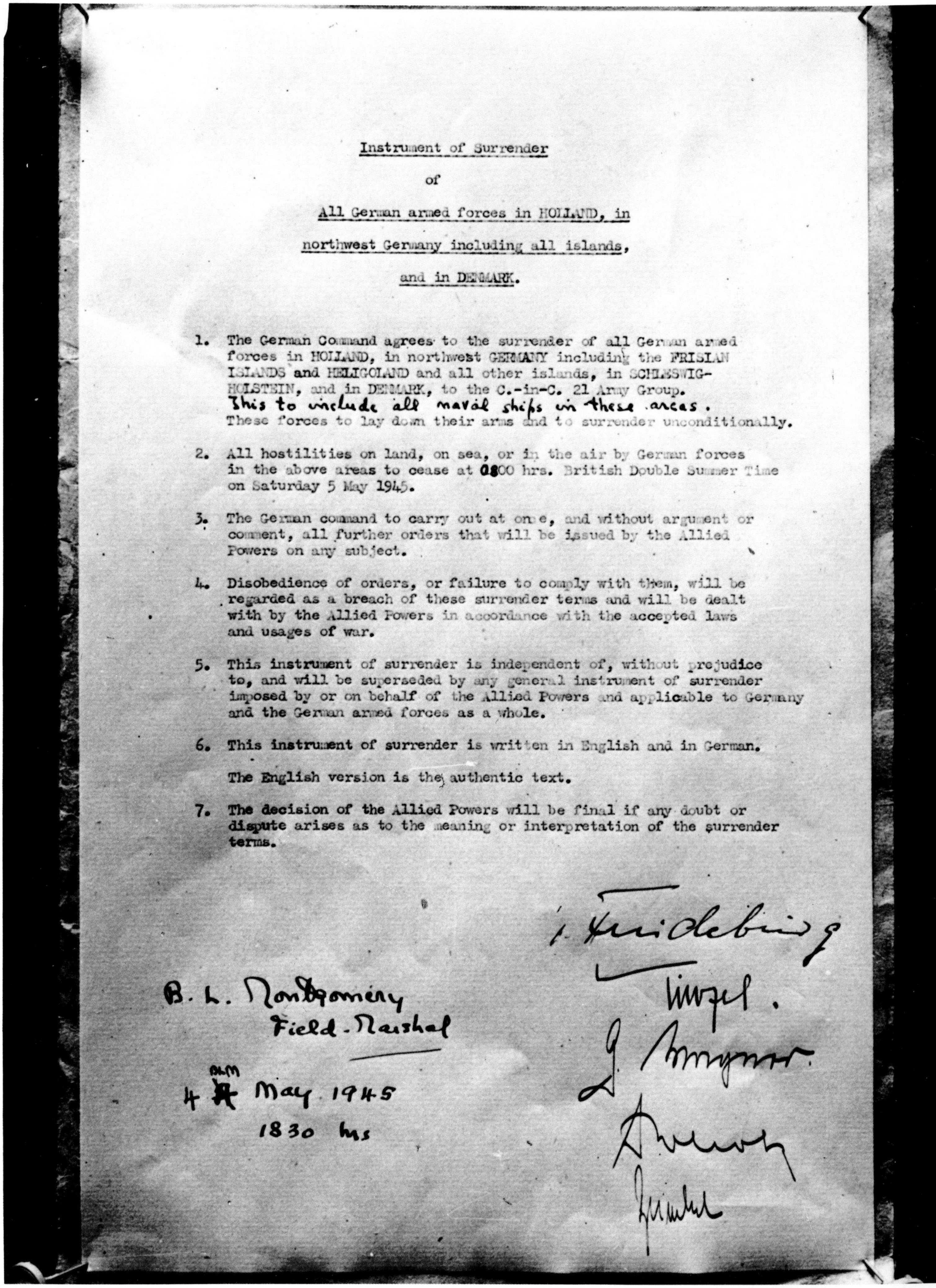

Instrument of Surrender

of

All German armed forces in HOLLAND, in

northwest Germany including all islands,

and in DENMARK.

1. The German Command agrees to the surrender of all German armed
   forces in HOLLAND, in northwest GERMANY including the FRISIAN
   ISLANDS and HELIGOLAND and all other islands, in SCHLESWIG-
   HOLSTEIN, and in DENMARK, to the C.-in-C. 21 Army Group.
   This to include all naval ships in these areas.
   These forces to lay down their arms and to surrender unconditionally.

2. All hostilities on land, on sea, or in the air by German forces
   in the above areas to cease at 0800 hrs. British Double Summer Time
   on Saturday 5 May 1945.

3. The German command to carry out at once, and without argument or
   comment, all further orders that will be issued by the Allied
   Powers on any subject.

4. Disobedience of orders, or failure to comply with them, will be
   regarded as a breach of these surrender terms and will be dealt
   with by the Allied Powers in accordance with the accepted laws
   and usages of war.

5. This instrument of surrender is independent of, without prejudice
   to, and will be superseded by any general instrument of surrender
   imposed by or on behalf of the Allied Powers and applicable to Germany
   and the German armed forces as a whole.

6. This instrument of surrender is written in English and in German.

   The English version is the authentic text.

7. The decision of the Allied Powers will be final if any doubt or
   dispute arises as to the meaning or interpretation of the surrender
   terms.

B. L. Montgomery
Field-Marshal

4 May 1945
1830 hrs

Friedeburg
Kinzel
G. Wagner

Corps had captured the islands of Akyab and Ramree in January, and then fought an epic battle at Kangaw at the end of that month, when the Japanese counterattacked. Priority for air resupply, however, was concentrated on supporting the drive to Rangoon, for which the airfields on Akyab and Ramree were invaluable.

With the prize so near, Slim determined to fight on regardless of the monsoon. An Indian parachute battalion was dropped 20 miles south of Rangoon on 2 May, meeting no opposition, and simultaneously 26th Indian Division landed from the sea. Two days later Rangoon fell.

While mopping up in Burma continued, preparations were made for the invasion of Singapore and Malaya, Operation Zipper, an ambitious plan involving large-scale amphibious and airborne landings. Just as it was about to be mounted, the atomic bombs were dropped on Hiroshima and Nagasaki, and the war was over.

Just over three and a half million men and women had enlisted in the British Army during the years 1939-45, rather less than in 1914-18, and the casualties were proportionately lower, with 144,000 killed, 240,000 wounded and 152,000 taken prisoner. The main difference between the two world wars had been that the second did not have the long bloody slogging match of France and Flanders. In addition the increased complexity and sophistication of the conduct of war meant that the administrative tail required to support the fighting man, be he gunner, tankman or infantryman, was inevitably very much longer than in the Great War. The fighting generation of 1939-45 was also more imaginative and better educated than its fathers and demanded more of the comforts of life. Com-

bined with the fact that the higher commanders had experienced at first hand the horrors of trench warfare, this made it seem that the British soldiers did not have the same sticking power as their fathers. Battalions were withdrawn from combat after suffering significantly lower casualties than 25 years earlier. Yet the British soldier fought just as well. The conditions in Burma, Italy, Tunisia and Normandy were often just as bad as they had been in the trenches. In spite of bewildering reverses, tenacity and courage still shone through. Indeed, perhaps the most outstanding quality was that an army, far less prepared for modern war than its predecessor had been, by 1943 had recovered and become highly professional, able to fight and turn defeat into victory.

Above: Closing up to the Rhine. Men of the 6th Cameronians (52nd Division), January 1945.

Opposite: Victory at last.

Below: 7th Armoured Division, the Desert Rats, parade before Churchill, Berlin, 21 July 1945. The tanks are Cromwells.

THE RECENT YEARS

Previous page: Royal Ulster Rifles (now Royal Irish Rangers), Sibu, Sarawak, 1964, during the Borneo Confrontation.

The problems facing the British Army of 1945 were the same as those of November 1918 – demobilisation and over-commitment. The lessons of 1919 had been taken to heart with regard to demobilisation, and a plan had been evolved toward the end of 1944 which took into account both the need to get the country back on its feet and the status of the individual service-man in terms of age and length of service. Those urgently required in reconstruction work were categorised as Class B and were given priority, but were liable for recall should they leave their trade. The remainder were in Class A, with every two months' service being equivalent to a year of age. Thus a man aged 40 with two years' service would be released at the same time as a man of 30 with three years and eight months of service. Great emphasis was also placed on resettlement – retraining for civilian life – many more oppor-tunities being given than in 1919. As before, every man was issued with civilian clothing, the 'demob suit', and he was given eight weeks' paid terminal leave. Great efforts were also made to get home those who had served overseas for a long time. Python, as the scheme was called, had already begun in 1944, those with four years' service or over overseas (later dropped to three

years) being sent home to serve in Europe. There was nevertheless understandable impatience, but not the same unrest as in 1919.

The British Army's commitments were very much larger than in 1919. In Europe it was not merely a question of garrisoning the bridgehead at Cologne, but the whole of northern Germany and a large part of Austria as well. Germany especially was physically devastated by the end of the war, to a far greater extent than in 1918, and the Allied troops had to set up the necessary infrastructure for the German people to survive. Each ally had its own zone of occupation and set up a military government to run it. There was also the need to screen the population, sur-rendered members of the German Wehrmacht and civilians alike, for those possibly guilty of war crimes. Hundreds of thousands of displaced persons (DPs), many survivors of the concentra-tion camps and others who had fled from the Russians, had to be looked after. One consolation was that the troops took over the Wehrmacht's excellent barracks, many of which are still used by the British Army of the Rhine (BAOR). Initially there was a very strict rule of no frater-nisation with the Germans, but this was impos-sible to maintain. The British soldier, with his

Below: The end of the Raj. Troops patrol the streets of Calcutta in August 1946 in the face of mounting civil unrest.

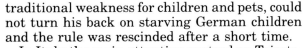

Left: The worst Jewish terrorist act. The blowing up of the King David Hotel, Jerusalem, 23 July 1946.

traditional weakness for children and pets, could not turn his back on starving German children and the rule was rescinded after a short time.

In Italy the main attention centred on Trieste, which President Tito was claiming for Yugoslavia, and at one time it was thought that fighting might break out between the British troops and Tito's former Partisans for possession of this city. Luckily a major clash was averted. In Greece, too, there was a potential source of conflict, and indeed civil war was to erupt once more in 1946 with British troops becoming embroiled. Cyprus, Egypt, Libya and Palestine still required garrisons, the last-named quickly becoming another trouble spot. India, her people now agitating even more determinedly for self-determination, was another problem, as was Burma, which together with Britain's other Far East territories formerly under Japanese occupation required a major reconstruction programme.

Large military garrisons overseas were therefore inevitable for the foreseeable future, and to reduce the Army to its prewar strength would in no way provide sufficient manpower to meet these varied commitments. Clement Attlee's Labour Government, which had come into power after the General Election of July 1945, had no alternative but to keep conscription. Initially it wanted a term of just one year, but this created running problems. By the time the National Serviceman, as he was called, had received his basic training and had been sent out by troopship to far-flung parts of the world, it was almost time for him to come home again. When Field Marshal Viscount Slim became CIGS in November 1947, one of his first tasks was to persuade the Government to lengthen the term, and this was done, first to 18 months and then, in 1950, to two years. The Government still wished, however, to see the strength of the fighting arms reduced, and the 138 infantry battalions of 1939 fell to 73 by 1947, the old two-battalion Cardwell regimental

system being abandoned in favour of geographic groupings.

The British Army at home was inevitably condemned, given the country's severe economic problems in the aftermath of the war and the resultant age of austerity, to live in draughty barracks, many of them temporary wartime hutments. Montgomery, whom Slim had succeeded as CIGS, made his top priority improving the lot of the soldier, especially his living conditions. 'Why,' he asked, 'should not a soldier have a bedroom light to enable him to read in bed?' While his policy was generally welcomed by the Army, the money was not available to implement it and what little could be spared was to the detriment of equipment and training. Another problem was the complicated pay structure including a mass of complex allowances which had grown up during the war years. In an effort to simplify this a new pay code was introduced in 1946. Officers were now merely entitled to marriage and ration allowances, as well as extra pay for certain technical qualifications such as being a pilot or parachutist. Pay for other ranks, however, was based on a star system related to trade qualifications, rank and service which proved just as difficult to understand, and eventually Royal Army Pay Corps detachments had to be deployed with every unit, a practice which still continues. Before the war officers were not entitled to marriage allowance below the age of 30, and those who married under age were jokingly deemed to be 'living in sin'. For other ranks the minimum age was 25. These rules were dispensed with during the war, but it was now announced, as part of the new pay code, that after 1 July 1946 only officers of 25 years and over and other ranks aged 21 and over would receive the allowance. Consequently there was a stampede by those below the new minimum age to get married before this date so that they could continue to receive the allowance, which was greatly valued since pay was well below that of the

Right: Korea, 1950. A 7th Royal Tank Regiment Comet moves up to the front line.

Below: Malaya. Members of 22 SAS on board a Beverley transport ready for a hazardous drop into the jungle.

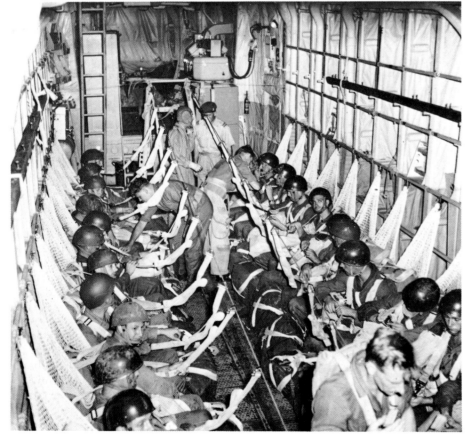

civilian market (National Servicemen received only a fraction of the pay that was given to Regular soldiers).

The Labour Government came to power in 1945 pledged to grant independence to India, but this did not prevent continuing widespread unrest in the country. The British Army units stationed there, their structure disrupted by Python and the men impatient to return home, were very stretched. Lord Louis Mountbatten arrived as Viceroy in February 1947 with the pledge that the country would be split into two, reflecting the religious differences between Moslems and Hindus, and that independence would be granted to each by June 1948. This immediately created a wave of inter-religious strife, aggravated by the decision a little later to bring independence forward to August 1947. There were mass migrations across the borders of India and what was about to become Pakistan, and numerous massacres, often on board trains. Where British troops were present violence was generally prevented, but they were too few to have much effect. It was therefore with feelings of relief that the Army finally left the country to end an association that had lasted over 200 years.

For the British officers in the old Indian Army it was, however, a time of tragedy. Many of them regarded India as more their home than Britain, and the prospect of beginning afresh in the drabness of postwar life did not appeal. Nevertheless, while a few were able to stay on temporarily as advisers to the new Indian and Pakistani armies, the majority were faced with the stark choice of transfer to the British Army or retirement. Only one link with the old Indian Army was saved. In 1946 it had become apparent that the new Indian Army was prepared to take over only a proportion of the Gurkha regiments, and Wavell suggested to the British Government that the residue be transferred to the British Army. This was an attractive proposition, being the best way to retain political links with Nepal and also providing a solution to the problem of balancing Far East military commitments with the one-year conscription term. Consequently, after lengthy negotiations with the Nepalese and future Indian governments, it was agreed that four two-battalion regiments, 2nd, 6th, 7th and 10th Gurkha Rifles, would be transferred, and would be based in Malaya under 17th Division.

Nearer home, the British Government persuaded the Americans to take over responsibility for Greece, so that the British troops there could be withdrawn. Palestine, however, proved a more intractable problem. By the end of 1945 the British Army had two divisions there, 1st Infantry and 6th Airborne, whose primary role was to provide the strategic reserve in the Middle East as the Gurkhas would do in the Far East. Jewish immigration had been restricted since

Right: A 3-inch mortar crew, Korea, summer 1952.

Below: Korea. President-elect Eisenhower with General West, commanding the Commonwealth Division.

1939 so as to prevent Arab resentment erupting into another revolt, and this restriction was maintained after the war. Vast numbers of Jews from Europe, their lives shattered by the events of the past decade, were desperate to make a fresh start in their ancestral land, but many of the refugee ships were turned back by the British. This was too much for the Jews already in Palestine and at the end of October 1945 the Irgun, a Jewish underground army, launched a bombing campaign on economic targets in the country. There was a spate of rioting, followed by attacks on British troops. Reinforcements were rushed from Germany to fight what had now become a very unpleasant counterinsurgency campaign of a type which was to become all too familiar to the British soldier in the postwar years. Thousands of illegal weapons were found in cordon and search operations and many Jews were arrested on suspicion of terrorism, for this was what the Irgun were practising. Their worst atrocity was blowing up the King David Hotel in Jerusalem, used for military and government offices, claiming the lives of 90 people.

Eventually, in November 1947, the United Nations (UN) stepped in and partitioned the country between Jew and Arab. The result was an Arab backlash, and by Christmas a virtual civil war was raging. The British Government having declared that its mandate would end in May 1948, the British Army tried to achieve an orderly withdrawal. This was not easy, with both Jew and Arab now attacking them. By the end of April 1948 the Jews had become confident enough to take their war against the Arabs into the few remaining British enclaves around Jaffa, Haifa and Jerusalem. Tanks and artillery had to be used against them, which at least demonstrated that it was not worth taking on the

British Army in conventional warfare. The last two weeks were quiet, and the Army withdrew to leave the newly created state of Israel to fight for its own survival.

No sooner had the troops withdrawn from Palestine than trouble arose in another quarter. On 16 June 1948 young Chinese killed three rubber-estate managers in various parts of Malaya to mark the beginning of a counter-insurgency campaign which was to last for 12 years. These attacks had been instigated by the Chinese-run Malayan Communist Party which believed that the time was ripe for revolution. The jungles, together with the mountains which ran down the centre of the country, provided the ideal terrain for the terrorist, and the atrocities rapidly increased. By March 1950 the Communists had killed some 850 civilians, 325 policemen and 150 soldiers, and although 2000 terrorists had been killed, captured or had surrendered, new recruits ensured that their strength was not reduced. A month later Lieutenant General Sir Harold Briggs arrived as Director of Operations. He realised that the terrorists must be isolated by moving the thousands of Chinese supporters living in villages on the edge of the jungle. He also found a lack of worthwhile intelligence and instituted committees, of military, police and government at every level. The administration of the country lacked the will, however, to co-ordinate the relevant agencies, and after the assassination of Sir Henry Gurney, the High Commissioner, in October 1951, General Sir Gerald Templer was appointed as High Commissioner and Director of Operations combined.

Some 45,000 troops were under Templer's command, including British, Gurkhas, Australians, New Zealanders, Fijians, East Africans and the Malays themselves, whom Templer encouraged to take an increasing role. Security force and

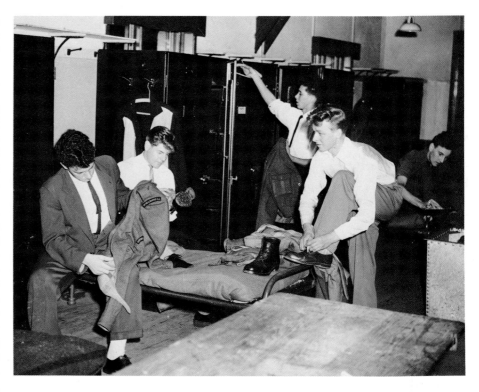

civilian casualties began to fall, while those of the terrorists, especially surrenders, increased. On 31 August 1957, the independence of Malaya, now to be called Malaysia, was declared amid popular rejoicing, removing any hope that the terrorists might achieve their long-term aim. Nevertheless it was three years before they were finally chased across the border with Thailand, from where they have continued from time to time to cause trouble.

While the Gurkhas, whose permanent base the country now was, undoubtedly provided the backbone of the British Army's effort, many British battalions proved themselves expert jungle fighters. As in any counterinsurgency

Above: National Servicemen during their first few days in the Army.

Above right: Kenya. Members of a 'counter-gang' recruited from the Kikuyu tribe to help track down the Mau Mau terrorists.

Above, far right: Suez. 3 Para dropping on the El Gamil airfield, 5 November 1956.

Left: Patrol in the Aberdare Forest, during the latter part of the Mau Mau campaign.

Right: General Sir Walter Walker, centre, a jungle expert, who masterminded the campaign in Borneo.

campaign, the need for constant alertness was paramount: a soldier might undergo days of 'jungle bashing' without seeing any sign of his enemy. Then suddenly there would be a burst of fire. To overcome the terrorist in this situation required superlative weapon handling and marksmanship, which was one of Templer's priorities. Intelligence, too, was vital, and it was this that enabled the Security Forces to become increasingly successful in laying ambushes for the enemy. During 12 years, some 11,000 terrorists were accounted for at a cost of 3000 civilian lives and almost 2000 of the Security Forces, including police, the Army's share of the losses being 350 British and 159 Gurkha soldiers. The Malayan counterinsurgency campaign provided many lessons for the British Army, which were quickly applied to similar situations.

The onset of the Cold War, especially the breakdown of negotiations between the Western Allies and the Soviet Union over the future of Germany, events in Eastern Europe and the Berlin Blockade, which began in June 1948 and lasted for a year, led to the formation of the North Atlantic Treaty Organisation (NATO) in April 1949. This was aimed at dissuading the Soviet Union from embarking on any military incursions into Western Europe. Her most likely objective was seen as West Germany, so the occupation troops there had to be turned speedily into an operational force. For BAOR this meant that the equivalent of two divisions now had to be transformed into five, with the necessary logistic support to wage general war. It was this which forced the Government to increase the National Service term to two years in 1950, so that by 1952 the Army had a strength of 442,000 men.

A further call for manpower came in June 1950 with the start of the Korean War. The invasion of South Korea by her communist-ruled northern neighbour resulted in the quick deployment of United Nations troops. Britain's initial contribution was two battalions sent from Hong Kong, 1st Argyll and Sutherland Highlanders and 1st Middlesex, but it quickly grew to the equivalent of two brigades. In July 1951 these were combined with the Australian, New Zealand and Canadian

troops present to form the Commonwealth Division. After the initial invasion the North Koreans were driven back to the Yalu river. This precipitated Communist China's entry into the war and during the winter of 1950-1 the United Nations troops were now in their turn pushed back beyond the 38th Parallel. It was towards the end of this retreat that the 1st Battalion, The Gloucestershire Regiment carried out an epic last ditch stand on the Imjin river. Totally sur-

rounded and many times outnumbered, the Glosters fiercely resisted the Chinese for four days and nights. Eventually, their ammunition exhausted, the survivors were ordered to break out by their commanding officer Lieutenant Colonel James Carne. Only 46 officers and men out of 622 reached the UN line, the remainder being killed or captured. For this the Glorious Glosters, as they became known, were awarded the US Presidential Distinguished Unit Citation, the riband of which is still worn on the right upper arm by all serving members of the regiment; and no less than 24 individual decorations for gallantry, including two VCs, one to Lieutenant Colonel Carne. He and the others who were captured endured two years of harsh treatment, including brainwashing. The Army subsequently introduced special training in techniques for resisting interrogation after capture.

Efforts during the first half of 1951 to drive the Chinese back resulted only in stabilisation of the front along the 38th Parallel. For the next two years, against a background of almost continuous truce negotiations, the war became static, but fierce fighting continued as both sides tried to seize local points of advantage. British units were sent to Korea for tours of one year and experienced both the bitter winter and scorching summer of that country. The last major fighting when the Chinese and North Koreans launched another offensive, came two months before the truce was eventually signed at Panmunjon at the end of July 1953. Much of the fighting was centred on the hills to the west of the River Samichon, and 1st Battalion, The Duke of Wellington's Regiment had an especially fierce battle on a hill called The Hook, which degenerated into hand-to-hand combat amid the bunkers and tunnels which honeycombed it.

The British casualties during the three years of the Korean War amounted to 793 killed and 2878 wounded and missing. A number of regiments had taken part and all had distinguished themselves.

In 1952 trouble also erupted in East Africa. Elements of the Kikuyu tribe in Kenya were agitating for the return of what they deemed tribal lands. Two battalions of the King's African Rifles were all that was available at the time, so in October a British battalion, the Lancashire Fusiliers, was flown in from Britain. As the murders of loyal Kikuyu and European settlers mounted, more troops had to be brought in, until there were two British brigades together with African troops. The Mau Mau, as the dissidents were known, operated from the forests, and large-scale sweep operations, very reminiscent of those used in the later stages of the Boer War, were initially employed against them. These, however, were relatively ineffective until the Security Forces were concentrated on one area at a time. This concentration, together with the harassment of the Mau Mau's supply lines and the integration of police and military intelligence staffs, as well as the setting up of a small War Cabinet – all lessons from Malaya – enabled the back of the Mau Mau to be broken by the spring of 1955. Thereafter the lead was taken over by Special Forces, consisting of British officers and terrorists who had been 'turned', who tracked down and destroyed the remaining bands.

While the Mau Mau campaign was winding down, another insurgency campaign was starting up, this time in Cyprus. On 31 March 1955 there was a series of bomb explosions in Nicosia caused by a movement calling itself *Ethniki Organosis Kuprion Agoniston* (National Organisation of Cypriot Fighters, or EOKA for short), which was agitating for the union of Cyprus with Greece. Apart from the strategic importance of the island to the British, this move would also have been anathema to the substantial Turkish minority on the island. The British garrison at the outset consisted of just two infantry battalions, an artillery and an engineer regiment, and as the violence increased this was clearly not enough. By January 1956 no less than four brigades were deployed, and Field Marshal Sir John Harding, who had commanded in Malaya during the early days, was appointed Governor. He organised a number of large-scale operations in the Trudos Mountains, from where the EOKA bands, led by Colonel Grivas, were operating. A number of the bands were broken up but Grivas himself remained at large, although he had one or two near escapes. The campaign was, however, interrupted at the end of July 1956 when Colonel Nasser, Egypt's Premier declared that he was nationalising the Suez Canal.

The last British troops had left Egypt in March 1956, and Nasser's declaration took the British and French Governments by surprise. Prime Minister Eden believed that troops might well be

required to make Nasser back down, and his military planners considered that a corps would probably be required. The problem was that Britain lacked both the sea- and air-lift capacity for such a force. In any event, because of the Cyprus emergency and the fact that King Idris of Libya refused to allow 10th Armoured Division, then stationed in that country, to move across the border into Egypt, the troops would have to come from Britain. In order to bring the regiments at home up to strength no less than 23,000 reservists were immediately called up and almost overnight a large number of military vehicles changed from their normal green to a sand colour. A corps headquarters under General Sir Hugh Stockwell was brought across from Ger-

Above: The Radfan, 1965. Men of the Royal Sussex Regiment (now part of the Queen's Regiment) with A41 company/platoon radio.

Below: Aden, 1967. Royal Northumberland Fusiliers sieze a suspect in the notorious Crater district.

many, but then there was a delay caused mainly by US opposition. Eventually a plan was concocted in collusion with the Israelis, who would invade Sinai while the British and French landed in the Canal Zone masquerading as peacekeepers. The operation was finally launched at dawn on 5 November 1956 when French and British paratroops flying from Cyprus dropped on Port Said, to be followed by an amphibious landing by two Royal Marine Commandos and a third flown in by helicopter, the first British airmobile operation. Fighting was sporadic and by midnight the following day a ceasefire had been imposed, largely thanks to international pressure. The British had lost 11 killed and 92 wounded, and the French 10 killed and 33 wounded. For the next two months British and French troops garrisoned the Canal until the UN took over. The enterprise had been politically unsatisfactory and had revealed severe military shortcomings. For the troops mobilised it had been a frustrating few months, many of them never even getting as far as Malta.

After the interruption caused by Suez, the British Army concentrated once more on Cyprus, and by 1958 virtual peace had been restored to the island. Much negotiation with the Cypriots, Greece and Turkey was still required, however, before the violence was finally ended, and it was not until 1 August 1960 that the Republic of Cyprus came into being after 82 years of British rule. Britain, however, retained two Sovereign Base Areas at Dhekelia and Akrotiri, as well as a number of radar and radio sites elsewhere on the island.

During this time small forces, especially the SAS, who had been reactivated for Malaya, were helping the Sultans of Muscat and Oman to foil Saudi Arabian designs on their oilfields. The climax came in January 1959 when the SAS, supported by elements of the Life Guards, managed to capture the Saudi-backed rebel base in the Jebel Akhdar, a sheer limestone massif 40-50 miles in length and rising to 10,000 feet, which was widely considered to be impregnable.

The Suez episode and the widely held belief that any future major war in Europe would 'go nuclear' from the start resulted in a dramatic change in British defence policy. Harold Macmillan, who had succeeded Eden as Prime Minister, believed that there was no longer a

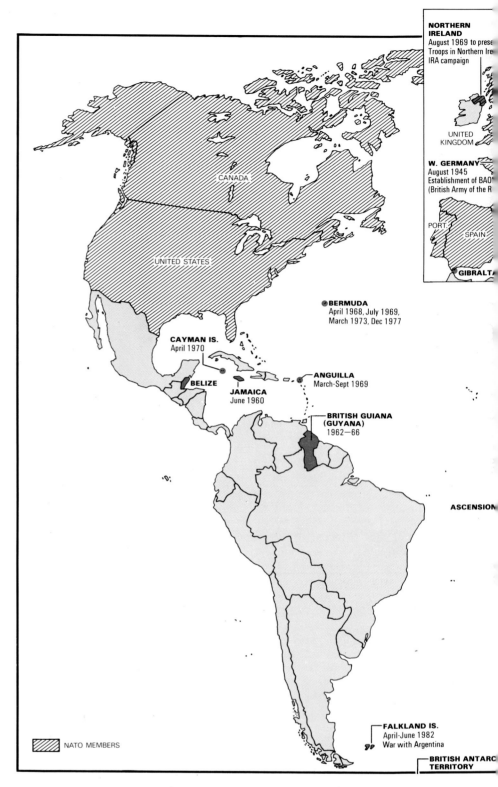

NORTHERN IRELAND
August 1969 to prese
Troops in Northern Ire
IRA campaign

UNITED KINGDOM

W. GERMANY
August 1945
Establishment of BAO
(British Army of the R

PORT. SPAIN

GIBRALTA

CANADA

UNITED STATES

●BERMUDA
April 1968, July 1969,
March 1973, Dec 1977

CAYMAN IS.
April 1970

ANGUILLA
March-Sept 1969

BELIZE

JAMAICA
June 1960

BRITISH GUIANA
(GUYANA)
1962—66

ASCENSION

FALKLAND IS.
April-June 1982
War with Argentina

BRITISH ANTARC
TERRITORY

NATO MEMBERS

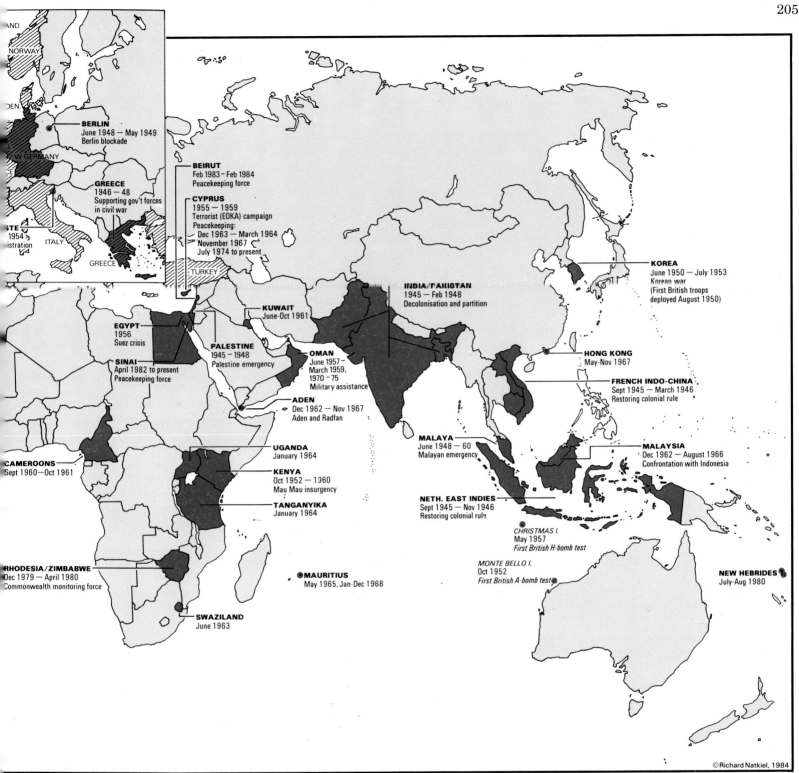

The map shows major and minor British military commitments since 1945.

BERLIN
June 1948 — May 1949
Berlin blockade

GREECE
1946 — 48
Supporting gov't forces
in civil war

BEIRUT
Feb 1983 — Feb 1984
Peacekeeping force

CYPRUS
1955 — 1959
Terrorist (EOKA) campaign
Peacekeeping:
Dec 1963 — March 1964
November 1967
July 1974 to present

KOREA
June 1950 — July 1953
Korean war
(First British troops
deployed August 1950)

INDIA/PAKISTAN
1945 — Feb 1948
Decolonisation and partition

KUWAIT
June-Oct 1961

EGYPT
1956
Suez crisis

PALESTINE
1945 — 1948
Palestine emergency

OMAN
June 1957 —
March 1959,
1970 — 75
Military assistance

HONG KONG
May-Nov 1967

FRENCH INDO-CHINA
Sept 1945 — March 1946
Restoring colonial rule

SINAI
April 1982 to present
Peacekeeping force

ADEN
Dec 1962 — Nov 1967
Aden and Radfan

CAMEROONS
Sept 1960—Oct 1961

UGANDA
January 1964

KENYA
Oct 1952 — 1960
Mau Mau insurgency

TANGANYIKA
January 1964

MALAYA
June 1948 — 60
Malayan emergency

MALAYSIA
Dec 1962 — August 1966
Confrontation with Indonesia

NETH. EAST INDIES
Sept 1945 — Nov 1946
Restoring colonial rule

CHRISTMAS I.
May 1957
First British H-bomb test

RHODESIA/ZIMBABWE
Dec 1979 — April 1980
Commonwealth monitoring force

MAURITIUS
May 1965, Jan-Dec 1968

MONTE BELLO I.
Oct 1952
First British A-bomb test

NEW HEBRIDES
July-Aug 1980

SWAZILAND
June 1963

©Richard Natkiel, 1984

Above: The map shows major and minor British military commitments since 1945.

Left: Northern Ireland, 1972. Paras making arrests in the aftermath of a riot.

requirement to keep large conventional forces in Europe and that operations overseas could be carried out by moving troops by air from Britain rather than maintaining large overseas garrisons. BAOR was therefore reduced in strength from 80,000 men to 55,000, its current total, and would have been reduced even more but for West German and American objections. Furthermore conscription was to end in 1960, and the Army, after lengthy debate, was to be pegged at a total strength of 180,000.

The end of National Service was greeted with approval by both the Army and the civilian population. While many National Servicemen had, at least in retrospect, enjoyed their time in the Army, especially since it enabled them to come in contact with other strata of society, others had resented both the interruption to their lives and the military discipline, or 'bull' as they called it.

While the Regulars had found the endless training of conscripts tedious and had often been hard put to keep them gainfully employed, the National Servicemen had fought alongside their Regular counterparts in Malaya, Korea, Cyprus and Kenya and proved themselves just as good soldiers. They also provided a large pool of reservists on which the Army could call in time of war, having to carry out a limited period of training with the TA each year for three years after they had left the Colours. An all-Regular army, on the other hand, has only a small number to call upon, and many of them, with little or no training liability, are often very out of touch, as the Army found during exercises Crusader and Lionheart, two major reinforcement exercises carried out in Germany in 1980 and 1984.

The contraction in the Army meant that fewer units were needed. The infantry fell from a post-

Above: The Brigade of Guards rehearsing for the Trooping of the Colour, nearest the camera are men of the Coldstream Guards.

Below: The Life Guards Squadron of the Mounted Regiment Household Cavalry with Standard, outside Buckingham Palace.

Opposite: In contrast, The Falls Road, Belfast.

war high point of 85 battalions in 1951 to 60 by 1960. The Royal Armoured Corps lost seven of its regiments, the Royal Artillery 20 and the Royal Engineers four. Serious consideration was given to abolishing the traditional regimental system in the infantry by forming a Corps of Infantry, but regiments were amalgamated instead. Faced with much lobbying by colonels of regiments and retired officers, the Army Council decided that regiments should be selected for amalgamation on a basis of seniority (foundation date), historical links and roles, and territorial proximity. The infantry regimental depots were also abolished in favour of brigade depots. It was a sad time for many, but the regiments which had to amalgamate soon settled down together.

While Macmillan's 'wind of change' in Africa reduced garrison commitments as colony after colony was granted independence, the British Army still remained heavily committed over-

seas. In 1958, King Hussein of Jordan, who had been educated in England, and had been an officer cadet at RMA Sandhurst, faced a revolt in his country and asked for British help. The 16th Parachute Brigade was flown to Amman and spent nearly four months there. In June 1961 Iraq threatened Kuwait, which also appealed to Britain, and a hastily made-up brigade sweltered there in the desert heat until October.

In December 1962 there was an Indonesian inspired revolt against the Sultan of Brunei. It was quickly crushed by the Queen's Own Highlanders, 1/2nd Gurkha Rifles and 42 Commando Royal Marines, which were quickly dispatched by Headquarters 17th Division in Malaya. President Sukarno retaliated by sending parties of irregulars across the border into Sarawak and Sabah (formerly North Borneo) to harry the authorities. Later in 1963, after Sarawak and Sabah had joined the Federation of Malaysia set up in September, Sukarno declared virtual open war and Indonesian troops began to make incursions. For the next three years the British Army found itself involved in another jungle campaign, and the old skills of Malaya and Burma were quickly revived. The British soldier, however, quickly learnt not to underestimate the Indonesian Army. They were as skilled in the jungle as the terrorists in Malaya, and were often prepared to fight it out rather than immediately withdraw. Clashes therefore often resulted in casualties on both sides. General Walter Walker, himself widely experienced in jungle fighting in both Burma and Malaya as a Gurkha battalion commander, was in command for most of the campaign and soon decided to take the war to the enemy's side of the border. Because Indonesia and Britain were not officially at war, this had to be done in great secrecy, and was given the code name of Operation Claret. Patrols penetrated as much as 10 miles into Indonesian territory and laid often highly successful ambushes. The SAS, operating in four-man patrols, spent months at a time on Claret operations, befriending border villagers and sending back invaluable intelligence. On the home side of the border company base camps were built, complete with bunkers and trenches and 105-mm pack howitzer guns

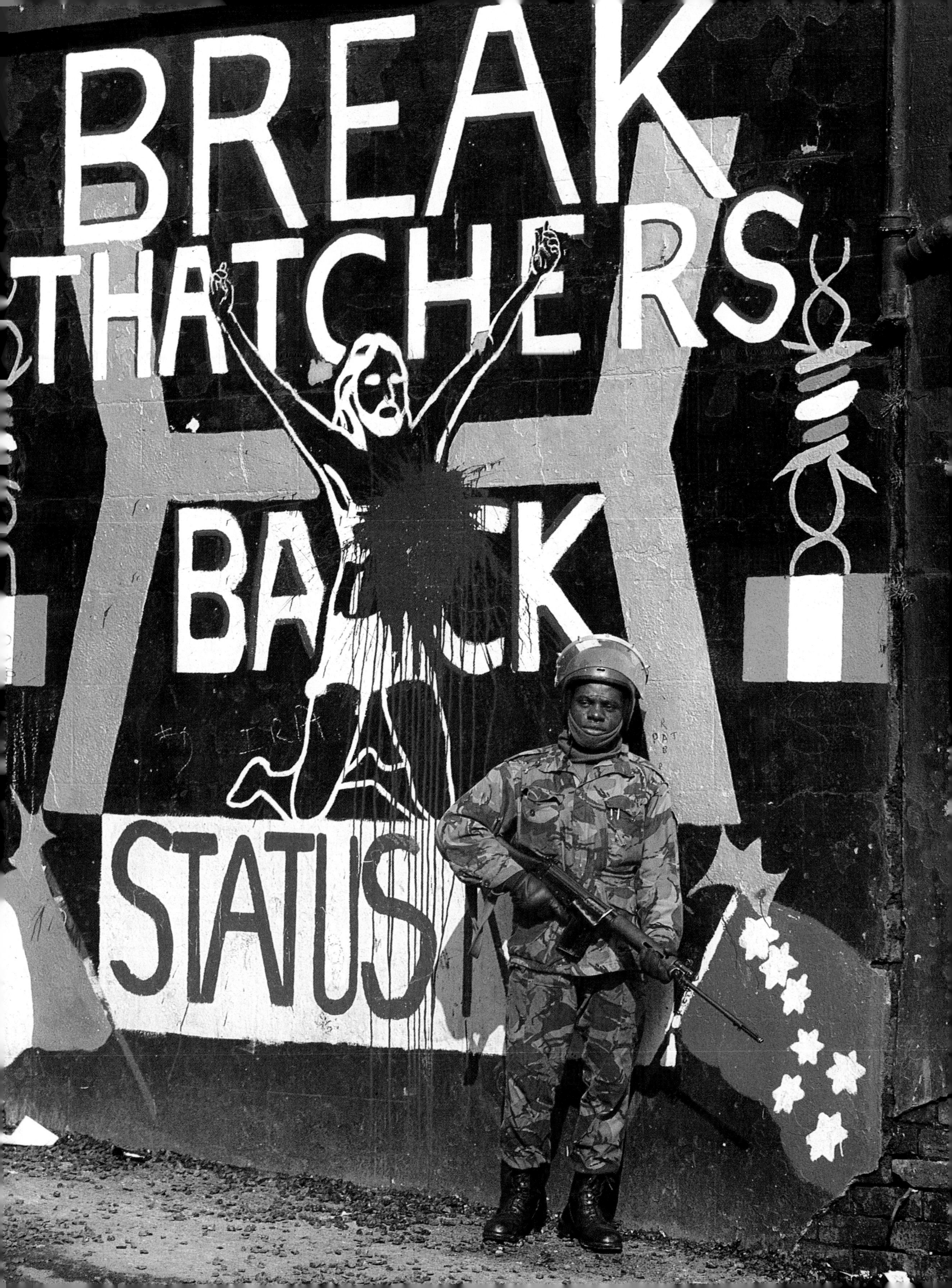
BREAK
THATCHERS
BA K
STATUS
IRA

Above: A typical riot scene from the early 1970s, Northern Ireland.

ready to support any patrol which found itself in difficulties.

Gradually the Indonesians were worn down, and unrest within the country led to the virtual deposition of Sukarno by early 1966. Peace feelers were put out and in August an agreement was finally signed in Jakarta. While, as in Malaya, the Gurkha battalions had borne the brunt, 15 British infantry battalions served tours in Borneo, along with armoured car regiments, artillery and Royal Engineers, as well as Australian and New Zealand contingents. Total Commonwealth casualties were 114 killed and 180 wounded compared with well over 600 Indonesian dead. It may have taken time to achieve a satisfactory conclusion but, as Labour Defence Minister Denis Healey said, it was 'one of the most efficient uses of military force in the history of the world.'

For the British Army, though, there was little time for congratulation. Trouble erupted once more in Cyprus when Greek Cypriots attacked Turkish Cypriots, and it seemed as though the British would be caught in the middle of a civil war. Elements of 3rd Division, based on Salisbury Plain, were sent out to the island early in 1964, but in March the UN accepted responsibility for keeping the peace. A British contingent was offered, and continues to this day to wear the

UN's blue beret on the island. In the same year there was unrest in Aden, which Egypt wished to become part of the newly formed Republic of Yemen. To take charge of operations, 39 Infantry Brigade Headquarters was flown out from Northern Ireland, where it had been supporting the Royal Ulster Constabulary against the Irish Republican Army in the Border Campaign of 1956-62. The insurgents were operating from the mountainous Radfan in the north, and a punitive expedition made up of the 1st East Anglian Regiment, 3rd Battalion, the Parachute Regiment and 45 Commando Royal Marines defeated the rebels, suffering only 18 casualties. The violence, however, did not cease, and 1965 was marked by an increasing number of bombing incidents in Little Aden, where the major port facility so important to the British was situated. The following year the Wilson Government declared that the British would withdraw by 1968, but this merely served to exacerbate the violence of the rival factions, most prominent of which were the Marxist National Liberation Front (NLF) and the Front for the Liberation of Occupied South Yemen (FLOSY). In the notorious Crater district of Aden Town the sound of shots, as British troops exchanged fire with NLF and FLOSY members, became commonplace, and casualties and atrocities mounted. Finally, at the end of 1967,

Aden achieved independence and the troops were withdrawn. The three years of conflict had cost the Army 600 casualties, including 90 killed.

The year 1968 was the only one since 1945 in which a British soldier was not killed in action somewhere in the world: poetic justice perhaps when the Vietnam War was at its height. The explanation was the Labour Government's switch in defence policy so as to give priority to NATO in Europe, all garrisons east of Suez apart from that in Hong Kong, which had now become the base for the Gurkhas, being withdrawn. The rise of Colonel Gadaffi in Libya meant that the garrison there, although little more than a battalion, also had to be removed.

The result was that the Army, which through its recent overseas commitments had grown to 196,000 men was reduced by the early 1970s to 166,000. Once again the number of battalions and regiments had to be cut. The infantry was left with 41 battalions, including the SAS and the Parachute Regiment, and the Royal Armoured Corps 13 cavalry and four Royal Tank Regiment units. The Royal Artillery now had 21 regiments and the Gurkhas were reduced to five infantry battalions. Some regiments preferred to disband rather than amalgamate and one or two famous names such as the Cameronians (Scottish Rifles) disappeared from the order of battle. Large

regiments were also formed from those with the same historical role. Thus the Light Infantry represented all the old light infantry regiments and the Royal Regiment of Fusiliers the fusilier regiments. For regimental administration the infantry was split up into a number of divisions, with divisional rather than brigade depots.

There was also a major reorganisation of the Territorial Army, which for too long had been reliant on obsolete World War II equipment. There was no money to re-equip the equivalent of 11 divisions and a modern force could be created only by drastic cuts. Many of the old county titles were abolished and new ones substituted, such as the Wessex Regiment, Highland Volunteers and Mercian Volunteers. The Yeomanry were cut to one armoured car regiment, although a second was raised a little later, and the infantry reduced to 37 battalions. At the same time the TA was combined with the Army Emergency Reserve to form the Territorial Army & Volunteer Reserve (TAVR). The TAVR was split into two categories, those with a reinforcement role to BAOR which were given priority in equipment, and home defence units. Recently the TA has regained its old title.

In the early 1960s there had been a major re-organisation at the top of the three services, largely inspired by Lord Louis Mountbatten,

Above: Belfast, July 1970. Women protesting against a curfew imposed on the Falls Road. In some ways, Northern Ireland has been the British Army's sternest test.

then First Sea Lord. He advocated greater merging under a single Chief of the Defence Staff (CDS), and this came into being in 1964, Mountbatten being appointed the first CDS. The old titles of the Admiralty, War Office and Air Ministry were abolished, and all three merged into the Ministry of Defence (MOD), the separate departments being known as MOD(Navy), MOD(Army) and MOD(RAF).

The Lee Enfield rifle had given way to the 7.62-mm Self Loading Rifle (SLR) in the late 1950s. This, together with the General Purpose Machine Gun (GPMG) and the 7.62-mm version of the old Bren, are now being replaced by the new 5.56-mm SA80 family. The workhorse of the Royal Armoured Corps, the Centurion tank, which had been in service since the closing stages of the war, was gradually replaced by Chieftain with its 120-mm gun, and some of these are now being superseded by Challenger. The infantry, too, went from being motorised to being mechanised with the introduction of the FV432 Armoured Personnel Carrier (APC), now being joined by the Warrior MCV-80 Mechanised Infantry Combat Vehicle (MICV) with its 30-mm Rarden gun. Most guns in the Royal Artillery are now self-propelled, being made up of the obsolescent 105-mm Abbot on the FV432 chassis, which will be replaced by the German/Italian/British 155-mm SP70, and the US 175-mm M107, 155-mm M109 and 8-in M110. Air defence guns have given way to missiles, Rapier and the handheld Blowpipe and Javelin. Likewise the Anti-tank Guided Weapon (ATGW) now plays a vital part. The first of these, introduced in the early 1960s, was Malkara, which gave way to Swingfire and Vigilant, the latter now replaced by Milan. The importance of the helicopter has been long recognised. It is the responsibility of the Army Air Corps, although heavy-lift helicopters are still flown and controlled by the RAF. There have also been radical developments over the last 20 years in surveillance aids and communications, especially to increase security.

Another major reform introduced in 1970 was that of the military salary. In order to equate the pay of the armed forces more closely to that of civilians, the marriage allowance was removed and all servicemen were paid the same, whether married or single. The single man living in barracks, however, would now be charged for his food and accommodation in the same way that the married man had always had to pay rent for his married quarters. In recognition that military life was often more disruptive, an extra percentage, usually about five per cent, was added to the serviceman's pay to give him some financial advantage over his civilian counterpart.

Great efforts were also made to improve living conditions in barracks under a programme called Operation Humane. The traditional barrack-room gave way to comfortably furnished smaller bedrooms with not more than four soldiers in each. The quality of food, too, has dramatically improved since the days of National Service, so much so that Egon Ronay, editor of the *Good Food Guide*, has recently commented that the quality of catering in the Armed Forces is generally of a significantly higher standard than in civilian life.

Left: The 5.56mm Individual Weapon System, part of the new SA-80 small arms family, which is now replacing the 7.62mm SLR and General Purpose Machine Gun in the British Army.

Opposite, top: An M109 155-mm howitzer of 39 Medium Regiment, Royal Artillery on exercise in Germany.

Opposite, below: Peace keeping. Ferret scout cars of the British contingent of the Multinational Force in war-torn Beirut, 1983.

Below: Members of the British Monitoring Force in Zimbabwe, 1979.

Left: Falklands, 1982, walking wounded of 2nd Scots Guards about to be lifted back by a Scout helicopter, after their epic fight for Tumbledown. An SAS man, distinguishable by his US M16 Armalite rifle, on right.

Below left: The Falklands operations.

Right: NATO's Northern Flank. Soldiers of the Royal Scots on exercise in Norway. The vehicle is the Swedish-made over-snow Bv202.

Below right: The 1980s infantryman. A Royal Anglian Regiment General Purpose Machine Gun gunner.

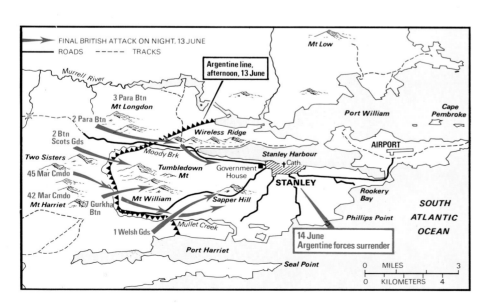

In August 1969 British troops were deployed on the streets of Belfast and Londonderry in Northern Ireland to deal with civil unrest which the Royal Ulster Constabulary (RUC) could no longer cope with. This marked the beginning of what has become the British Army's longest continuous campaign. Space prohibits a detailed description of the course of events over the following years. Suffice to say that the Army was first welcomed by both Protestant and Catholic, but in the squabbling between them the troops were caught in the middle and were for a time the target of the paramilitaries on both sides. It soon emerged, however, that the real enemy was the Provisional Irish Republican Army (PIRA) and its sister organisation the Irish National Liberation Army (INLA). Both are determined to remove the British presence in Northern Ireland by force, and they have waged an unceasing campaign of bombings and shootings against both the RUC and the Army.

Many of the lessons of colonial counter-insurgency campaigns were quickly found not to apply to Ulster, and for the first time, like the Americans in Vietnam, the Army found itself under the watchful eye of the media. New techniques had to be learnt, such as controlling riots where the traditional use of aimed live ammunition has been ruled out, and even dealing with on-the-spot media interviews. The soldier, too, since martial law has never been declared in the province, is under the law of the land and any wrongful action can lead to criminal charges being brought.

Until the mid 1970s, while the RUC reorganised, the Army took the lead, and its strength in the province reached a peak of over 20,000 in the summer of 1972, and for some years never fell below 15,000. Troops had to be sent not only from the mainland but also from Germany. This created problems in the disruption of training for general war, especially since Royal Armoured Corps and Royal Artillery units often found themselves acting as infantry and had to be trained in new skills. Some units serve in permanent barracks in Ulster for two-year tours, taking their families with them. They are known as 'resident' battalions. The majority, however, have been sent on four-month, later increased to four-and-a-half-month, emergency tours, and are called 'roulement' units.

Northern Ireland has provided the Army, especially the junior officers and NCOs, with one of its toughest tests. The basic tactical unit is the four-man 'brick' led by a junior officer or NCO, who can often find himself in a position where he has to make a split-second decision, knowing that if he acts wrongly he can bring trouble not just to himself but to the image of the Security Forces as a whole. Many attempts have been made to vilify the British Army in Ulster, and the conduct of individuals has sometimes been questionable. Nevertheless in the overwhelming majority of instances the Army has acted impeccably. It is hard to imagine any other army which could have stood this test of discipline, fortitude and patience for so long, especially since it has long been realised that Ulster is not a winnable military campaign. All the Army can do is hold the ring for as long as it takes the politicians to hammer out a workable political solution.

Yet Ulster has brought benefits to the Army. Nowhere was this better illustrated than during the Falklands campaign of 1982. Apart from the incredible speed with which the Task Force was organised and sent 7000 miles to the South Atlantic, the conduct of both the soldiers and the Royal Marine Commandos won worldwide admiration. The epic feats of the 2nd Battalion the Parachute Regiment at Goose Green and the 3rd Battalion on Mount Longdon, which gained for each a posthumous Victoria Cross, and of 2nd Battalion Scots Guards on Tumbledown, were in the highest traditions of the British Army, especially in the way the junior leaders and the individual soldiers conducted themselves. Much of this is directly attributable to the Ulster experience. In a different setting, the conduct of squadrons of the Queen's Dragoon Guards and the 16th/5th Lancers as part of the Multi-National Force in the Lebanon during 1983-84 is a further example of the British soldier's ability to cope with the most difficult situations, as is the work of the force sent to supervise the Lancaster House Agreement in Zimbabwe in 1979.

The British Army of 1985 is just as busy as ever. I(BR) Corps, with three armoured divisions in place and an infantry division in the United Kingdom, still provides a major contribution to NATO ground forces in the Federal Republic of Germany. The troubles in Northern Ireland continue, as does the allocation of the British contingent to the UN in Cyprus. For the past 15 years a British force has been stationed in Belize (formerly British Honduras) to protect the country against a long-standing Guatemalan claim. British garrisons remain in Gibraltar, Cyprus, Brunei and Hong Kong, although the last will be given up when the colony is handed back to China in 1997. It is also necessary to maintain a garrison in the Falklands. Military assistance teams are present in a number of African and Middle East countries, and British officers and NCOs continue to serve on secondment with the armies of some of the Gulf states. It was here during 1970-76 that the Sultan of

Oman's troops fought a highly successful campaign with British support against Yemeni incursions in Dhofar. Small specialist teams, mainly Royal Engineers, are constantly at work on civil relief programmes throughout the Third World.

Yet while there have been many changes, often dramatic, in the past 300 years, there has been no radical alteration in the basic nature and character of the British soldier. Whatever the challenges of the future, they will be met with the same steadfastness as in the past. Indeed his spirit is exemplified in the song sung by Marlborough's soldiers on campaign in the Low Countries 280 years ago:

'The Queen commands and we obey,
Over the hills and far away.'

Above: Falklands. 2 Para and their Regimental Flag.

Left: Paras about to land on the Falklands.

Above right: Challenger, Britain's latest main battle tank.

Right: 2 Para bury their dead after their victory at Goose Green.

Far right: 3rd Royal Tank Regiment Chieftain on Exercise Lionheart in Germany, 1984.

Appendix 1:
British Army Campaigns

Dates	War	Campaigns	Medals Awarded
1660-84	Against Moors	Tangier	
1685	Monmouth's Rebellion		
1689	Scottish		
1689-91	Against James II	Ireland	
1690-97	War of the Grand Alliance	Low Countries	
1701-13	War of the Spanish Succession	Low Countries Spain	
1715	Against Old Pretender	Scotland	
1739-42	War of Jenkins' Ear	South America	
1741-48	War of the Austrian Succession	Flanders Germany India N America	
1745-46	Against Young Pretender	England Scotland	
1756-63	Seven Years War	Germany Canada West Indies India Mediterranean	
1776-83	American War of Independence	N America West Indies Gibraltar	
1771-1819	Maharatta Wars	India	First India Medal (17 bars)
1793-1815	Napoleonic Wars	Low Countries West Indies Mediterranean Egypt South America Portugal/ Spain India South Africa Waterloo	Gold Medals and Cross (officers only) Seringapatam Medal Military General Service Medal (GSM 23 bars – sanctioned 1847) Waterloo Medal
1812-14	American War	N America	Military GSM (3 bars)
1814-16	Nepalese War		First India Medal (bar)

Dates	War	Campaigns	Medals Awarded
1824-26	First Burma War		First Burma Medal
1824-31	Ashanti War	W Africa	
1834-35	Kaffir War	S Africa	Medal for South Africa
1839-42	First Afghan War		Medal for Capture of Guznee Jellalabad Medal Canadahar, Guhznee and Cabul Medal Medal for the Defence of Kelat-I-Ghilzie
1841-42	First China War		China Medal
1843	Subjugation of Sinde	India	Sinde Medal
1843	Gwalior Campaign	India	Star for Gwalior Campaign
1845-46	First Sikh War	India	Medal for Sutlej Campaign (4 bars)
1845-47	First Maori War	New Zealand	New Zealand Medal
1846-47	Kaffir War	S Africa	Medal for South Africa
1848-49	Second Sikh War	India	Punjab Medal (3 bars)
1850-53	Kaffir War	S Africa	Medal for South Africa
1852-53	Second Burmese War		India GSM (1854) (1 bar)
1854-56	Crimean War		Crimea Medal (4 bars)
1856-57	Persian War		India GSM (1854) (1 bar)
1857-58	Indian Mutiny		Indian Mutiny Medal (5 bars)
1857-60	Second China War		China Medal

Dates	War	Campaigns	Medals Awarded
1860-70	Second/Third Maori Wars		New Zealand Medal
1863	Umbeyla Expedition	India	India GSM (1854) (1 bar)
1866	Fenian Raid	Canada	Canada GSM (1899) (1 bar)
1867-68	Abyssinian Expedition		Abyssinian Medal
1873-74	Ashanti War	W Africa	Ashanti Medal
1870	Red River Expedition	Canada	Canada GSM (1899) (2 bars)
1878-80	Second Afghan War		Medal for Afghanistan (6 bars) Kabul to Kandahar Star
1870-80	Minor expeditions India	Bhutan Looshai Jowaki Nagaland	Each a bar to India GSM (1854)
1877-79	Zulu War		Medal for South Africa (6 bars)
1880-81	Basutoland/ Transkei Expeditions		Cape of Good Hope GSM (2 bars)
1881	First Boer War		
1882	Egyptian Campaign		Egyptian Medal (2 bars) Khedive's Star
1884-89	Sudan Campaigns		Egyptian Medal (11 bars)
1885	Van Riel's Rebellion	Canada	North-West Canada Medal (1 bar)
1885-87	Second Burmese War		India GSM (1854) (1 bar)
1888	Sikkim Campaign	India	India GSM (1854) (1 bar)
1882-92	Operations NE Frontier of India and Burma	Burma 1887-89 Hazara 1888 Chin-Lushai 1889-90 Burma 1889-92 Lushai 1889-92 Samana 1891 Hazara 1891 Hunza 1891 NE Frontier 1891 Chin Hills 1892-93 Kachin Hills 1892-93	each a bar to India GSM (1854)
1891-98	Central Africa		Central Africa Medal (1 bar)
1893	Matabele War	East Africa	Chartered Company of South Africa Medal (1 bar)
1894-95	Waziristan Campaign	India	India GSM (1854) (1 bar)
1895	Chitral Campaign	India	India Medal (1895) (2 bars)
1895-96	Third Ashanti War	W Africa	Ashanti Star
1896-97	Rhodesia		Chartered Company of South Africa Medal (2 bars)
1896-97	Expeditions in Nigeria	W Africa	Royal Niger Company's Medal (1 bar)
1896-98	Sudan		Sudan Medal
1897-98	Indian Frontier Expeditions	Malakand 1897 Samana 1897 Punjab Frontier 1897-98 Tirah 1897-98	Each a bar to India Medal (1895)
1897-98	Operations in Uganda and Somaliland		East and Central Africa Medal (3 bars)
1899-1902	Second Boer War	S Africa	South Africa Medal (Queen's) (28 bars) King Edward's South Africa Medal (2 bars)
1900	Boxer Rebellion	China	China Medal (3 bars)
1900-20	Numerous small expeditions in West and East Africa		Africa GSM (1902) (43 bars)
1901	Ashanti Rebellion	W Africa	Ashanti Medal (1 bar)
1901-02	Waziristan	India	India Medal (1895) (1 bar)
1903-04	Tibetan Expedition		Tibet Medal (1 bar)
1906	Zulu Rising	S Africa	Medal for Zulu Rising in Natal (1 bar)

Dates	War	Campaigns	Medals Awarded
1908	North-West Frontier of India		India GSM (1908) (1 bar)
1911-12	Abor Expedition	NE Frontier of India	India GSM (1908) (1 bar)
1914-18	First World War	France/ Flanders S West Africa S East Africa China Dardanelles Egypt Palestine Mesopotamia Salonika Italy Russia NW Frontier India	1914 Star 1914-15 Star British War Medal Victory Medal
1919	Third Afghan War		India GSM (1908) (1 bar)
1919-20	Russia		
1919-20	Mahsud Expedition		India GSM (1908) (1 bar)
1919-21	Arab Insurrection	Mesopotamia	GSM (1919) (5 bars)
1919-21	Ireland		
1919-21	Waziristan		India GSM (1908) (1 bar)
1921-22	Malabar Rebellion		India GSM (1908) (1 bar)
1930-31	Waziristan		India GSM (1908) (1 bar)
1930-32	Burma		India GSM (1908) (1 bar)
1933	Mohmand Expedition		India GSM (1908) (1 bar)
1935	NW Frontier of India		India GSM (1908) (1 bar)
1936-39	Arab Rebellion	Palestine	GSM (1918) (1 bar)
1936-39	NW Frontier of India		India GSM (1936) (2 bars)
1939-45	Second World War	Norway France Flanders 1939-40 East Africa 1940-41 North Africa 1940-43 Greece/Crete	1939-45 Star Africa Star Italy Star Pacific Star Burma Star France and Germany Star Atlantic Star Defence Medal
1939-45		1941 Hong Kong 1941 Iraq/Syria 1941 Malaya/ Singapore 1941-42 Burma 1942-45 Sicily/Italy 1943-45 NW Europe 1944-45	Victory Medal
1945-46	South-East Asia	Indo-China Dutch East Indies	GSM (1918) (1 bar)
1945-48	Palestine		GSM (1918) (1 bar)
1948-60	Malaya		GSM (1918) (1 bar)
1950-53	Korean War		Korean Medal UN Service Medal
1952-56	Mau Mau Rebellion	Kenya	Africa GSM (1 bar)
1954-60	Cyprus		GSM (1918) (1 bar)
1956	Suez Expedition		GSM (1918) (1 bar)
1957-59	Muscat and Oman		GSM (1918) (1 bar)
1962	Brunei Revolt		GSM (1918) (1 bar)
1963-66	Borneo Campaign		GSM (1962) (3 bars)
1964	Cyprus	UN Peacekeeping	UN Peacekeeping Medal
1964-67	Aden/Radfan		GSM (1962) (2 bars)
1969-	Northern Ireland		GSM (1962) (1 bar)
1979	Zimbabwe		Zimbabwe Medal
1982	Falklands Campaign		South Atlantic Medal
1983-84	Lebanon	Multi-national Force	GSM (1962) (1 bar)

Bars are awarded for particular battles within a campaign and for campaigns themselves.

Appendix 2: British Army Regiments and Corps 1985

(In order of precedence)

Household Cavalry
Life Guards
Blues and Royals (Royal Horse Guards and 1st Dragoons)
The Mounted Regiment (one squadron of each regiment)

Royal Armoured Corps
1st The Queen's Dragoon Guards
The Royal Scots Dragoon Guards (Carabiniers and Greys)
4th/7th Royal Dragoon Guards
5th Royal Inniskilling Dragoon Guards
The Queen's Own Hussars
The Queen's Royal Irish Hussars
9th/12th Royal Lancers (Prince of Wales's)
The Royal Hussars (Prince of Wales's Own)
13th/18th Royal Hussars (Queen Mary's Own)
14th/20th King's Hussars
15th/19th The King's Royal Hussars
16th/5th The Queen's Royal Lancers
17th/21st Lancers
1st Royal Tank Regiment
2nd Royal Tank Regiment
3rd Royal Tank Regiment
4th Royal Tank Regiment
The Royal Yeomanry (TA)
The Wessex Yeomanry (TA)
The Queen's Own Yeomanry (TA)
The Queen's Own Mercian Yeomanry (TA)
The Duke of Lancaster's Own Yeomanry (TA)

Royal Regiment of Artillery
Royal Horse Artillery
Royal Artillery
Honourable Artillery Company (TA)

Corps of Royal Engineers
Royal Engineers
Royal Monmouthshire Royal Engineers (TA)

Royal Corps of Signals

The Infantry
(Each Regiment is a single battalion unless otherwise specified)

The Guards Division
Grenadier Guards (two battalions)
Coldstream Guards (two battalions)
Scots Guards (two battalions)
Irish Guards
Welsh Guards

The Scottish Division
The Royal Scots (The Royal Regiment)
The Royal Highland Fusiliers (Princess Margaret's Own Glasgow and Ayrshire Regiment)
The King's Own Scottish Borderers
The Black Watch (Royal Highland Regiment)
Queen's Own Highlanders (Seaforth and Cameron)
The Gordon Highlanders
The Argyll and Sutherland Highlanders (Princess Louise's)
51st Highland Volunteers (TA) (three battalions)
52nd Lowland Volunteers (TA) (two battalions)

The Queen's Division
The Queen's Regiment (three Regular and two TA battalions)
The Royal Regiment of Fusiliers (three Regular and two TA battalions)
The Royal Anglian Regiment (three Regular and two TA battalions)

The King's Division
The King's Own Border Regiment (one Regular and one TA battalion)
The King's Regiment (one Regular and one TA battalion)
The Prince of Wales's Own Regiment of Yorkshire
The Green Howards (Alexandra, Princess of Wales's Own Yorkshire Regiment)
The Royal Irish Rangers (27th (Inniskilling) 83rd and 87th) (two Regular and two TA battalions)
The Queen's Lancashire Regiment (one Regular and one TA battalion)
The Duke of Wellington's Regiment (West Riding)
Yorkshire Volunteers (TA) (three battalions)

The Prince of Wales's Division
The Devon and Dorset Regiment
The Cheshire Regiment
The Royal Welch Fusiliers (one Regular and one TA battalion)
The Royal Regiment of Wales (one Regular and two TA battalions)
The Gloucestershire Regiment
The Worcestershire and Sherwood Foresters Regiment (29th/45th Foot) (one Regular and one TA battalion)
The Royal Hampshire Regiment
The Staffordshire Regiment (The Prince of Wales's)
The Duke of Edinburgh's Royal Regiment (Berkshire and Wiltshire)
The Wessex Regiment (TA) (two battalions)
Mercian Volunteers (TA) (two battalions)

The Light Division
The Light Infantry (three Regular and three TA battalions)
The Royal Green Jackets (three Regular and one TA battalions)

Airborne Forces
The Parachute Regiment (three Regular and three TA battalions)
The Special Air Service Regiment (one Regular and two TA regiments)
Army Air Corps

The Brigade of Gurkhas
2nd King Edward VII's Own Gurkha Rifles (The Sirmoor Rifles) (two battalions)
6th Queen Elizabeth's Own Gurkha Rifles
7th Duke of Edinburgh's Own Gurkha Rifles (two battalions, but one about to disband)
10th Princess Mary's Own Gurkha Rifles
The Queen's Gurkha Engineers
The Queen's Gurkha Signals
Gurkha Transport Regiment

Services
Royal Army Chaplains' Department
Royal Corps of Transport
Royal Army Medical Corps
Royal Army Ordnance Corps
Royal Electrical & Mechanical Engineers
Royal Military Police
Royal Army Pay Corps
Royal Army Veterinary Corps
Small Arms School Corps
Military Provost Staff Corps
Royal Army Education Corps
Royal Army Dental Corps
Royal Pioneer Corps
Intelligence Corps
Army Physical Training Corps
Army Catering Corps
Army Legal Corps
Queen Alexandra's Royal Army Nursing Corps
Women's Royal Army Corps

INDEX

Acknowledgements

The author and publishers would like to thank David Eldred, who designed this book and Ron Watson who compiled the index. Picture research by Wendy Sacks and Jean Martin, Editor Donald Sommerville. The agencies and individuals listed below kindly supplied the illustrations on the pages noted.

Marquess of Anglesey/NT: 66-7
Army Museums Ogilby Trust/NAM: 42 (bottom)
BBC Hulton Picture Library: pages 28 (top), 40 (top left), 46 (top), 49 (bottom), 53 (top), 80 (bottom), 84-5, 101, 132, 133, 134-5, 136, 137 (both), 138 (centre), 138-9, 140-1 (all 4), 142, 180 (bottom).
Bison Picture Library: pages 12, 82 (top), 120, 124-5, 125 (top), 157, 192.
Blackman Harvey Ltd: page 35 (bottom)
Bristol Museum & Art Gallery/NAM: page 94 (bottom)
British Museum: page 14 (bottom).
Anne S K Brown Military Collection: page 80 (top).
Bundesarchiv: page 160 (top).
Coldstream Guards/NAM: page 69 (top)
Dorset Military Museum/NAM: page 28 (bottom)
Earl of Dartmouth/NAM: page 19 (top)
John Freeman: page 206 (bottom).
John Frost Newspapers: pages 99 (top right), 113 (top), 147 (bottom), 168 (top), 185 (top).
Impact Photos/Alain Le Garsmeur: page 207.
Imperial War Museum, London: pages 4-5, 7, 8-9, 102-3, 104, 106 (both), 109 (both), 110, 111 (both), 113 (bottom), 114-15 (all 3), 116-17 (all 4), 118 (bottom), 119 (top), 121

(bottom), 122-3 (all 4), 124 (top), 126 (both), 127 (both), 128 (top right and bottom), 130-1 (both), 138 (top), 143 (bottom), 144 (both), 145 (both), 146, 148-9 (all 4), 150 (both), 151 (bottom), 152 (top), 153 (both), 154 (bottom), 155 (both), 156-7, 159 (both), 160 (bottom), 162-3 (both), 164-5, 166, 167 (both), 168-9 (bottom), 169 (both), 170 (both), 171, 172, 174-5, 175 (top), 176, 177 (both), 178-9 (all 4), 180 (top), 181 (both), 182, 183 (both), 184, 185 (bottom left and bottom right), 186-7 (all 3), 188 (both), 189 (both), 190-1 (all 3), 193 (both), 194-5, 197, 198 (both), 199 (both), 200 (bottom), 201 (all 3), 202 (both), 203 (top), 204, 212 (top).
Mansell Collection: pages 1, 17 (bottom), 29 (top left), 40 (top right), 44-5, 52 (bottom), 60, 63 (top), 72, 76-7, 89 (both), 90 (top), 91 (bottom right), 97 (top right), 108 (bottom), 112.
Duke of Marlborough/NAM: page 6 (top)
Duke of Marlborough (photo: Jeremy Whitaker): pages 25 (bottom), 26 (both), 27 (bottom).
MARS/A Moore: page 215 (bottom right).
Middlesex Regimental Museum/NAM: page 57 (bottom)
MOD (Crown copyright): page 215 (top).
National Army Museum, London (NAM): 2-3, 6 (bottom), 10-11 , 13 (both), 17 (top), 20-1, 22, 23 (top & bottom), 24 (both), 28-9 (bottom), 29 (top right), 30, 31 (all 3), 32-3, 34 (both), 35 (top), 36 (top), 37 (bottom), 38-9 (both), 41 (top), 42 (bottom), 43, 46 (bottom), 47 (both), 48 (top), 49 (top), 50-1, 52 (top), 53 (bottom), 54-5 (all 3), 56 (bottom), 57 (top), 58 (top), 58-9 (bottom), 59 (bottom), 60 (bottom), 61 (both), 62 (both), 63 (both), 64 (top), 65, 66 (top), 67 (top), 70-1, 73 (bottom), 74 (both), 78,

79, 81 (both), 82 (bottom), 83 (bottom), 87 (top), 88 (both), 90 (bottom), 91 (top and bottom left), 94 (top), 95 (both), 98 (top), 98-9, 99 (top left), 100, 119 (bottom)
National Maritime Museum, London: pages 36 (bottom), 37 (top).
National Portrait Gallery, London: page 15 (bottom).
Richard Natkiel (maps): pages 27 (top), 39, 56 (top), 68, 83 (top), 97, 107, 121 (top), 129, 158 (both), 167, 174, 204-5, 212 (both).
Peter Newark's Historical Pictures: pages 14 (top), 15 (top), 16, 25 (top), 41 (bottom), 42 (top), 64 (bottom), 73 (top), 86-7, 87 (bottom), 92 (bottom left and right), 93 (both), 173.
Private collections/NAM: pages 23 (centre) Loan: Dr R J Rabett, 75 (top), 78-79, 154 (top)
Duke of Roxburgh/NAM: page 19 (bottom)
Royal Anglian Regiment/NAM: 74-75 (bottom)
RMA Sandhurst/NAM: 68-9 (bottom)
Royal Ordnance Factories, MOD: pages 210 (top), 211 (top), 213 (bottom).
TPS/Central Press: pages 104-5, 105 (bottom), 139 (top).
South Wales Borderers Museum/NAM: page 92 (bottom)
TPS/Fox Photos: page 96.
TPS/Keystone: pages 108 (top), 128 (top left), 147 (top), 151 (top), 152 (bottom), 196, 200 (top), 203 (bottom), 209.
TPS/3L Photos: pages 107 (top), 143 (top), 158 (bottom).
HQ UK Land Forces: pages 210 (bottom), 211 (bottom), 214 (both), 215 (bottom left).
Ulster Museum: page 118 (top).